Kid Dynamite

Kid Dynamite

The Gerry James Story

by

Ron Smith

OOLICHAN BOOKS
FERNIE, BRITISH COLUMBIA, CANADA
2011

Library and Archives Canada Cataloguing in Publication

Smith, Ron, 1943-

    Kid Dynamite : the Gerry James story / Ron Smith.

ISBN 978-0-88982-276-4

1. James, Gerry, 1934-. 2. Football players--Canada--Biography. 3. Hockey players--Canada--Biography. 4. Hockey coaches--Canada--Biography. I. Title.

GV939.J34S65 2011   796.335092   C2011-901007-0

We gratefully acknowledge the financial support of the Canada Council for the Arts, the British Columbia Arts Council through the BC Ministry of Tourism, Culture, and the Arts, and the Government of Canada through the Canada Book Fund, for our publishing activities.

Published by
Oolichan Books
P.O. Box 2278
Fernie, British Columbia
Canada V0B 1M0

www.oolichan.com

Printed and bound in Canada by Friesens

For Gerry and Marg

And, as always, for Pat

❧

I offer this book in memory of Robert Kroetsch who was killed tragically in a car accident on June 21, 2011. Bob was a cherished friend for over forty years. His willingness to read this book in an earlier draft was typical of his generosity and kindness. Enthusiasm, well, that defined his character. "No kidding" or "You don't say" may have been his favourite expressions, especially as he responded to the ideas of other people. He was always prepared to be surprised or astonished. Thanks, Bob, for the many unforgettable memories.

Only when nothing is unexpected of you can you really do what you want.

—John Cage

❧

Will it be a likeness?
Probably not, but I still have to answer the question.
Why?
Because how we see each other strengthens us. Adds to our individual and collective story.
And that's a good thing?
Yes.

Contents:

Preface / Announcing Gerry

Kid Dynamite.

It could be the title of a "B" film starring Jack Nicholson or Gene Hackman.

It could be any one of a number of heroic sports films where a superb athlete sets amazing records as a professional, but whose stellar career is cut short by injury. We think this is the end, but no: he becomes a successful hockey coach in a tiny rural backwater and his story continues.

We'll set this drama on the prairies. There, with his wife and growing family, he leads a team of young men, not unlike himself, through season-ending hardships and past seemingly insurmountable obstacles towards the finals and, the ultimate goal, a silver chalice.

Along the way the plot twists, of course. We've all seen some variation of this story. The boys' parents are dubious, the town council is corrupt, the equipment is second-rate, and the coach himself has his own demons — but he struggles against them all to personal and collective triumph. The kid from the other side of the tracks becomes the town hero. Everyone rejoices.

Oh, and there is a reporter who, whether at the dawn or sunset of his career, recognizes the depth of the man and tells his dramatic tale.

I've seen this film. And every time I see it, I want to say, Come on, show me the sacred, or, well, at least the down and dirty of the sporting world.

But then I remind myself, this is not what really happens. Not quite. What happens on celluloid is always dressed up; is, by definition, illusory. Whereas Kid Dynamite is real: he's my friend Gerry James. His life doesn't quite follow the plot of that film we've all seen — the details are a lot more raw — but he was an amazing athlete and successful coach, and he is a family man and a sporting legend. *Kid Dynamite* is his story.

❦

When I first decided to write this biography, I knew Gerry as a golfing mate. I also knew him as someone who for a period of his life had played professional football and hockey for a living. In my mind he was not yet an iconic figure, or his story the sort of material out of which films were often scripted. Occasionally we would discuss sports, usually in response to games we had recently watched. On occasion we talked about people and performances we remembered and admired. Rarely did Gerry speak about his own career. Mostly we talked about our golf swings, chided each other about missed shots. Nit-picked and nagged. Okay, we trash talked, as golfing buddies often do.

As our friendship grew and I decided there might be a story here, I first turned to Bob Ferguson's *Who's Who in Canadian Sport*. Knowing that I could never extract it from Gerry himself, I needed the sort of career summary that Ferguson's book provided. This is what Ferguson wrote:

> James, Gerry (football/hockey); b. 22 Oct 1934, Regina, Sask; given name: Gerald Edwin; m. Margaret Petrie; c. Debra, Tracy, Tara, Kelly, Brady; ret'd hockey exec., hotelier, storekeeper, property mgr; HS football to youngest in CFL at 17; CFL Winnipeg, Sask. '52-64; 63tds, 143 cvts, 40fg,

21s for 645 pts; 995 carries for 5554 yds (5.6 yd avg), 57 tds; twice rushed for 1000+ yds single season; record for tds scored rushing with 18 '57; scored 1 other on pass same season to tie Pat Abbruzzi; twice Dave Dryburgh Trophy as WFC scoring leader, once runnerup; twice WFC all-star; twice Schenley top Canadian award; offered contract by NY Giants (NFL); at 16 mem. Winnipeg Monarchs '51 Memorial Cup finalists; Toronto Marlboros '55 Memorial Cup champions; rw Maple Leafs '54-59/60; 149 scheduled games, 14g, 26a, 15 playoff games, 1g; competed in 2 major ntl finals within 6 months '59 Grey Cup, '60 Stanley Cup; mem. 6 Grey Cup finalists 4 winners; coached in Switzerland '63-64, owner/coach/player Yorkton Terriers, Sask. Jr. HL (Tier 2) '66-69 4 consec. Sask. titles; coached 3 all-star teams; 2 coach-of-year awards; coached SJHL, WHL teams 19 yrs; 2 Sask. Titles; 7 all-star coach awards; organized/coached Weyburn Special Olympics Floor hockey team; nicknamed "Kid Dynamite"; election to Canadian Football Hall of Fame provided grid shrine with (Eddie "Dynamite" James) 1ˢᵗ father-son combination; mem. Cdn Football, Man., Blue Bombers, Sask, Yorkton Sports halls of fame; res Nanoose Bay, B.C.

Here was a list, filled with abbreviations, almost in code, that provided something between a sketch and a doodle of the man about whom I wanted to write. Ferguson's was a stick figure that didn't tell you the man, but did set down some essential facts about a person named James. From those I could build my story. I had to admit that the facts alone were fairly seductive. Even though Ferguson got Gerry's given name wrong, here was a skeleton outline on which to hang my version of Gerry's story. All I needed to do was decode the bits and pieces and attempt to get the man himself to flesh out the summary with details. In that way I hoped to take the reader on a journey into the person.

When I approached Gerry about writing the book, he was receptive to the idea, but how willing he would be to open up and talk about himself, well, that was still in some doubt. He was quick to praise others but getting information from him about himself was akin to squeezing a lemon for a large glass of juice. You needed to get past the thick skin, the rind, to get to the fruit.

In 1991, Gerry was invited to the 40th Anniversary, Conn Smythe Sports Celebrities Dinner. Listed in the program were all those who joined him as guests at the head table. They included: Jeff Adams, Joe Carter, Wendel Clark, Mike "Pinball" Clemons, Whitey Ford, Bill Gadsby, Althea Gibson, Gordie Howe, Ferguson Jenkins, Red Kelly, Ron MacLean (host), Bob Mathias, Zeke O'Connor, Johnny Padres, Maurice Richard, Marlene Stewart-Streit, Tony Trabert, Johnny Unitas, Kaye Vaughan and Lucille Wheeler. This was illustrious company.

I dug the program out of a dusty cardboard box of memorabilia that had survived Gerry's yearly purging of the past. Even as I closed in on the final lap of this book, I was not sure why he was so reluctant to talk about his own accomplishments. He is modest, that much I had determined, but clearly there had to be moments in his life that remained significant and special, justifiably so, moments that gave him pleasure and made him proud. Otherwise, why save his program which he had asked each of the other head-table guests to sign? I thought this was revealing. After working with him on this project for over a year, I suspect he really does not count himself an equal in this company. This sort of doubt, this sense of potential failure, is not unusual among the most accomplished athletes. It's what pushes them to keep striving game after game, enabling them to excel.

Slowly I gathered together the tools and materials to construct a book. Whether a consequence of time, faulty memory (Gerry kept telling me he was going to donate his brain to medicine in light of recent discussions about brain trauma and concussion), or natural reticence, some rather significant details had been slow to emerge. For example, well into the project, he let drop, as an aside to some other point, the following crumb of information. He had been runner up for the Lou Marsh award for Canada's top athlete in 1957. I guess placing second didn't matter because I had not run across this detail in any of the internet write-ups I had read about Gerry. Nor in any of the books that provided career summaries. Here is what Jim Hunt wrote in one of the major newspapers, the *Toronto Daily Star*, on Tuesday, Feb. 18, 1958.

Headline: Marsh Trophy for The Rocket
Sub headline: He's Unanimous Pick Over James, Balding

Hockey's greatest scoring machine — Maurice (The Rocket) Richard — is the 1957 winner of the Lou Marsh Trophy, it was announced today.

The Montreal Canadiens' winger, who passed the 500-goal milestone last October, was the unanimous choice of the board of judges for the award which goes annually to Canada's outstanding athlete — amateur or professional.

There wasn't really much doubt about this year's winner. It was Richard all the way. In his 16th season in the NHL, The Rocket was headed for one of the greatest when an injury cut him down in Toronto, Nov. 13, but not before he had scored his 500th goal in regular NHL play.

Sub headline: Only Howe has Chance
It's a new record that may never be equalled. Only Gordie Howe, among players active in the game, has passed the 300-goal milestone.

Gerry James, the running star of the Winnipeg Blue Bombers, was the runner-up for the award. Gerry came back to the football wars this season after two years of toil with the Toronto Maple Leafs. He broke the Canadian pro scoring record, the Western Conference rushing mark and was one big reason his team was in Varsity stadium on Grey Cup day.

In Canada, placing second in the balloting for the Lou Marsh Award in any year should be a significant and celebrated moment in an athlete's career. Placing behind "Rocket" Richard in any sort of competition that recognizes athletic achievement is a major accomplishment. As we all know, sometimes the selection process is a crapshoot. Gerry undoubtedly would argue that "The Rocket" was the correct choice for 1957. But I have wondered, for example, how the judges chose between Steve Nash and Sidney Crosby? And with all due respect to F1 racing, how did Larry Walker lose out to a car?

In a way, meeting Gerry has been and remains a constant replay. The game goes on. Each encounter, whether a more formal type of interview or a conversation on a drive to a farm to pick up top dressing for my garden or a chat over a morning cup of coffee, adds a few more yards of text to the tale Gerry has to tell. Mixed in are the inevitable insults and the little attempts at one-upmanship. Gerry loves verbal jousting. Rather quietly and reluctantly he talks about his celebrity life. Actually, as I say, he has little sense of himself as a celebrity. Whenever asked to play the role, as a guest at a father/son banquet for example, he mocks the attention with some self-deprecating comment, such as, there must be someone better known still drawing a breath who could have rolled over for this gig.

He's a guy who played football and hockey, who loved

both games passionately and still likes to tell a tale or two out of class. He has criticisms, some of which I have noted, but overall he respected everyone he played with and against. Yes, he wanted to beat them if they were the opposition, but everyone did something in their lives to which he had a connection; they were all participants in two games he continues to esteem.

Writing someone else's story is both daunting and a joy; after all, a person's story constitutes something approximating the truth of who they are and measures within limits the value of what they've done. When Gerry James played professional football and hockey, he thought he was one of the luckiest people on the planet. What kid wouldn't agree with him? 'Playing' for a living — it's every kid's dream.

Not until many years later did Gerry stop to think about his accomplishments. Like any athlete with marketable skills, and he had those in abundance, he was providing for his family. But he also knew that his time was limited. Playing was not a magic carpet that was going to carry him into the land of plenty. Even offers to play for the New York Giants didn't alter his future prospects. Like most professional athletes of his day, at the end of his career he knew he would have to find another occupation. He would have to work for a living. In the meantime, he got to live out what many people, certainly many young men, would have seen as the fulfillment of their most cherished fantasy.

Mark Twain suggested biographies cannot be written. They are in essence merely the coat and buttons of a man. And John Arbuthnot lamented they are the new terrors of death. But these days there are no rules; a person's story can go viral on the internet in milli-seconds. Perhaps the most appropriate comment for my purposes comes from Phillip Guedalla who said that "Biography, like big game hunting, is one of the recognized forms of sport, and it is as unfair as only sport can be."

In our case, Gerry's and mine, I hope we have achieved a bit more than Twain suggested is possible and that the game I've attempted to catch has been fairly treated. I like to think I've captured a likeness of the man in the pages that follow but I wouldn't for a second claim that this is a complete portrait. To borrow John Berger's term, it is a photocopy. After all, the subject is constantly shifting, in and out of view through time. That's what makes the challenge intriguing. What I do know is that I have had the good fortune to become a friend of one of the great sportsmen of the twentieth century.

About his sporting days, Gerry and I have had many conversations, some that ran directly to the point, others which wheeled about the room gathering in distant points of light which seemed at the time quite inconsequential but that later proved illuminating. When I asked him about appearing in the most CFL post-season games, thirty-six, he wasn't even aware of the record. That sort of notoriety seemed unimportant to him but when I realized those extra games totaled up to slightly more than two additional seasons of play my question seemed to me noteworthy. In a way, I told him, you played thirteen, not eleven seasons in a major professional sport. That's amazing. To my surprise he appeared unimpressed, almost sheepish.

He is an honest man who I'm sure has kept his distortions of truth to a minimum and I am a writer who has attempted to control the overwhelming temptation to embellish or fictionalize. Thus I hope we've recounted a small bit of history with reasonable accuracy.

Absolute accuracy, admittedly, is a challenge, for whenever people tell hockey or football tales, exaggeration creeps in. People in communities across the country gather around rinks and fields to watch sons and daughters at play, but later, assembling around a fire or pot-bellied stove to warm their feet and bullshit over a beer, they'll revel in having been there and turn to great performances they have witnessed or great victories they have won. Small details will become larger; larger details will swell. Being there is important.

The riots that followed Rocket Richard's suspension in 1955 were large but as tale-teller's memories become more distant, the crowds grow.

The fog bowl of 1962 is another such memorable contest, one Gerry played in. Fans of the sport who were not in attendance at the game itself remember where they were that afternoon. But perhaps most significantly, the five o'clock morning practice at the local rink illustrates best who we are; it is a ritual many Canadian families embrace as a defining part of their heritage. Huddling together in the stands, outdoors if you're serious, whether football or hockey, from short sleeves at the beginning of the season to parkas at the end, through hot muggy days, torrential downpours, blizzards, fog and what seems like endless deep freezes, has helped to shape our character.

I don't think Gerry's modesty is merely caution or insecurity, but it may be. To have played in two major sports in one's lifetime at the highest level is a notable feat. To have learned enough to coach successfully in one of those sports for twenty years is equally momentous. To have remained humble in the light of such achievements seems to me admirable, especially when I reflect on the end zone antics of today's crop of gridiron stars. All that fist pumping! All that posing! All that crazy dancing on steroids. You would think they had solved some great medical puzzle rather than satisfying some primal need for play that we all appear to have; that we apparently share with our chimp relatives.

What I do know is that Gerry had a remarkable career, one we should all take some pleasure in sharing. His description of a particular touchdown or goal can, if we let it, put us in mind of one of our own achievements, whether on a sandlot, pond, or while standing on the sidelines watching our kids at play. It just might also remind us of being there and being young.

After one of Gerry's silly quips or after he breaks wind when we're out golfing, usually in the middle of one of our back swings, Peter Brooks, one of our golf foursome, often shakes his head and says, "At seventy-five he still behaves like a damn kid." Then he pauses and smiles, a bit of the devil's light in his own eyes. "But that's what we love about him, isn't it?"

1 / A few first words

When I told a friend of mine, the fine BC/Saskatchewan writer Alan Safarik, that I was writing a book about Gerry James, he said, "Really, *the* Gerry James, the old Winnipeg-Blue Bomber and Toronto Maple Leaf player?"

"Yes," I said, and I could hear him blowing air out at the other end of the phone line.

"Wow," he said, "no kidding, really, wow! He was my childhood hero. Do you have any idea how many records that guy set. How good he was?"

Alan has an encyclopedic knowledge of many subjects, amongst them sports trivia.

"And for him to have played two sports at a major league level," he continued. "Wow. He was incredible. Others have done it, but not as well as he did. There was Deion Sanders but he was always injured and Bo Jackson, who really didn't amount to much."

"And," I added, "Michael Jordan, who tried his hand at baseball, as well as John Ferguson and Jack Bionda who played both hockey and lacrosse, although lacrosse is hardly a major sport. A great game but not big league."

"No," Alan said, "and the thing that sets Gerry James apart from all of them is that he played in a Grey Cup and a Stanley Cup in the same season. Now that's impressive. Really, he played two gruelling sports, two sports that were hellish on the knees and head, not to mention the entire body. And he played at a time when football players often played both offence and defence."

"Not Gerry," I replied. "But," I added, almost apologetically, "he was a kicker."

"And he was tough," Alan said, "a scrapper. That would have doubled up the punishment on his body."

Alan, I should point out, was a first-class soccer talent on the Vancouver scene and brings a certain amount of personal athletic prowess to his admiration for Gerry. As a kid, Alan lived close by Empire Stadium and walked down to watch the Lions and visiting teams practice. The team he looked forward most to watching was the Bombers, in particular, one Bomber, Gerry James.

Larry Robertson, in charge of Stats and History at the CFL, corrected Alan's and my knowledge of two-sport athletes when he informed me that Lionel (The Big Train) Conacher, won a Grey Cup with the Toronto Argonauts in 1921 and successive Stanley Cups with the Chicago Black Hawks in 1934 and the Montreal Maroons in 1935. Of course this does not detract from Gerry's accomplishments. To share the spotlight with Canada's greatest athlete of the first half century (20th) is clearly an honour. Robertson noted that Elwyn (Moe) Morris also played both pro hockey and pro football.

A response like Alan's to the mention of Gerry's name is not unique. When Gerry and I have been together, I have heard many men my age ask: Are you the Gerry James who used to play for the Winnipeg Blue Bombers? Or the Toronto Maple Leafs? The question depends very much on which sport they were a fan of when they were growing up, where they lived, or which sport they played themselves. Some actually remember his career in both sports. I have to say right here that Gerry never invites these inquiries. In fact, he is quite modest about his career. When we're golfing and someone joins the group and eventually gets around to the inevitable question that men ask of each other on a golf course, what do or did you do for a living, Gerry will usually mention one of the businesses he had. He might relax and let out that he owned one and coached several junior hockey teams.

But for the most part, if a person doesn't respond to his name, he remains mum. If someone starts to talk football or hockey, he might add his two-bits worth but only if he has something to say that has to do with a game shown the previous day on TV. I've never heard him say, well, when I played…we did this or that. He might laugh or shake his head at some observation one of the group makes, but he'll never boast or launch into a litany of his own credentials. In fact, he can often be self-deprecating to a fault. I have to say that in recent years I've wondered about this because it's difficult to miss the large ring he wears on one finger showing and celebrating the four Grey Cup winning teams he played on. It's a lovely gold ring embossed with a massive "W" sparkling with diamonds.

Recently when we were visiting a garden centre and came to the counter with our purchase of several plants, the woman running the cash register, who was quite chatty, spotted the ring and asked, "Did you actually play for them, for the Bombers?" Gerry answered, "Yes, but that was a long long time ago." "Oh," she said, "that doesn't matter. It must have been fun and the ring is beautiful. Good for you, that's quite an accomplishment. You should be proud." As we walked out of the place I could see that he was a bit chuffed. Gerry is a complicated man but the simple things amuse and please him.

If someone does know he played ball or hockey and they encourage him to talk about his career, he'll usually come up with an anecdote or two about someone else. He'll tell you about the backup QB, Joe Zaleski, who, when called on to replace Indian Jack Jacobs, grabbed his helmet from where it sat next to the heater — the game was being played at around twenty below zero — pulled it over his balding head and almost roasted his brains. The helmet had turned into a small oven. Or he'll tell you the story about the same QB who, with only a quarter left to play, was sent in when Winnipeg was losing 42 to 0, stopped midway onto the field, ran back to the sidelines and asked Coach Trafton, a bit bashfully, if he wanted him to just tie the game or go all out for a victory?

If Gerry says something about himself he'll likely mention the time he shanked a kick so badly it ended up in the stands behind the visitor's bench. This happened when he was invited to perform the ceremonial kickoff at a Grey Cup playoff game. Or he might mention his one Stanley Cup playoff goal, one in a four-year career. Toronto was playing Detroit in the 1955 semi-finals and on one of his few shifts, Gerry blocked a Gordie Howe shot, broke away on the Detroit goal and scored on none other than "Mr. Goalie" himself, Glenn Hall. He recalls: "All the way down the ice I could hear Howe gaining on me, his skates making a unique rasping sound, probably from dragging his toes…and, yes, I put the puck past one of the great gentlemen of hockey."

Gerry's admiration for these two giants of hockey is understandable, but from the way he tells it, you would think he was the kid on the sidelines dreaming of what's possible. His gruff modesty is coloured by the image of a kid caught with his thumb in a homemade plum pie.

Occasionally I've been with him when he's met someone who played on an opposing team, often as a defensive lineman, and this former hulk will say something to Gerry, shake his hand and they'll chat about the "good old days." Later, when I ask Gerry about the person he's just met, he says, "I don't remember him. I never wanted to know the names of the people I was playing against. I didn't want to know anything about the person who was trying to stop me from scoring. I felt if I knew their name it somehow became personal and I didn't want that."

In spite of this comment, I've noticed one thing they all seem to share in common: none of these old players moves with ease. As someone has commented, in his heyday Gerry ran like a gazelle on the gridiron, but now he lurches about like a character from the Munsters. Years later, after many collisions on the field and the ice, the damage done to his joints has taken its toll.

So why the fuss? Why this book? What exactly did Gerry James accomplish in his eleven-year career in what has become the Canadian Football League (CFL), and his four-year career in the National Hockey League (NHL)? For those readers unfamiliar with this great sporting era or for those who might simply want a quick catalogue of Gerry James's achievements and who don't want to be bothered searching through the more important events of the man's life, here is a summary of his major sporting statistics and accomplishments.

In a letter dated February 28, 1952, Gerry was invited to summer camp by the Blue Bombers. He received this letter at the ripe old age of seventeen. They offered him fifty dollars a week, which he thought was pretty good; he would be getting paid to play one of his favorite sports. For a kid still in high school this was like winning the lottery. He figured that by the end of camp they would separate the wheat from the chaff, the big boys from the young, and he would be amongst the chaff. As it turned out, though, they kept him on and he became the youngest player ever to play in what was then called the Western Inter-provincial Football Union, the WIFU, later to become part of the CFL when it was formed in 1958.

During that first season, he and Tom Casey were used primarily to run back punts, Gerry maintaining a fairly respectable average of 9.9 yards and Casey an average of 10 yards per return. Gerry is quick to point out that this was in the days before blocking was allowed on returns, as if in some way this qualifies or lessens the achievement. In my view, it would make this particular statistic even more remarkable. Into the season, on October 13 of his rookie year, he was given the chance to play halfback against Saskatchewan. He scored two touchdowns in that game, nine days short of his eighteenth birthday.

By 1953, Gerry was beginning to show that he had something special to offer his team and the league. He was a clutch player. He would be instrumental in Winnipeg's triumph over Saskatchewan by a score of 60 - 23 in the two-game, total-point semi-final. In the second game of the Western best-of-three final against Edmonton, he was used primarily as a punt returner. He touched the ball five times: for 38, 35 and 9 yard returns. With a stiff wind behind him, he punted the ball 70 yards for a single point and near the end of the first half recovered a teammate's fumble. Not a bad day for a kid of eighteen. By winning the third game, Winnipeg earned the right to face Hamilton in the Grey Cup. In the 12 to 6 Grey Cup loss against the Tiger-Cats, Gerry scored Winnipeg's only touchdown, a touchdown set up by his own long kickoff return.

Inspired by the moniker of Gerry's dad — Eddie "Dynamite" James — the well-known sports announcer, "Cactus" Jack Wells, nicknamed Gerry, "Kid Dynamite." It was a nickname that would stick with him throughout his career, and rightly so. In what is obviously a rare occurrence, father and son would eventually end up side-by-side in the Canadian Football Hall of Fame. Although all of the honours Gerry has received are special, this may be the one that pleases him most.

During the 1954 season, the league established a Schenley award for the best non-import—an odd way of saying most outstanding Canadian—player in Canadian pro football. Gerry James was the first recipient of this award.

In the second game of the 1954 semi-finals against Saskatchewan, at a critical juncture in the game, he returned a kickoff eighty-seven yards for a touchdown, giving the Blue Bombers the lead in a two-game, total-point series they would go on to win 27 – 25. Edmonton would beat them in the final.

When he completed his football season that year, he went off to join the Toronto Marlboros in their quest for the Memorial cup, which they won in the spring of 1955, Gerry's final year as a junior. Over the next four years he played right wing with the Toronto Maple Leafs and competed in one Stanley Cup final. While he chuckles when he tallies his hockey stats for you—in 175 games he scored only 14 goals and had 27 assists—his love of the game shines through.

"I wasn't there to score goals," he'll tell you with a wry smile spreading across his face, "I was hired to defend," and, he will admit somewhat self-consciously, "I was an enforcer. At those two jobs, I was pretty good."

His smile broadens even further when he tells you how many penalty minutes he managed to tally. Even today his hands are big and rough and his knuckles gnarled. Mostly they are like this from tending his lush garden — he has a passion for ornamental grasses — but each hand is scarred with a memory or two of hockey brawls.

The following football season, the fall of 1955, proved to be one of Gerry's most successful and memorable. He rushed for 1205 yards and was named All-Western running back. But just as he was getting going, he had to stop. After signing a two-year contract, the Leafs demanded that he sit out the 1956 football season if he intended to play hockey.

By 1957 he had come to a new arrangement with the Leafs and he returned to play with the Blue Bombers. This may have been his greatest season. He again rushed for over 1000 yards, (1192 in fact) and, more significantly, he scored 18 rushing touchdowns, a record that stood for forty-three years. Finally, in 2000, one of the longest-standing records in the CFL was broken when Mike Pringle of the Montreal Alouettes carried the ball across the goal line 19 times. In a game devoted to the pass option, both men demonstrated how important the ground game is to a well-rounded offense. To add to his accomplishments, Gerry was also the league's scoring leader that year. At age 22, when most athletes are just graduating from university and preparing for their respective drafts, there was no question that Gerry James's name belonged in the football pantheon alongside Jackie Parker, Hal Patterson, Normie Kwong, Johnny Bright, Leo Lewis and Sam Etcheverry. To add to this claim, in 1957 Gerry was again honoured as the All-Western running back and, for the second time, with the Schenley Most Outstanding Canadian Award.

As any diehard Winnipeg Blue Bomber fan can tell you, from 1958 to 1962 were the glory years at Winnipeg Stadium. They were a genuine dynasty in sporting parlance. In four out of five seasons, in 1958, 1959, 1961 and 1962, under the guidance of Bud Grant, the team won four Grey Cups. Gerry James was a serious cog in that amazing football machine that included several greats: Kenny Ploen, Charley Shepard, Cornel Piper, Leo Lewis, Frank Rigney and Herb Gray, to name a few. Perhaps one of the most remarkable feats of that Bomber era, Gerry told me, was that through 1958, 1959 and into 1960, the Bombers won 25 straight road games.

"That's incredible," he said.

And it is, I reflect. Home field, after all, is supposed to

be an advantage to the home team. Obviously someone forgot to explain this theory to the Bombers. But if you know Gerry James and multiply his determination and intensity by several equally determined and intense teammates, you'll understand why such records are not surprising. Most importantly, Bud Grant knew how to exploit those qualities in his players.

As John Chaput wrote in his book *Saskatchewan Sports Legends*: "On September 6, 1958, in a Labour Day Weekend game at Winnipeg Stadium, Gerry James of the Winnipeg Blue Bombers caught a short option pass from fellow running back Leo Lewis and was tackled by Jack Hill of the Saskatchewan Roughriders after a six-yard gain. It looked like a routine collision until James remained on the grass with a broken tibia and fibula. Suddenly, one of the most amazing athletic careers in Canada was in jeopardy." While not career ending, this injury would slow Gerry down, but only slightly. He continued to compile impressive stats, win scoring titles, and play a major role in Winnipeg winning four Grey Cups. By the end of the 1962 season, though, Winnipeg had become more dependent on Leo Lewis for their running attack and Gerry was released.

The legacy of Gerry James or any other athlete cannot be summed up in a few numbers but for the record here they are: James rushed 995 times for 5,554 yards and scored a total of 645 points on 63 touchdowns, 143 converts, 40 field goals and 21 singles. It is important to note that until 1956, a touchdown was worth only 5 points.

Jude Kelly gave a more comprehensive summary of Gerry's career when he wrote a piece entitled **Secret** for the Yorkton paper.

There's a guy in town here and I'm sure many of you don't realize just how great a football player he was.

During his playing days they called him "Kid Dyna-mite," as his explosive moves left defensive players clutching air as he zigged and zagged his way to racking up over 18 Canadian Football League records.

That's right, 18 CFL standards.

Gerry James "was something else," according to my pops, Ellison Kelly, who knew a good gridder when he seen one. Dad told me Gerry James was the talk of the league during James' 11 seasons (10 with Winnipeg Blue Bombers, one with Saskatchewan Roughriders) in the league.

Using the 1984 CFL official record manual as my source, I spotted James' name dotting the pages of the 180 page booklet so many times I wondered why he hasn't got a street or a park named after him like all the other great stars of other sports.

Elected to the Canadian Football Hall of Fame Jan. 5, 1981, "Kid Dynamite" could also do other things with the football besides rush with it.

Did you know James owns CFL career playoff records for kicking converts, field goals and single points?

"I was pressed into service," James laughs explaining his kicking abilities. "Nobody else wanted to do it."

Among his other accomplishments, James led the CFL in scoring in 1957 with 131 points, the same year he wrote the book on rushing touchdowns, with 18. He was also western conference scoring leader in 1960, with 114 points, one point back of Toronto's Kent (Cookie) Gilchrist.

Did James feel he was a standout player back then?

"Oh sure," he says modestly, "I knew I was good. I was play-ing with some pretty good teams and had some great blocking."

Although the great George Reed owns virtually every rushing record to date, Gerry James was no slouch in that department, either.

Twice a member of the CFL's 1000 yard club, James also rushed for 10 100-yard games with the Blue Bombers.

It was during playoffs, however, that the 6'-0" 190 pound halfback was at his best. It seemed James performed better under the gun as his seven playoff records will attest. Among others, he's seventh on the all-time playoff rushing list carrying the ball 202 times. He's 11th in total playoff rushing with 799 yards and his 74 yard gallop back in 1961 is the 5th best ever in playoff action.

"I was pretty lucky in the playoffs," James says as he recalls the 1962 Grey Cup game against Hamilton in which he was successful on all four of his convert attempts while Hamilton's Don Sutherin missed twice allowing Winnipeg to escape with a 28 – 27 victory.

"That was the difference."

James played in six Grey Cup games, winning four, and not only that he found time when he wasn't on the field to play pro hockey with Toronto Maple Leafs of the National Hockey League.

He toiled with the Leafs for four seasons during the winter months.

The highlight, perhaps, of James' football-hockey career came in 1959 – 60 when he played in the Grey Cup game and the Stanley Cup finals just five months apart. Something which had never been done before and likely never will again.

But football was his sport. James won the Schenley Award twice ('54, '57) for most outstanding Canadian.

The oft-controversial James even has a separate footnote devoted exclusively to him in the CFL record book.

It says: "Gerry (Kid Dynamite) James is the only player in the history of the Schenley Awards program to win one of the awards the first year it was presented (1954 Most Outstanding Canadian Player) and then win that award again (1957) during his career."

My dad was right. Gerry James was "something else."

After the 1962 season and feeling a need for change, Gerry decided to explore a career in agriculture and enrolled in St. Paul's College at the University of Manitoba. He did well in four out of his five subjects but he had some "difficulty" with physics. While the idea of tilling the land had enormous appeal, he couldn't quite see the relationship of physics to agriculture. He couldn't reconcile what seemed to him incomprehensible abstract theories with growing acres of wheat or running a dairy farm. Ironically the programme dropped physics as a prerequisite the following year. But by this time, Gerry had moved on. Even today he has a surplus of energy that needs to be satisfied by direction, by purpose. Otherwise he feels adrift. In part, this explains his focus and determination on the gridiron and the ice.

During the summer of 1963, when he sensed that his football career was on the wane, Gerry went to Davos, Switzerland, as player-coach for Hockey Club Davos, the renowned team in the Swiss first division and the home of the Spengler Cup. While this was not a wholly satisfying experience — the team did not perform as he or the owners expected, largely because many of the best Swiss players were called up to perform National Service — he did get a taste for coaching, a job he fell in love with.

In 1964 he returned to Canada and signed on with the Saskatchewan Roughriders, but with nagging knee problems—after each game team physicians needed to drain fluid off his knee — he was unable to perform at a level that pleased him or, for that matter, the team. "In a league that was always trying to juggle and balance imports and home bodies," Gerry explained, "they saw this as an opportunity to fill my spot with another Canadian. Rightfully so." After half a season and as a veteran of eleven years in the Canadian Football League, Gerry James, age 29, shifted his attention to hockey. Years of double duty had taken their toll.

Following his experience in Davos, Gerry was keen to try coaching full time. While he maintains that coaching and playing at the same time are almost impossible to do if you want to achieve a balance between consistency and fairness, he took on both roles with the Yorkton Terrier seniors, a team that topped the league four times and won three provincial titles. After this success he then moved on and coached junior hockey in Yorkton, Melville, Estevan and Moose Jaw. He was voted all-star coach seven times in the Saskatchewan Junior Hockey league.

He was also instrumental in setting up the first bursary system for scholarships in the SJHL. "I wanted kids to know that education was as important to them as their hockey." For a man who went straight from high school to professional sports, this was an important admission. When I asked him "why", he looked at me as if I were as dumb as a common post.

"Because, while playing sports is exciting, is a rush," he answered, "it will never be enough to fill your life. I wish I could have convinced all the kids' parents that this is the case. People tend to be blinkered by the sport's pot-of-gold, especially these days. When I played, it was a living, nothing more. The big bucks still lay off in the distance. One year, when I was in New York with the Leafs, I had a meeting with the New York Giants. They offered me a contract but they paid less in those days than I could earn in the CFL. While there might have been more fame or recognition with an NFL club, the idea of dislocating my family for essentially the same wage didn't make sense."

I think Gerry would have been a sensation in a league where the running game was premium.

This brings me to the last Gerry James short-order stat, his work coaching Special Olympians, a responsibility he took on with considerable joy and pleasure until 1996-97.

"They were always eager to play and eager to please," he said. "We treated them the same way as we treated other athletes and they responded very well. They put everything into it. They didn't hold anything back. And they were always on time. I liked that and their enthusiasm."

These days, Marg, his wife, drags Gerry along to the soup kitchen at the Salvation Army once a week and every Christmas he stands outdoors for a couple of weeks during the afternoon rush hour at a Petro Canada station on the main island highway, attending to his Salvation Army kettle. He cajoles, insults, berates, flatters, and embarrasses, whatever works, anyone and everyone to give a donation. Sometimes you wonder if the ex-football/hockey player masquerading as Santa Claus might not lose it and tackle or board some unsuspecting citizen to mine their wallet or purse. This is unlikely though — Kid Dynamite has a heart of gold. Who would have thought?

When I asked Gerry about his dual career he said, "I played in the days before the big money in sports and I looked at it as a way to support my family. Marg and I had three children by the time I signed to play two sports, and our family kept growing. I think I had a certain amount of leverage to negotiate better contracts, too, because I was playing two sports. I played one sport against the other. And I'd have to say that I was probably the last athlete in Canada to do it. The seasons are longer now in both football and hockey and the shift from one sport to the other wouldn't be as easy. The seasons overlap too much." In a rather massive understatement, he went on to say, "I doubt the clubs would allow it anymore anyway."

Dick Duff, one of his teammates on the Leafs, once asked Gerry how he, Duff, could earn more money and Gerry, always quick with a response, said, "Learn how to play football, Dick."

Gerry James, I think, has always delighted in the little ironies that are so much a part of all of our lives. I'm sure he enjoyed telling Duff to turn over a new leaf.

This is the bare bones of Gerry James's career, but what he has to say about his teammates, today's athletes, and about professional sport in general is intriguing. He knows this world inside out. While he can be quite forthcoming and forthright, he can also be enigmatic, not because he wants to be coy but because he is genuinely modest. He is straight and he is honest, sometimes brutally so. I don't think the word discretion exists in his vocabulary. At times this can lead to embarrassing moments, not only for those at the other end of a barb, but for Gerry himself. One could say that he does not tiptoe anywhere, least of all through and around social conventions. He also has little time for those who live in the past. Every day has too much to offer for him to sit back and dwell on past accomplishments. In a way I think he sees that backward glance as an indulgence, as a form of self pity, and he abhors self pity. It is a weakness. He would rather celebrate life.

2 / First Meeting

Gerry and I first met on the practice putting green at Fairwinds Golf Club, located in Nanoose Bay, BC. Since then, for the past ten years or so, he and I have played golf on a weekly basis.

At that first meeting I showed up for what I thought was a scheduled round of golf only to be told by the group I expected to play with, a group known as "The Legends" by members of the club, that they already had two foursomes and I was not included. One member of the group took me aside and, in a rather condescending fashion, told me that I was a spare for the group and I couldn't expect to play with them on a regular basis. Only when one of the long-standing members was unavailable would they consider inviting me in as a replacement. I had just retired and, he whispered, I couldn't expect to be included in their draw. I had to earn my stripes. For a moment, I thought I was being interviewed for acceptance into some sort of top secret society — would there be initiation rites, a secret handshake, vows of silence, perhaps even clandestine manoeuvres whereby we discovered pin placements in advance of other members of the club? Then it struck me to ask why in god's name had one of them invited me to join them in the first place?

"Mistake, it had been a mistake," he said, looking around to see who was listening. Someone had obviously thought they were one player short. He would speak to that person and make sure this sort of thing did not happen in the future. As I recall, Gerry overheard this conversation and invited me to play with his gang; they were only a three-some. He chuckled as he talked and generally seemed quite amused by the way I had been treated; or dressed down.

At first, I think Gerry was a tad annoyed by the name "The Legends" had given themselves and I think he wanted to make a point about their self-proclaimed status. At this stage, I was pleased to have his support. As we moved about the green, awaiting our tee-time, he took a few potshots at the Legend who had taken me aside. Most of Gerry's shots missed the target as The Legend dodged about the green like an old, broken-down running back doing his best to avoid us. In addition, as I recall, he might have been partially deaf. The image of the three of us hobbling about the green, at-tempting to look casual, still strikes me as amusing if not a bit pathetic.

What I did not realize at the time is that I would become known to Gerry's group as "the spare," a nickname he took some delight in giving me but one, thankfully, which as the season wore on the other two found tiresome. Gerry per-sisted until he, too, grew weary of the game and the name. Besides, he had moved on to other more immediate subjects for his derision. Our swings. Our putting strokes. Our dress. Our violations of golf etiquette (but only when it affected his swing or putt). He got particularly annoyed when some-one stood on or near his sight lines. We were relieved when he directed his thunderbolts at something or someone else, such as a news item he'd heard or some ridiculous decision by the golf club's management. These were frequent enough to keep him fully occupied.

The most upset I have seen him is when the then man-ager of the club demanded Gerry remove the large, beauti-ful grass specimens he had on display on his property along the edge of the golf course. A few of these exquisite plants crossed the boundary between the two parcels of land, but none of them interfered with play in any way. After Gerry had proposed a couple of reasonable compromises, the manager showed up on his doorstep, letter in hand, and demanded all the offending plants be removed. Or else. Gerry was given a strict time-line for their removal or he would face legal action. Well, this incident confirmed two things I already knew about Gerry: one — as on the golf course so in other aspects of his life — he would abide by the rules, no matter how silly they were; and two, he did what he had to do with bullish resolve. The request was stupid and the day sad.

Since the removal of these plants — their flowers or seed heads no longer showing the wary golfer the shape of the wind — that six to ten foot area on both sides of the property line, tended by no one, looks like a wasteland, a rock pit. What, I wondered at the time, was why this wasn't happening elsewhere on the course where clearly the separation between private property and golf course had been breached. Somehow the issue had become personal. I think it might have had something to do with the wording on the "Keep Off" sign Gerry had nailed to one of the trees on the front of his property where golfers often strayed in search of their balls and from where they often even hit their ball. The fact is, Gerry employed slightly more colourful epithets than a warning against trespass, but sometimes these wayward golfers were twenty feet off the course, well beyond the out-of-bounds markers. Not only did they think it was their right to propel their ball back onto the course from the middle of Gerry's and Marg's garden, but often, in a fit of temper, they'd also take a wide swath of Rhododendron or azalea in the process.

Of course, whether friend or foe, if Gerry were to catch

you taking a mighty swing, a "colorful" verbal assault would rain down from the deck above. No doubt, some were upset by the foul tongue of the buffoon who spoke from his perch in the sky. Blind to the out-of-bounds markers and keen to retrieve their expensive ball, these black sheep would stumble about and bleat some incomprehensible excuse back at him.

Since our first encounter on the practice green and over the years, I have learned that Gerry gets some perverse pleasure from giving people a hard time, from "sticking it to them," and while on occasion his persistence can test anyone's patience, he does finally get the message and know when to stop. Mind you, he stores away whatever it was that got under your skin for future use, and he can unleash these barbed insults on you in the most absurd moments, for the strangest reasons — usually when he has been caught out himself or feels he has "lost" in some way. If this is a sample of the sort of trash talking he practised on the field or on the ice, then ultimately it is harmless. A little uncivilized perhaps, but innocuous, if not meaningless. This said, his verbal jousting can be a lot of fun, if not a little annoying. This is his goal, of course, and you can see where it would have annoyed the hell out of his opposition in all the sports in which he participated.

When we were finally called to the tee the day we met, I was none the wiser about Gerry James. Frankly, if I had heard his name while I was growing up in Vancouver, which I'm sure I must have, it hadn't registered. Certainly, I would not have been a Bomber fan. Like most males of my age raised in Vancouver, I followed the BC Lions and, from week to week, I knew where they were in the standings and who played for them. This knowledge belonged in the standard survival package. I remembered the names of Jim Carphin, Pat Claridge, Ted Hunt (he was my favourite rugby player), Willie Fleming, Joe Kapp and By Bailey, to name a few, and

I knew a few players from other CFL teams — in particular Jackie Parker who owned a pool hall in downtown Vancouver even though he played for Edmonton — but Gerry James didn't belong on my limited CFL roster, either then or as we were about to tee off.

I was drifting into my teens when football arrived on the west coast and I was more interested in well-established sports like rugby, lacrosse and soccer, even cricket. While I knew Empire Stadium was where the football teams played, in my imagination the stadium remained primarily the site of the Commonwealth games and the home of the Miracle Mile, the duel between Bannister and Landy, and the amazing marathon finish of Jim Peters. It was difficult for me to visualize the grass field inside the cinder track at Empire Stadium as a football field.

The picture of the British official grabbing Peters as he struggled toward the finish line still remained vividly in my mind. I think both men thought he had crossed the line but poor Peters was so dehydrated on that hot day, my eleventh birthday, he had no idea where he was. Sadly, he was so far out in front of his competitors he could have taken a nap. Unfortunately Peters was disqualified because he received assistance before finishing the race. Ironically, it was subsequently learned that the course was 27 miles long and that Peters had in fact completed the official distance and therefore the race. Peters was later presented with a special medal struck by the Duke of Edinburgh to commemorate his valiant run.

But seeing the field being used for football took a long time for me to register and accept. When Gerry later told me how poor the field was to play on, like a bog he remarked, I was disappointed. Certainly some of the shine disappeared from my personal memories of this important Vancouver landmark.

On that first meeting, as Gerry and I walked towards the tee, he introduced me to the other two members of the day's foursome, Bruce Wylie (who still belongs to the group) and Peter Turner (who has since been replaced by Peter Brooks). Immediately the gauntlet was thrown down. We would be playing for twenty-five cents for each nine and twenty-five cents for the eighteen. That's right, we would be competing, and this is the operative word, for the grand total of seventy-five cents—times three if you lost all three matches. It would be medal play, simple and straightforward. Not big stakes, at all. Gerry made it very clear that he preferred it that way. Being the newcomer I was happy to go along with whatever wager made the others feel comfortable.

That first round began under a partially cloudy sky and ended on the eighteenth hole in brilliant sunshine, the sort of sunshine you get occasionally on the west coast which gives an extra edge of clarity to everything around you; which makes everything look as though it's backlit. The sky was an intense, vibrant, cerulean blue against which the green of the trees seemed surreal. Everything had a glow about it. But mostly what I noted before we walked off the eighteenth green that glorious day was the dynamics of the group.

The banter was endless and spirited. Peter Turner liked to review every game he'd watched over the weekend — and that was most of them. In addition to weekly golf tournaments, we were in the middle of what seemed like interminable hockey and basketball playoffs. The boys of winter do-si-doed around the boys of summer. Peter wasn't interested in what Bruce or I thought about a game, if we'd seen it, but he solicited Gerry's opinion on every controversial play. When I interjected what I thought was an insightful observation, it was dismissed, which I have to confess after a few holes began to miff me. What was I, chopped liver? Bruce was too busy in the bushes looking for his stray ball to notice. His disposition is such that he would not have cared in any case.

At some stage, Peter finally made it clear why my opinion mattered not a pinch. As we walked together up a fairway — Gerry and Bruce were in the wilds, in amongst the broom, brambles and salal — he finally asked me if I knew who Gerry was.

I had to admit, "No, not really. Should I," I asked?

"Hey," he said, "Gerry James," as if this were self-explanatory. "He played for the Winnipeg Blue Bombers and the Toronto Maple Leafs, at the same time! In Grey Cups and Stanley Cups, for god's sake!"

What planet had I been living on, he seemed to be asking?

For the second time that day I felt inappropriately chastised. Later in the round when I questioned Gerry about what Peter had told me, he seemed more reticent or annoyed than anything. He confirmed that, yes, he had played for both teams, but that was it. He clammed up.

I decided I would get the lowdown from my wife when I got home. In her teens she had been a Winnipeg Blue Bomber fan, largely because her parents had been Edmonton Eskimo fans. The corollary for this might be when we are driving and I suggest we take the next exit, she invariably continues on. Presumably there is logic here, by the way, with which I still struggle.

Overall, I liked the group and hoped they would invite me to play with them again. Peter enjoyed talking, Bruce was totally caught up in his game, Gerry was the master of the occasional crude one-liner and I fell in the middle somewhere.

Our skill levels ran the full gamut. Bruce had a swing longer than John Daly's, a swing that took the club head well past his ankles, well past three hundred and sixty degrees, into the realm of a second rotation. We all shook our heads and looked elsewhere when Bruce swung. I was in awe. I would hurt myself with that sort of swing. If I didn't tie myself in knots, I would most certainly need some form of medical assistance later.

Peter, on the other hand, had a beautiful swing, smooth and clinically picture-perfect. His timing and tempo were pro-like. And he knew it. His shades were the perfect complement to his swing. He was also left-handed which made his swing impossible to imitate.

Gerry played like a lot of hockey players. He could swing, as the cliché goes, inside a phone booth. If you blinked, you missed his swing. His swing was really a slap shot, short, quick, beautifully timed, and, for its length, powerful. It was mostly arms, probably because the rest of him couldn't make any sort of turn. He usually hit the ball straight but not very long. While he couldn't make most par four and five greens in regulation, he was a deadly chipper and putter. When he parred a hole, Peter would call it a Gerry James par which I was convinced Gerry took as a put-down while I think Peter intended it as a compliment. If Gerry made a par after someone else had hit a particularly long drive and then messed up their chip or missed their putt, Gerry would razz them ceaselessly with, "Good drive though. A really good drive," he would repeat. "Great drive. You can sure hit that ball a long way but...." And if he won the hole, he would sing, "Cream, cream always rises to the top." This was my first inkling that Gerry was competitive with a capital C.

At the end of that first round I was to learn just how competitive Gerry James could be. The four of us shook hands and stood off to the side of the green while Peter tallied up the scores and calculated who owed how much to whom. Gerry was the loser and owed me under a dollar. I wasn't prepared for what happened next. He reached into his pocket, hauled out some change, removed what he owed me, and flung it on the ground. Then he turned and shuffled off without a word, back down the eighteenth fairway, toward his house. While the others took little notice of this display, I was gobsmacked. As he walked away, I thought, what a first-class a-hole. Who needs that? What a poor sport, a sore loser, I thought.

In spite of this, I joined the group, and over the next few weeks I saw that, for Gerry, there were moments of joy — he won money — and moments of borderline angst — he lost money. In one sense, he measured his skill level on any given day against the amount of money he won or lost, but on a more fundamental level, he simply hated to lose. The money was purely symbolic. Slowly it dawned on me that competition was what drove the man. I realized two things: love of the game was important, but "winning" was his creed and obsession. If he didn't win, clouds formed and you could almost see them gather over his head, like they did over Joe Btfsplk in *Lil Abner*.

From others I learned bits and pieces about Gerry's career, especially from those who admired what he had achieved. While Bruce respected what Gerry had done, he seemed otherwise indifferent. For Peter, on the other hand, his response to Gerry seemed almost a form of adulation. While I thought that perhaps he was a little over-zealous, I respected the whys and wherefores of his deference. I picked up very little information about his careers directly from Gerry himself; he refused to talk about what he considered his past. For the most part, he seemed stuck in the moment, intent on his golf game.

In those early days of our acquaintance, Gerry spent hours on the practice green, hunched over a chip or putt. Often, when others turned up to practice, he would challenge them to a putt or chip off. Even in a heavy west coast downpour, he seemed the happiest of men bent over an eight foot putt. I was quick to learn that this sort of focus was characteristic of the man. He was intent on becoming a better chipper and putter — anything that would improve his game and give him the upper hand in the competition of the moment; and the new competition was not football or hockey but golf. I realized that everything he did, whether it was golfing, gardening, exercising, or dieting, was done with the same degree of intensity.

Towards the middle of August, Gerry and Marg hosted a dinner for our new foursome and their spouses. My wife, Pat, was looking forward to this occasion, partly to demonstrate to Gerry her football knowledge but, in particular, her Bomber knowledge. We were lounging on the deck, eight of us, when Pat suddenly said, "You know Gerry, I was a Winnipeg fan in the early 1960s when I was growing up in Edmonton — my parents were Eskimo fans, of course, so I couldn't root for them — and I remember Kenny Ploen, Leo Lewis, Cornel Piper, Farrel Funston, Ernie Pitts and, of course, Bud Grant. And my favourite player, Charlie Shepard. But I don't remember your name. I don't remember a Gerry James." And then in a voice that betrayed a hint of apology and considerable confidence, she said, "Sorry."

Gerry looked back at her. After a prolonged and, I have to say, embarrassingly uncomfortable silence, perhaps for me more than anyone else, all of us waiting for him to snap back at her, he said, "Charlie was my roommate when we were on the road. He was the punter, I was the kicker."

Then he said nothing more. A few moments of awkwardness followed, Pat laughed uncomfortably and had the good sense to keep quiet. Conversations resumed. At some point Gerry slipped unnoticed indoors and when he returned and sat down, it took a short time before we all realized that he was wearing a Bomber's jersey with his number, 28, and his name on it. As our laughter died down, he said, "When I first started playing my number was 98 but then they changed the rules so that it would be easier for the referees to identify positions by number."

He looked directly at Pat and said, "You do recognize the jersey?"

She nodded and left well enough alone, thankfully.

Surprisingly, after one rotation around the social wheel, we were all invited back to Gerry's and Marg's for another delicious dinner. I knew by then that at least two desserts, one a pie, preferably raisin, would likely top off the feast. What I didn't anticipate was Pat revisiting her previous *faux pas*.

Mid-way through the evening, when everyone had consumed enough of Gerry's homemade libation to be feeling warm and charitable, Pat said, "I've been thinking, Gerry, and I do remember your name. I remember now. Leo Lewis would carry the ball all the way down the field, and then you would take it the final yard for the touchdown. You see, I do remember."

Whether or not it was the alcohol, she looked around somewhat bewildered by the response this revelation was receiving. We all sat in stunned silence, wondering what Gerry would say. He was quick, I have to admit, saying, "One-yard James, that's what you're calling me? One-yard James."

Pat, realizing her blunder, her indiscretion, a bit too late, muttered, "Well, yes. I'm sorry, but that's what I remember."

At least by this stage we had established to Pat's satisfaction that Gerry had indeed played for her favourite Bombers. Gerry seemed satisfied with this little success, although for some time, with a certain doggedness whenever in Pat's company, he would refer to himself as "One-yard James."

Ironically, a few years later, at yet another social gathering at the James' household, Pat pulled a newspaper clipping out of her purse and handed it to Gerry. "I found this in one of my old scrapbooks, Gerry, from a 1961 edition of the *Vancouver Sun*, when the Bombers won the Grey Cup.

It has a photograph of you and the article makes it sound as though you won the game almost single handedly. All these years that article has been sitting amongst my memorabilia. Had I only known."

Gerry accepted the gift and indirect apology gracefully, much to everyone's surprise. But then, after the event, was it so surprising?

Most interesting people are a mass of contradictions. The running back who didn't want to know the names of his opponents, the thugs on the other side of the line, is complicated. The man who played two sports in which he was so dependent on his teammates to guard his back fears intimacy. On the one hand, he has to appear ruthless, like a warrior or gladiator, on the other he is horrified when he sees a woman's face cut up by a wayward puck. He copes by being honest to a fault, which invariably leaves him open to disappointment. Oh yes, he can be a jerk, but there is a side that is perceptive and, perhaps, dare I say it, sensitive. I can feel Gerry cringe at such a charge.

By the end of the season, shortly after the golf club's annual Rye Door Cup matches, we all decided that friendship was more important than competition and all bets were off. Gerry noticeably relaxed. By this time I was beginning to understand that in addition to his raw athletic ability, his will to win combined with his inexplicable desire to compete at everything, in many ways defined him as person. He told me once that he refused to play cards because he hated to lose.

I know it's a sports cliché, but Gerry's most serious competition is himself. Quietly he can and does beat up on and berate himself, more than anyone else. This may be why Marg is both his biggest critic and his most devoted fan. She has learned to walk that tightrope between scorn and praise with the agility of a world-class gymnast; she knows how important it is to keep Gerry in balance.

In a way, he gardens with the same tenacity, obviously not to win but to be the best he can be and to know as much as he can possibly know. Thus he reads voraciously about grasses and regularly consults a couple, Dale and Kathy Olson, who run a nearby nursery devoted to grasses. When I've visited the nursery in his company, he will hobble around after Dale, asking him questions, giving him advice, challenging him, ribbing him, always in search of some new tidbit of knowledge. Kathy, happily, has a special gift; she knows exactly when to pull Gerry's chain and delights in his jesting. On the serious side, both once commented that they had never seen so many ornamental grasses in one garden, so beautifully laid out and tended. At the core, everything Gerry does receives this sort of attention and commitment.

Yes, Gerry James is obsessed, perhaps because he fears rebuke or rejection. Or perhaps because belonging is a form of self-definition and proving himself to himself at the highest level is an antidote to alienation. Perhaps this explains why in his mid-seventies he probes a universe of ideas through a world of books that almost passed him by because athletics dominated his early life.

3 / Early Years

Edwin Fitzgerald (Gerry) James was born on October 22, 1934, in Regina, Saskatchewan. Most articles and books that refer to Gerry get his name wrong; they refer to him as Gerald Edwin James. But his first name is Edwin, after his father, and his second name is Fitzgerald, his mother's maiden name. He expresses surprise when people who write about him don't at least get his name correct. Many spell Gerry with a "J".

Shortly after his birth, his parents, along with his brother, four years his senior, moved to Winnipeg, to be near other members of the family. In particular they would be close to Charles, his paternal grandfather, his Aunt Lil, and his Uncle Percy and Aunt Bessie, all of whom would have a major impact on Gerry's early years.

Strangely and inexplicably, Gerry spent the first year of his life in the care of his Aunt Irene and Uncle Brian who lived in Broadview, Saskatchewan. Uncle Brian was from the maternal, Fitzgerald clan. Years later his Aunt Irene, a tall, buxom blonde, would wow the entire Blue Bomber team when she turned out, dressed to the nines, to greet Gerry and cheer him on as the team travelled through Broadview, a main terminus for the train, on their way to a game in Regina. This was in August of 1952 — Gerry's first road trip. When his teammates asked Gerry who the gorgeous woman was who had just planted a big sloppy kiss on his cheek,

Gerry, aged seventeen, ducked his head, looked pleadingly at Tom Casey for help, and then blurted out that she was his aunt. The reply caused a major uproar. Of course she was, of course, that lovely, tall, long-legged, sexy woman was his aunt, they teased. Who else? "Your aunt," they repeated while shaking their heads, all the way to Regina.

But in November of 1934, Gerry was quite unceremoniously "dropped off" in Broadview as the rest of his family headed east across the chilly prairie landscape to Winnipeg. Why he was placed in the care of these relations was never explained, although Gerry speculates that it was to enable his father and mother to build the family a new home, free from the worry of child care, either on the James' family acreage on the edge of the city or somewhere nearby. Grandfather Charles, Gerry was to learn later, was a bit of a control freak; he insisted on having the entire family living close at hand. Whatever his other motives might have been, there is no question that the tribe's safety and security came first and that the family lived at the centre of his heart.

Understandably, Gerry has no memories of his first couple of years, but can there be any doubt that this immediate separation from his family, his mother in particular, had serious ramifications for the infant Gerry James? Certainly it had a long-term impact on his competitive relationship with his older brother, Don. It might explain why Gerry feels that his Grandfather Charles always seemed to prefer Don to him, although Gerry is quick to point out that his grandfather was kind and generous towards both of them. But clearly Don had an advantage as the first grandchild to take up a position on the old man's radar. It might also explain why Gerry James is so determined to prove himself. When you think you are playing second fiddle in a two-piece orchestra, you can be driven to try to play your way to first.

The move to Winnipeg was made in the middle of the

depression when food was scarce. Luckily his Grandfather Charles owned an egg farm and had a large vegetable garden. This garden kept them all well fed, not only through the latter days of the depression but throughout the war. The garden plot was bountiful, filled with every conceivable vegetable, from cabbages to peas, from beans to lettuce, plus tomatoes, cucumbers, carrots, radishes, beets, onions, spinach, turnips, squash, and hills of new potatoes — still one of Gerry's favourite foods — everything a garden can provide. Fruit trees abounded — apple, pear, plum, cherry — alongside rows of raspberries. All found their way into preserves for the winter months. It's interesting to reflect on the extent of self-sufficiency in a time of extreme hardship.

The house itself, with its two verandas, piano and stately wooden banister, was two stories plus an attic, an impressive old wooden structure that stood like a fortress against the frigid Manitoban winters.

At Christmas the entire family gathered in the living room of the massive old house, where a huge, decorated tree reached to the full height of the twelve foot, sculpted-tin ceiling. It was a festive occasion which Gerry recollects as a merry time for everyone. Only years later did he learn that his Aunt Lillian, who always seemed to wear a happy and contented face, had broken off her engagement, the marriage ceremony imminent, at the insistence of his Grandfather Charles. Grandfather Charles's wife, Lil's mom, had died and the old man needed someone to care for him; someone to look after the house and cook his meals. For the rest of her life, Lil toiled for her father, the uncompromising patriarch of the James clan. When the old man died, she stayed on in the house, knowing no other life. Poor Aunt Lil died a spinster, spending her last days roaming the many empty rooms of the large house that had lost its purpose. She never complained, never uttered a word against Grandfather Charles, but Gerry wonders to what degree her parental devotion was voluntary. His grandfather could be incredibly persuasive if not intimidating.

The portrait Gerry paints of his grandfather is one of a complicated man, some would suggest cold and rigid, more a product of the 19th century than the 20th, but he was also compassionate and caring. He was a man who enjoyed the company of children. Gerry was always happy to join his grandfather on his egg delivery runs into the city, outings which inevitably ended with a treat. While his grandfather never played games, he would idle away an afternoon watching Gerry pretend he was the master of a defunct old tractor that rested and rusted on the back lawn. Man and boy imagined the fields they ploughed, heard gears shifted, listened to an engine purr as smoothly as a sleeping cat — Gerry providing all of the necessary sound effects. Boy and man merged into an imaginary world where age mattered not a hoot.

On another occasion, Gerry recalled finding a crow's nest with four chicks huddled down in amongst the twigs, bark, animal hair and moss. When he asked his grandfather if he could turn one into a pet, perhaps train it, his grandfather said yes, but they would have to cut out the bird's tongue. He wasn't about to be bothered listening to a bird cawing all day and into the night. Unfortunately, while his grandfather was performing the surgery he held the bird too tightly and strangled it and the pet crow project came to a quick and macabre end. Both Gerry and Grandfather Charles were devastated by the experience and today Gerry wonders why he wanted to take a perfectly happy wild bird and cage it for his own pleasure.

For Gerry, climbing into the attic of the old wood-frame house, in amongst the head-bumping rafters, was one of his favourite pastimes, and rummaging amongst all the keepsakes that had been stored away there was an endless source of entertainment. These objects were the family heirlooms, the bits and pieces of past lives that were being saved to pass along to the next generations. For a young boy it was a place to escape to, to avoid chores, but Gerry also spent plenty of time looking through boxes of old photographs, letters, and books. He could wile away a summer afternoon up there, lost in the plot of a good book or daydreaming about the lives of the people whose faces filled the photographs. Those photographs were a map to his past. Where had his family come from and how had they ended up in Winnipeg?

Oddly, what leaps to his mind today most vividly is all the lamps that were stored away up there, along with other old furniture. The attic was also a repository for junk, "stuff" that someone had decided was no longer needed. When Gerry was eleven, squirrels moved in and over one winter they chewed through everything, creating such a dirty and untidy clutter that his hideaway was no longer inviting. Feathers from old quilts covered the place. One of his favourite haunts had become a smelly and filthy mess.

Marg, who helped clean out the attic when the big old house was sold years later, testifies to the mess the squirrels had made. But what caught her attention, she says, were the old clothes, the family Bible — which unfortunately Gerry gave away — and a settee with a framed photograph of four people standing behind it. Definitely turn of the century, she says. Were these images of Gerry's grandparents? Who knows? Perhaps the most interesting things were the boxes of financial records. Father and daughter had saved every bill they had ever paid. It was an astonishing record of survival from the early part of the century, through the depression into the post-war period, but no historical society was interested in it at the time and letters, records, bills, clothes, photos, books, all ended up in the dump. Marg remembers a couple of truckloads rumbling away from the house down the road, an ancestral record heading towards oblivion. Sad but true.

By contrast, the white clapboard house his father and mother built in the Sir John Franklin district, a modest place at 570 Beaverbrook Street, in the four-square-block area between the Canadian National (CN) and Canadian Pacific (CP) tracks on the western outskirts of Winnipeg, was tiny, especially for a family of four. It was about seven or eight hundred square feet, Gerry guesses, including the sun porch. The house had one bedroom, a living room, dining room, bathroom and kitchen. Even though there was a furnace in the basement, the only really warm room in the house during the deep freeze months was the kitchen, and it was warm because they turned on all the stove elements and oven and hung a blanket between the living room and kitchen to hold in the warmth. While their father was away, the kitchen was where Gerry and his brother dressed and undressed and huddled to fend off the winter cold.

Gerry claims that his absolute favourite memory was taking a bath. "A simple bath, can you imagine?" he asks. "Warmth is a precious thing, an almighty luxury, especially for someone who grew up on the prairies. Soaking in the tub was the only time I felt really warm. You'd take a bath," he says, "and then run like a jackrabbit back to the kitchen.

"I'm told we were poor," he continues, "but it didn't seem that way at the time. We had all the vegetables we needed from my grandfather — I'm not sure what we would have done without his contribution — and my mother worked. She was also a fantastic cook. For extra income she baked cinnamon rolls, topped with swirls of icing, and hot cross buns, butter rich, which my brother and I were told not to touch, an almost impossible command, and then she sold them out from under us to the neighbours."

The aromas still lurk in his memory and today whenever he sees cinnamon rolls or hot cross buns amongst the baked goods, the scents ambush his taste buds.

As with most families during the depression, food was always an issue. His mother bought the cheapest meats — liver, heart, tongue, kidneys — for pennies a pound, cuts which some would consider delicacies, but which Gerry hated. "I would gag at first swallow," he says, "and I still do, although curiously I don't mind their scent when they're cooking. But the texture, once the meat is in my mouth, turns my stomach. Fortunately we had two dogs, Oscar and Skipper, and as the cliché image goes, after a couple of hours sitting at table, my plate would be clean and the dogs sleeping contentedly in front of the stove. Every country boy needed his best friend."

Gerry's own occasional offering to the family feast during the winter months was rabbit. He found an old clothesline and unraveled the wires to make snares. He then developed his own trap line, an idea he either picked up from his grandfather or, more likely, from the folklore that was in general circulation around the neighbourhood. He would set the loops along the paths left by the rabbits in the bushes at the back of the house and hope they would run into them, which they did. His method was a bit primitive but did the job. "The improvised snares worked perfectly." Often his prey was still alive when he got to them and he recalls the trapped rabbits crying like newborn babies, an eerie and disturbing sound, which almost turned him off the hunt. But he was hungry and his mother made delicious rabbit stew, a special treat.

For the first few years in the clapboard house, his brother slept alone on a hideaway bed in the living room while Gerry slept on a cot in his parent's bedroom, until his father's return at the end of the war. After his father's safe homecoming, Don was forced to share his hideaway bed with Gerry during the winter months. In late spring, much to everyone's relief, when it was finally warm enough, Gerry was moved to his cot out on the screened-in porch. During the months they had to sleep together, the brothers did everything conceivable to make each other's life and sleep miserable. While his parents hoped that separate sleeping arrangements would provide peace and quiet for themselves as well as for the two warring factions — with a sort of DMZ or "firewall" zone between the two — according to Gerry, brother Don was quick to take advantage of his parents' attempts to create a neutral space. He did everything he could to provoke his younger brother. He would hide out and attack Gerry from behind. He would get his school chums to tease Gerry.

All of these failed attempts to bring peace between the two brothers most certainly explains the growing and life-long tension and conflict between Don and Gerry. In the first instance Don was probably jealous that Gerry got to sleep in the same room with his mother, and then, when his dad returned home, Don was forced to accept Gerry into his territory, into his den. Suddenly he had to share his private space — with a younger bother. Sibling rivalry then took on all sorts of new twists and turns.

When they fought, their mother would stop them, clear the furniture out of the way, and then tell them to get on with it. She had no idea how to control them. There was nothing playful or friendly about these skirmishes: "They were all-out war," Gerry explains, and, until he got older, Gerry was always on the losing end of a good thrashing.

"My brother kicked the crap out of me at least once a day," he recalls.

"Why?" I ask.

"I don't know," he replies.

Then somewhat cynically, he says, "Perhaps it was because we didn't have any toys."

He pauses. "To be honest, Don had serious asthma and

was unable to compete in any sports. He had no stamina at all. I think when he saw that I could do all the things he couldn't do, he was jealous. I think he feared that I would become Dad's favourite. He did all sorts of things to make up for what he thought were his inadequacies. He was always trying to prove himself, often by creating a public spectacle."

If nothing else, Don was instrumental in teaching Gerry how to defend himself. Who knows, but these brotherly disputes, these daily differences of opinion, might explain, at least in part, some of those future major minutes in the penalty box. They might help to explain Gerry's role and reputation in hockey as a tough guy.

One of the many games Don dreamt up was a shooting game, with Gerry as the target. "He treated me as if I were an animal," Gerry says. The idea went like this: Don and a friend had a BB gun and they needed big game to hunt, preferably game that moved. They decided that Gerry would be their dupe, their big game, and they forced him to run back and forth between the garage doors. This was not a matter open for debate. As long as Gerry was moving, he was fair game, but, they agreed, at least Don and his friend did — this was their one concession to Gerry — that there would be no shooting if Gerry wasn't moving. Dodging BB pellets is probably excellent, albeit dangerous training for any aspiring CFL halfback.

The first memorable event that he can recall and the one that obviously disturbed him most at the time was his father's departure for the war. He even remembers saying goodbye to him late in the evening. Nevertheless, when pressed to wander the memory paths of his first six years, there are earlier memories. He recalls being four or five when his father asked him if he wanted to go for a ride in his old Model T. Gerry loved the car and being with his father.

Then the memory turns a bit sour as he remembers that

his father only went about two miles down the road to the St. James Hotel where he spent the afternoon drinking beer. Gerry was left in the car and made to wait. Why he didn't walk home he doesn't know. When I suggest that he was only four or five and two miles was a long haul by foot, he says, "I know, but I never learned. When Dad next asked me if I wanted to go for a drive, I hopped in the front seat, as eager as ever. And at the end of the two mile journey, I faced yet another afternoon of waiting and disappointment. I never learned."

Another of Gerry's early memories, although not an actual event, is a dream, one that still haunts him and causes him considerable anxiety. In this dream he is on a bridge. In the several variations of the dream, he falls off the bridge and plunges towards water — river, lake, ocean; it doesn't matter — and at the last second he wakes up.

"If I hit the water I know I'm going to die," he says.

I try to tell him that the old theory about hitting the water and dying isn't true but he isn't convinced. Even these days, his palms sweat and he can feel the terror in his gut whenever he has to drive over a bridge. This is yet another wrinkle in the character of a man who most know was fearless on a football field or in a rink. What I wonder is whether or not there is any connection between this dream and his father leaving for the war. A feeling or sense of loss can manifest itself in many ways; a terrifying dream is one possible and reasonable response I would think. Or perhaps the image of falling is a sign of being abandoned.

As a young boy, between the ages of six and twelve, Gerry measured the war years by the absence of his father. This was a diffficult time for a lot of young boys whose fathers had enlisted. Perhaps to soften the feeling of loss, Gerry's mother made a point of telling him that she and his dad had taken Gerry and his brother to all the Bombers' games in the mid-to-late thirties. He does remember going into the Blue Bomber dressing room on two occasions before he was seven, but this connection to his father remains foggy.

"I vaguely remember these outings but I didn't know the man. As I grew older," he continues, "while my dad was away during the war, I read all of his scrapbooks and learned all about the Blue Bombers back in the days when my dad, Fritzie Hanson and Bert Oja were the stars. This is when I knew I wanted to play football for the Bombers.

"And when I was finally old enough to tell people that I wanted to follow in my father's footsteps, they told me I'd be lucky if I were ever half the ball player he was, but what they said didn't discourage me, quite the opposite. Between my father's absence — I missed him a lot — and my developing dream of playing football and hockey, the desire to do both, to the exclusion of pretty much everything else, was seeded so deep down inside of me that I ached. I was determined to make it happen."

Perhaps the one saving grace for Gerry during the years his father was overseas was the closeness of the family. His grandfather's big house and his Uncle Percy's and Aunt Bessie's mink ranch were both in the Charleswood District, only three to four miles away from his parent's place in the Sir John Franklin District. For a young boy, this was an easy walk or bike ride during the late spring and summer months.

Gerry could escape his brother. He would bike or walk the gravel roads as far as the army housing and barracks of Fort Osborne, which was where his father received his training with the Princess Patricia Canadian Light Infantry regiment and then cut through the scrub bush of Tuxedo to Charleswood. Here the well-marked, two-foot-wide deer trails ran through the oak, poplar and willow stands. At the end of these trails, Gerry emerged, as if into his own Never

Never Land, at either his grandfather's, where he helped weed the vegetable garden, or at his uncle's.

His aunt and uncle had no children of their own and took great pleasure in spoiling both Gerry and Don. For doing a little work around the mink ranch, Uncle Percy would pay them twenty-five cents, plus a coke. Soon, Gerry started turning up on his own every Saturday during the summer. Uncle Percy's offer seemed like a pretty good deal although the work Gerry was given to do most often was shoveling shit from under the mink pens. But he didn't mind; with his father away Uncle Percy had become a surrogate father. In addition to the extra attention he received, Gerry also learned how to skin a rabbit from Uncle Percy by watching him skin mink when the pelts were ready for market. A little unpleasantness was worth the promise of spending an afternoon and perhaps having a meal with Uncle Percy and Aunt Bessie.

"They doted on us," he remembers, "they were great people."

Winnipeg winters were far too cold and snowy for much socializing, even with family, so Gerry stayed nearer to home at that time of the year despite the fact he felt isolated. During the winter, with Don on the warpath, Gerry spent much of his time at the Community Club which had a hockey rink, tennis courts and rough fields where kids could play organized sports or pick-up games of football and baseball. While there was a fee to join, the fee was waived if your family couldn't afford it. From age seven, the Club became one of Gerry's main hangouts. Through the winter he played hockey every chance he had.

When he received a new pair of hockey gloves at age nine he didn't know he needed to wear another pair of gloves under them. He was so excited about this new real-life equipment that he played all day, without a break. Arriving home he discovered that all of his fingers were frozen. There was no feeling left in them and they were beginning to change colour. He remembers crying like a baby until a neighbour heard him, took him inside and poured cold water over his hands to unfreeze his fingers. His passion for the game had numbed his brain. He confesses now that this may have been a lifelong problem — becoming too caught up in the game to take in the richness and variety of the world around him.

When summer rolled around again and the sun broadcast its golden glow onto the blue sky and the dust bowl below, he and his friends made up variations of field or street games that kids play worldwide. They named theirs "Yards" and "Can the can". In "Yards" the object of the game was to kick or throw a football over the goal line for a single point. Then you would start over again. Teams had to have the same number of players and, if there was a strong wind, you changed ends. Fairness was a code everyone honoured. If the other team caught the ball when you threw or kicked it, they were allowed to take three giant steps and then throw or kick the ball in the opposite direction, towards you. If they didn't catch the ball, they had to at least touch it and then kick or throw it from that spot.

Can there be any doubt that this is where Gerry's kicking career began? I can't imagine him throwing the ball once he learned he had a fairly good kicking leg.

Somewhat surprisingly "Can the can" had its origins in cricket. In this game, all a group of kids needed was six tin cans, two baseball bats and a ball. Three cans, separated by sixty feet or so and facing each other, were set up on a field, one can on top of two. Then you dug a shallow hole, about six inches across, two feet in front of the cans. The hole is where you rested your baseball bat and your partner faced you with his bat on the ready in the hole in front of him.

The opposition, two or more, would throw the ball and attempt to knock over the three cans. The batsman would try to protect the cans by hitting the ball away from the cans, in any direction. If you hit the ball, you and your partner would run back and forth between the cans, and each time you passed each other counted as a run. If your opponents knocked the cans down when you didn't have your bat in the hole in front of the cans, that was an out. Three outs and your innings was over.

Gerry was to become a fairly formidable baseball player and no doubt this was where it all began.

During the winter months, a favourite pastime for Gerry and his friends was to trek a mile and a half down to a spot where the sewer outflow ran into the Assiniboine River. There, where the icy waters of the frozen river met the sludge chugging out of the sewer pipe, they fished — after a fashion. They knew the suckers, a small fish, congregated there in the warmth and were easy to catch. They would snare them by hand and then take the live fish home and try to train them as pets, without much success. Assiniboine Park with its world-famous zoo was a constant destination for a daily outing. The gang of young boys would wind their way to the zoo and then spend the afternoon, first on the swings, and then riding what they called the "Monkey Paths" that ran along the river.

Occasionally they would get caught up in what Gerry and his friends thought were clever pranks, pranks that in retrospect were sometimes outright dangerous and stupid. One such prank was setting fire to dry prairie grass and then pulling the handle on the nearby fire box. At least they had the common sense to light these fires within easy reach of an alarm but they never gave a thought to the possibility that they might get caught in a backfire or that the fire might spread faster than the fire department could respond. The local cop, fondly referred to as "Speedy", would arrive on his bicycle at the scene about two hours after the fire department had doused the flames. He'd walk about, examine the evidence, and then turn to the boys who had hung around awaiting his arrival and ask, "Okay, who did it?" Of course, this was the moment they had waited for and each boy in turn would pull a look of incredulity and innocence.

"We did this," Gerry says, "but I'm not proud of it."

Another temptation was the Victory Garden situated right next to the CN railway tracks about three blocks from home. A gang of three or four of them would raid the garden at night, take their pick of corn, tomatoes and potatoes, and head for one of the many hiding spots they knew nearby. There, under the dome of a darkening sky, they would build a circle of stones, light a small fire, and nurture the coals until they were red-hot.

"If you've never tasted potatoes roasted over a prairie fire, charcoaled on the outside, hot and hard on the inside, and then sprinkled with salt, well you've never tasted one of the world's great gourmet delights. On the way home, we would top off our feast with an apple or crab apple dessert picked from one of the Garden's trees that hung out over the fence and sidewalk."

For entertainment, if he wasn't playing outdoors, he would curl up in front of the large cabinet radio in the living room and listen to the *Green Hornet* and *The Shadow*, two radio dramas that entertained kids for a couple of decades before television, but his favorite broadcast was "Hockey Night in Canada" with Foster Hewitt.

Hewitt's broadcasts inspired him. He knew, as he listened to the play by play, that one day he wanted to be a part of that down east show. Wherever the Gardens was, he wanted to be there. As he listened to the well-known announcer, he imagined himself playing every position on the ice.

Often, well after a game had been completed, he ran the play by play commentary in his mind. He fell asleep reviewing every little detail about the development of a play. He was Syl Apps breaking down the ice and scoring on Bill Durnam in the Montreal goal or he was Turk Broda, big in the Toronto net, shutting out Detroit once again in the playoffs. Probably a more accurate dream would see Gerry checking "Terrible" Ted Lindsay into the boards, at the same time clearing a path for Ted Kennedy to make a rush down the wing for a shot on goal. This was the action he desperately wanted, body hits, in particular, something, anything, his brother would understand. Gerry was getting bigger and more athletic with each year, closing in on that day when he would be his brother's equal or better. Now he had two goals, playing for the Bombers and playing for the Leafs.

What he didn't realize is how much these obsessive dreams would affect his school performance. On reflection, Gerry says, he didn't comprehend how one-dimensional his life was becoming and there was no adult in his world who thought to tell him otherwise. Not that he was about to listen to any lectures about the virtues of a little knowledge.

Although the records show that he was a bright kid, Gerry unexpectedly failed grade four. This was a blow but it didn't divert him from his big dreams. In fact, it probably intensified them. He then spent even more time on the ice and playing fields. His failure at school coupled with his brother's success compounded the problem. Being four years behind, Gerry was expected to live up to the reputation of his older brother, a brother who had artistic talent aplenty, especially in languages. Don wrote beautifully, while Gerry struggled to express himself. Don, who had a horse named Ruby, rode his horse up the stairs and into the school and was greeted and hailed with laughter by students and teachers alike, while Gerry was punished for the slightest misdemeanor. For a young boy, the injustice of these contradictions churned in his stomach and resentment towards his brother was reaching its critical mass. An explosion of some sort was imminent.

Over the years, during summer vacations, Gerry, Don, his mother, and after the war, his father, would travel to Grenfell, Saskatchewan, to spend time with his mother's family. She had three brothers and a sister, all of whom had stayed in the area. One of the brothers, Pat, ran a farm equipment service and repair shop. Young Gerry was keen to help his uncle, and Uncle Pat was quick to accommodate his young apprentice. Gerry enjoyed mucking about at the shop, getting his hands dirty, the dirtier the better, while learning what made an engine tick. He liked working with tools and he fell in love with the smell of oil and gas. He still enjoys tinkering.

But, more important, Uncle Pat had a cottage at Crooked Lake in the Qu'Appelle Valley and the entire family headed out there for picnics and dips in the cool, crystal-clear waters of the lake. This country of mixed prairie grasses, aspen groves and floating fens was idyllic, not the sort of place one would usually pick to settle a score.

In 1948, when Gerry was fourteen and his brother eighteen, their ongoing battle came to a head at Crooked Lake. The two brothers duked it out for the last time. Gerry, who now weighed more than his older brother, had moved past defense and was quite capable of parceling out his own punishment. He thumped his leaner, asthmatic brother, remorselessly. When the dust cleared, the two would never fight again. Don, who had wanted to follow in his father's footsteps and play football, was too small and too sickly to do so. Now his younger brother was poised to fulfill that dream. He had the size, skill and savvy.

The brothers barely spoke again for the rest of their lives

and, as if to reinforce the division, Don ultimately settled on the east coast, Gerry on the west coast. An entire country and a whole lot of silence separated them. Two months before he died, Don sent Gerry a brief note, his last words, to which Gerry did not reply. He hadn't expected to feel the loss he did. For Gerry this was a major learning experience. He's tried to pass this message on to his own kids who, like many of us, hadn't always seen eye to eye with their brothers and sisters.

"Patch up whatever differences you have and speak to each other," he has told them.

For the most part, Gerry and Don were latchkey kids. Their mother worked in an office and when his father returned from the war, he returned to his job in a pickle factory. With both parents out working every day, the two boys came and went as they pleased. Gerry's dad was not exactly impressed with the continuous and rancorous rivalry that had developed between his sons and on weekends attempted to set tasks for them that required cooperation. He insisted the two of them accompany him when he went looking for firewood in the scrub bush. They'd search out and gather fallen poplar, tie a few together and drag them back to the house. Then Gerry and his brother each took an end on a bow saw and cut the lengths into shorter pieces. Under the watchful eye of their father, they couldn't zig when the other zagged. This may be as close to harmony as they ever got. The temptation to torment the other was temporarily put on hold.

Although Gerry was not one for joining in things, unless they had something to with sports in some way, his mother insisted he accompany her to church. She had been raised on and was devoted to the teachings of Mary Baker Eddy. As much as Gerry always wanted to please his mother, the beliefs of Christian Science simply didn't hold his interest. Service and lessons bored him so he skipped out on both.

One day, shortly after his father had returned, Gerry got caught, he doesn't remember where, but not in church where he was supposed to be. Worse, he had spent the money he was instructed to put into the collection plate on a chocolate bar. He wasn't accustomed to looking out for a second parent. He knew where his mom was, she was in church, but his dad, who was not a believer, was unaccounted for. He was the unknown. Not yet a presence. He certainly was not where Gerry expected him to be. Gerry was "busted", holding onto the remaining, melting evidence of what should have gone to God. His father now forbade him to return to church, but more importantly for Gerry, he had disappointed his mother, something he was concerned never to do again.

Having his father back home was a mixed blessing for Gerry. On the one hand, he had a male figure — whom he admired — in his life on a day-to-day basis, but on the other his father had developed a serious drinking problem, a drinking problem that would worsen as he grew to resent the way people treated him on his return This sort of treatment was puzzling, but a not uncommon experience for returning soldiers. Soldiers, Gerry read, often felt unappreciated and somewhat alienated from their communities when they tried to reintegrate. At a time when he thought they should all feel blessed — after all, his father had returned home safely — Gerry saw his parents fight, verbally and physically, day and night.

Like a fighting hen and cock, they tore into each other in a way that seemed incomprehensible. Gerry remembers many occasions when he leapt on his father's back to try to stop him from striking his mom. His father was jealous of his mother and her friends, which caused him to drink even more. It was a vicious circle. Finally, in 1947 his parents got a divorce. And things improved. Eventually both would remarry. At long last Gerry would have an opportunity to get to know his father.

By this time Gerry was well on his way to growing up; to becoming an adult. His own sporting career was taking shape. Hockey dominated his life for at least six months a year and football, track and baseball competed for his attention during the summer months. It was becoming evident that he was a "natural".

In an interview with Arnie Tiefenbach in 1981, when Gerry was inducted into the Canadian Football Hall of Fame and Museum, Gerry says about his early sporting days:

"It was either sports or jail, one or the other," said James, who ultimately returned to school years after having left it. "Dad was overseas in the war and mother worked all day, and while we didn't live in a run down area, it was the west end and it was tough. I got in scrapes with the law a few times, as I suppose most kids do. Sports took me to where I wanted to go. Who knows where I would have ended up without it?

"I think by the grace of God sports gives a lot of people the chance to get out of some pretty tough spots."

While there is no doubt that an entire family had made a contribution to the development of one of Canada's premier athletes, an equal partner in this shaping was the landscape, a landscape of great beauty, but a landscape that, when in the mood, could be a harsh adversary. I'm convinced this is why today Gerry features grasses in his Nanoose Bay garden; they remind him of home. They represent his connection to the earth and to six generations of relatives.

Grandfather James, wearing Masonic colours.

Grandfather James's house in Charleswood, early 40s.

Eddie James at Crooked Lake, Qu'appelle Valley. Before war.

Gerry's dad, Eddie, standing by his old car at Crooked Lake.

Gerry looking guilty, 1939

"Dynamite" Eddie and buddy in England during war.

Gerry shows off tan, Victoria Beach, 1942

First bike, age 10

Gerry's mother, Moira James, Gerry and brother Don. During war.

Marg and Tracy, Gerry and Debbie, summer 1957

Family portrait, Yorkton, 1968. From left: KC, Tracy, Marg, Brady, Tara, Gerry and Debbie.

Yorkton Terriers win provincial Junior trophy, 1983.

4 / How Do You Grow an Athlete?

A friend of mine, the prairie poet and novelist Robert Kroetsch, asks in his beautiful, long poem, *Seed Catalogue,* several searching questions: "How do you grow a garden? How do you grow a gardener? How do you grow a lover? How do you grow a prairie town? How do you grow a past?" Finally, the most difficult question, "How do you grow a poet?" The answers, of course, are perplexing if not arcane. Each question presents its own set of problems but all require planting, nurturing and harvest. And as anyone who has spent time working the earth can tell you, seed of some sort is essential to the process. The garden, as Kroestsch goes on to say, gives us shape.

The question in Gerry James's case is, How do you grow an athlete? And in what sort of garden? A healthy seed is obviously crucial, as brother Don was to realize, but equally important is the nurturing process. Support, given with enthusiasm and belief, is likely to be the main fostering ingredient but a good ass kicking when deserved can be just as beneficial.

From what Gerry tells me, his mother had a talent for mixing all of these qualities; she knew exactly when to praise and when to criticize. She could be tough, she could be gentle. She nourished while cultivating discipline and raised Cain when Gerry wandered too far off the path. She was strict but loved a good time. She had a set of rules and regulations and they were to be obeyed. In short, she was a no-nonsense lady with a good sense of humour.

With Gerry as her project, an appreciation of high jinks, tomfoolery and farce would have been indispensable. On any given day he could be up to just about anything. There is absolutely no question that this petite, very attractive woman, who during the war had worked in an aircraft maintenance plant and in the post-war era as a secretary and office manager, was the dominant inspiration and influence in Gerry's life.

From the beginning, Gerry was a competitor-in-waiting. His mother saw to that. While he was still a youngster, she decided to teach him how to play crib. The game, she explained, was to be enjoyed but it was also to be won. She outlined the rules, including the counting, and then told him that if he counted wrongly or missed points in his hand that he had not played which she caught, and which she spotted, then she would peg those additional points for herself. There was no excuse for inattention or miscounting. "Get it right," she told him. Otherwise she might win the game outright with points he should have had himself. "You'll lose if you don't stay focused."

To some this might seem harsh but when you have survived polio and have lived through the 1920s and 1930s on the prairies, in that winter place, life's lessons have taught you both compassion and fortitude. You understand barbed wire in a land that runs right off the horizon into the setting sun. You either fence it in or nature will run amuck. Your prized potato patch could quickly become a bed of thistles. Then you lose. The lesson is simple: take control of your life and do your best, always within the rules.

This emphasis on competition runs through Gerry's early years. He tells a story about his mother and seven other women who formed a bridge club and played the game weekly at a very skilled level. As they entered their teens, Gerry and his friends, somewhat surreptitiously, set about learning the game themselves, partly by watching their mothers play and partly by reading the daily newspaper and books, such as the famous *Bridge Made Easy* by Charles Goren, which they found lying around the house. Then one day the gang he hung around with reached the stage where they figured they could challenge their mothers.

Gerry and Fred Marsh, close friends, were the first to toss down the gauntlet. Cocky as could be and confident they could win, they baited their mothers. Soon the game was on. Surprisingly, Gerry and Fred won. For the entire evening, they were dealt winning cards, hand after hand. With astonishing ease, they walloped their mothers. Then, when the women requested a rematch, repeatedly over several months, Fred and Gerry refused. They knew how lucky they had been, and Gerry had learned his lessons well. Quit while you're on top. Winning, his mother had taught him, was the end goal of any competition and till this day he can't stand to lose.

Inexplicably, Gerry's father was silent when it came to motivating or supporting either of his sons to play sports, whether at an amateur or professional level. The man who had torn up the rugby league, as football was known in the early years, as a running back in Saskatchewan and Manitoba, didn't much care what his sons did in sports. Perhaps because his favourite son, Don, had serious health problems, he neither discouraged nor encouraged them to follow his example in any athletic pursuit.

Clearly, in Gerry's case, his father, the famous Eddie "Dynamite" James, was an influence by example, especially in football, if not in every other sport in which he excelled. Undoubtedly Gerry was challenged by his family and his father's friends to equal his dad's success. They taunted and goaded him and he responded. He set out to prove he could be his father's equal, not out of any sort of disrespect; quite the contrary — he wanted his father's approval and blessing.

As far as Gerry knows, his father never attended any of his high school games, although he does remember him showing up for a few Bomber games before his death after surgery on December 26, 1958. It is likely that he witnessed Gerry participate in his first Grey Cup victory in November of 1958. The man who had excited fans with his two-way play, with his lunging runs and spectacular defensive acrobatics, ended up working as a carpenter building sets for the CBC.

Once again we have evidence of the disparity between the after lives of honoured and celebrated athletes from the past and those plying their trade and negotiating their "corporate" contracts in the twenty-first century. In this day of multi-million dollar deals, it seems odd and perhaps regrettable that those who set the stage, literally in Eddie "Dynamite" James's case, benefit so little from their pioneering work.

Because their relationship had been so sporadic, interrupted as it was by war and then divorce, his dad's death was a particularly traumatic experience for Gerry. Father and son had not seen much of each other for some time and had arranged to have Christmas dinner at Gerry's and Marg's house the evening before Eddie died. When news arrived of his passing, Gerry was shocked by the fact that he would never see his father again. The man he admired most in life had been more of an absence than a presence throughout his life. He had not received directly from his father the validation he sought.

Thirty years later he was to learn that his father had asked one of his drinking buddies, Dick Huffman, a giant lineman who had migrated north from the Los Angeles Rams to play with the Bombers, to look after Gerry. Apparently he made Dick promise he would make every effort to keep Gerry out of trouble. I suspect this is one of those pacts made with the devil. Reining in Gerry would have been like harnessing lightning to run your beer cooler.

But, just as his mother was the single, dominant force upon his life, so was she the most important influence upon his sporting career. There can be no doubt that he was closer to her than his father. In Gerry's eyes, she was the force to be reckoned with. As much as he respected and admired his father's accomplishments, she was the one who was there for him in a pinch. She was the one who kept a scrapbook of his achievements from his earliest mention in a newspaper column to his Schenleys. From the beginning, she instilled and nurtured in him a driving competitive spirit. Do your best for you, she would tell him, not for anyone else. Do it hard and do it fairly. Her nourishment was always positive.

By the time Gerry entered grade ten at Kelvin High School, he was already a bit of a sports celebrity in Winnipeg. He had joined organized hockey at the age of seven and organized baseball at nine. Early newspaper accounts repeatedly mention Gerry's contribution to a game, whether in hockey or baseball. Organized football lay off in the distance but around twelve he recalls playing a lot of pick-up games with as few as four players a side. Having a full complement of players was not essential. However, it was only in high school that he finally participated in organized football.

When I asked Gerry about school, he said it was great; he had a lot of fun.

"I loved playing sports and I enjoyed the company of girls," he said. A wry smile crossed his face as he repeated, "Especially the girls. It was a much more innocent time and our interest was platonic. We enjoyed each other's company." As an afterthought, he said, "Oh, and I appreciated my teachers and my classes." He savored every minute of the one year he spent at Kelvin where he played on any team that would have him, but most notably the football team.

An old Winnipeg acquaintance and friend of Gerry's, Al Abbott, who also attended Kelvin, told me Gerry was "one of a kind. We first met when we were around nine or ten, at the Christian Science Sunday School. I was raised in a Christian Science family and I think Gerry was there because of a family relation."

"His mother," I informed him.

"Oh," Al laughed, "that makes sense. And then when it was time to enter high school, we both ended up at Kelvin."

Kelvin was a classic, old, red brick building, three stories high, with a separate entrance for boys and girls. Someone, either the Principal or a misguided school board, wanted to keep the sexes apart, a delusional undertaking at best, but one that appears to have been practiced across the country by many mid twentieth century educators and institutions. Someone genuinely believed they were saving hormone-driven teenagers, as excitable as Rhesus monkeys, from themselves.

"Because of its location," Al remarked, "Kelvin drew on a broad section of the population. Gerry came from a poorer section of the city, I came from the lower middle class area, Riverview, and then there were those from Tuxedo, the wealthiest district. As I say, the student body was a well-balanced cross-section of the population and we got on well. It was a tightly-knit community. And many of us remain close friends until this day. I know Gerry and Marg continue to get together yearly with their particular group of friends. I think we were all very lucky, we grew up in a great period of history. It seemed that everything we did was done outside. There was no television and there were no electronic games to keep us indoors. Everyone participated in sports; I'm not exaggerating when I say sports pervaded our existence, no matter what our skills. I'm proof of that." Chuckling at the memory, Al added: "Winnipeg was simply a great city in which to be raised.

"From the beginning, Gerry was someone I enjoyed and admired. He did his thing and didn't seem to care what people thought of him. He was a hugely talented free spirit, who never boasted about his achievements. He was exceptional in that regard. He simply wouldn't toot his own horn. He was probably the best athlete to come out of the province, perhaps the country, in those days, but when it came time to select Manitoba's 'Athlete of the half Century', not Canada's you understand, but Manitoba's, the prize went to Fred Dunsmore, a fine athlete in his own right but nowhere near the quality and calibre of Gerry."

I asked Al why he thought this was the case, because being passed over is a recurring theme in Gerry's life, and he replied, "Well, you know Gerry."

"He can be a bit abrasive," I said, and Al laughed.

"Many of us who grew up in that era were puzzled by the selection. We knew Gerry had rough edges, and that sometimes he could irritate people, but having said that, there has never been a better natural athlete. And a nice guy, even when he was beating the bejesus out of you. I know from personal experience how good he was, I played hockey and baseball against him."

Alison North, another friend of Gerry's, much younger she hastened to add, also attended Kelvin and she echoed Al's comments about the school and city.

"Kelvin was a very popular school; it was the place to be," she said, "even with its two door policy, one for boys, one for girls. I didn't know Gerry well but I remember one day he came into the gym to talk to our basketball coach — I played on the junior girls' team — and when he entered, we all stopped and a hush fell upon all of the girls. That's still vivid in my memory. It was as though we were in a trance or in the presence of someone great. Then we started whispering, Oh my gosh, he's so cute. All of us. So cute. I can still hear it. I've never told him this story because it might go to his head but...you know it wouldn't. Because he was older than us, he was far more fascinating than boys our own age. And that he was such a good athlete, well, that excited and impressed us, too."

None of this adulation registered with Gerry; or, more accurately, didn't distract him. What he knew for certain was that he wanted to play whatever sport happened to be in season.

⁂

Jack Robertson, one of Gerry's closest and oldest pals, had several revealing stories to tell about his old buddy. The two lived in the same district, went to Kelvin, played midget and juvenile hockey on the same teams, and, most importantly, had remained friends over the years and in spite of living hundreds of miles apart. They often shared adventures although each was quick to suggest the other was prone to exaggeration, especially when the content was less than flattering, or betrayed a weakness.

"I don't know how Jack remembers all that crap," Gerry remarked. "I'm damn sure not all of it's true."

Anticipating Gerry's response, Jack had already written, "Gerry will likely deny such and such happened. He always does."

Most of Jack's stories were unrelated to sports but all told a bit about Gerry's character. Hanging out with Gerry always included a lesson or two and was never dull. Mind you, I get the impression Jack was more than a willing participant.

Jack's father was the district manager of Hoover Company in Winnipeg. His marketing area included Manitoba and North Western Ontario. On one occasion he was travelling to Port Arthur, Fort William, now called Thunder Bay, and he asked Jack and Gerry if they would like to camp out at Thunder Lake, which is about ten miles east of Dryden, Ontario. Gerry, who was fifteen, and Jack, sixteen, leapt at the opportunity to be away from home on their own. Jack's dad rented them a cabin and dropped them off on his way east. He would pick them up on his way back a few days later.

Emboldened by being on their own, they decided one night to head into Dryden to see if there was a dance on at the community centre. They hitched a ride into town in a lovely old antique car, attended the dance, and around midnight agreed it was time to get back to the cabin.

At that hour, though, no one was willing to pick them up and, needless to say, they had no cash. After standing at the side of the road into the early hours of the morning, Jack came up with another bright idea; he suggested that maybe the OPP (the Ontario Police) might assist them with accommodation. Sure enough, when they walked in and made their request, the constable on duty told them things were pretty slow that night and showed them the way to cells 1 and 2. This was not quite the reception they expected, nor were the "rooms" as cozy and the beds as comfy as they had hoped. Years later, when Gerry spoke at a father-and-son event in Dryden, he told them about his first visit to their town.

On that same trip, the two adventurers decided to try their luck at fishing. They borrowed a boat and Jack rowed them out to the middle of the lake while Gerry trolled with one of Jack's dad's best rods. As the two sat facing each other, Gerry suddenly cast his line backwards, without looking, over his shoulders. Unfortunately, as the line released out across the lake, the rod also shot out of his hands and sank to the bottom, a few yards away from the boat. Jack said Gerry looked like he had just spotted the ghost of Tom Thompson rising out of the water. The lake was only about fifteen feet deep where the rod sat on the sand below but it was also fall and the water icy cold. Gerry took off his shirt and was about to dive in. He knew how upset Jack's father would be.

"I suggested we first try using a heavy lure to drag bottom. After a few casts, we hooked the rod and raised it gingerly to the surface. I've never seen Gerry quite so relieved. I've always told Gerry that whenever I became involved in one of his harebrained schemes, I got into trouble. He, of course, claims it was the other way round."

Jack's sisters, Pat and Joyce, probably knew best. Apparently every time Gerry visited the house he pretty much cleaned out the fridge. He did not pocket anything, he simply ate non-stop, from arrival to departure.

On another occasion, Jack and Gerry decided to ride their bikes out of town for a campout. They took along cooking equipment but very little food. When they arrived at a good spot beside the Assiniboine River, they built a lean-to to sleep under and then headed out into a nearby farm field to see what they could scrounge up for dinner. Crawling through rows of vegetables on their hands and knees, they managed to gather up a few carrots, potatoes, tomatoes and lettuce. But someone saw them and called the farmer. Soon a posse had gathered and started after them.

Jack and Gerry made it back to the river and were then faced with the decision whether to give themselves up or swim for the other side where they figured they would be safe. The two boys stripped down to their underwear, hid their clothes in some scrub bushes and swam across the river. From the opposite side of the river, they watched the posse first find their clothes, then the campsite and then their bi-cycles. The jig was up so they swam back. In retrospect, the farmers were lenient. They scolded them, told them they were bad boys whose behaviour was headed in the wrong direction, but otherwise left it at that.

"Likely the scare was enough," Jack reflected. "What surprised me most, though, was that Gerry couldn't swim. At one point, I was terrified the current was going to take him down river. I was doing the breaststroke and Gerry was thrashing away trying to do the crawl, all the time losing ground. Finally he slipped into a back eddy that pushed him towards shore and he was safe.

"I was surprised by this because Gerry was one of those athletes who seemed to excel at every sport. I can remem-ber him bowling for the first time and getting nothing but strikes. When we played a pick-up game of baseball at the Robert H. Smith Junior High School, Gerry would stand at the plate and purposely redirect his hits at the school, the ball 'accidentally' breaking one of the windows. He had the power and the aim. It was amazing. He'll probably deny this one.

"And when we were at Kelvin, he represented the school at the Winnipeg high school speed skating race. Gerry had on a plaid shirt, torn blue jeans and size twelve hockey skates. Most of his competitors wore speed skating suits and speed skates. Gerry won the gold. Once he got out in front, they either couldn't pass him or were afraid to. His elbows had a fair reputation by then."

Some of Gerry's exploits, as Jack recounted them, were the same sort of tales one hears about young boys carrying out in schools everywhere — setting off stink bombs, get-ting the strap, letting insects or snakes loose to scare young girls.

Outside of school the twosome made a habit of attending Bomber games at the old Osborne Stadium by scaling a twenty foot wall and sitting on top. Attendants would yell at them and demand they come down while the boys in turn would razz them with "Come on up and get us." Of course, no one did because it was too dangerous. Gerry's and Jack's seats were uncomfortable but they saw a lot of great games. "In one game," Jack recalled, "Indian Jack Jacobs, the Bomber's quarterback threw a bullet pass on the run which was intercepted. Within a blink, Indian Jack tackled the guy, whammo, who a few moments later was stretchered off the field. That sure impressed Gerry and me."

Not long after this, in 1952, Gerry was playing on that same field, with Indian Jack Jacobs, one of his heroes. Jack Robertson summarized the beginning of Gerry's career in a few sentences. "Gerry went from Kelvin High School to a Toronto high school and excelled in football in both cities. He went to Toronto because the Toronto Maple Leafs wanted to monitor his hockey progress. Conn Smythe liked Gerry because he was a rough and aggressive player. When Gerry was only seventeen and fresh out of high school football the Winnipeg Blue Bombers brought him up for his first game as a professional. They were playing the Saskatchewan Roughriders. The Roughriders knew Gerry was a young rookie so they directed the opening kick at him. Gerry caught it and ran for a touchdown. I was at that game.

"A few years later, Gerry broke his leg and was sent to Winnipeg General to recuperate. When I went to visit him, he told me he was going to end up with one leg shorter than the other. I thought the doctor should have rebroken the leg and started over but Gerry said that with one leg shorter than the other he would be able to cut to the left easier and faster. When I told my assistant that I thought this story was funny, she replied, yeah, only because it's so stupid."

Until recently, major league scouting for baseball prospects north of the border was accidental at best. For some reason the border was a twenty feet high barrier of ice and snow that precluded any likelihood of finding kids playing baseball. Hockey, yes, baseball, no. So no-one bothered to look beyond the forty-ninth parallel. Besides, if baseball were played up here, in this northern wilderness, the season would be far too short for the proper and expected development of a player. The fact that players were making it into the majors from states which bordered on Canada, such as Minnesota, didn't penetrate this thinking. Consequently, only 217 Canadians have made it into professional baseball since its inception.

With the success of players such as Ferguson Jenkins, Larry Walker, Éric Gagné, Jason Bay, Justin Morneau, Matt Stairs and Terry Puhl, this attitude changed. The careers of Jeff Francis, Rich Harden and Ryan Dempster, for example, have been built on good scouting. My own son played against and then with Jeff Francis at UBC and there were always knowledgeable scouts at their games. But when Gerry James was playing baseball, no one was looking, or else, judging from contemporary newspaper accounts, someone would have taken notice of this kid who was repeatedly belting the ball out of the park. From the day he put his right-handed glove on the wrong hand and took it off to throw, Gerry was impressive. He was a southpaw with a mighty bat. While there were no local role models for baseball, it didn't matter because he loved the game.

From what I've heard from men who played youth baseball against Gerry and from what I've read, when he was asked to pitch, his fast ball was wicked if not slightly wild. Hitters were scared.

"They had good reason to be afraid," Gerry quipped, "I had no idea where the ball was going once it left my fingertips. But I could throw hard. And, of course, I was left handed."

Reporters of the day had this to say about the young James: "James Brilliant in Franklin Win: James smacks a homer and pair of singles." And "James Whiffs 17 in Sir John Win. He added to his own cause by banging out two singles." Further: "Gerry James and Al Elcombe hooked up in a brilliant mound battle with the only run coming in the fifth inning. James whiffed 11 and walked three in his winning performance." The tributes continued: "Gerry James tagged for only one hit by the Rosedales, hurled brilliant ball, striking out 12 and walking one." Finally, "James collected both the Frankie hits, and both went for extra bases. His first blow was a triple that drove in one run, followed up by a homer in the third inning with two mates aboard to account for all the Franklin runs driven in."

In an end of season contest, one writer reported, "Gerry James Sensational: Gerry James entered local baseball's Hall of Fame Friday night with a brilliant no-hit no-run game as Sir John Franklin racked up their 11th victory without a defeat in Bantam League competition, a 4-0 triumph over River Heights. James struck out 13 batters and slammed out one of four Sir John Franklin singles in his standout performance."

Today if a team representative or scout were to hear or read about a kid consistently performing this well, no matter where he was located, they would pack their bags and make a point of attending a game or two. Such plaudits are hard to come by and when they are directed towards a kid who's excelling in other sports at the same time, it's probably time to take notice. Spotting a hot prospect has its rewards these days.

In 1950, when Gerry stepped up to the Juvenile ranks, the accolades continued: "Around River Heights they expect to see Gerry James become the finest athlete produced by the Fort Rouge district. The son of the former great Blue Bomber, Eddie James, Gerry has starred in baseball and hockey and is expected to find his way in the grid game that was so much a part of his father.

"Moving up from Midget ranks, Friday night, he proved his prowess to the Juvenile Baseball league with a magnificent display of pitching.

"Gerry donned a Rosedale uniform and relieved Al Seymour after he had been touched for one hit and suffered a back injury. James took the mound in the second inning and proceeded to mow the Columbus Club down to the tune of 10-0 and didn't give up a hit while doing it.

"James whiffed ten and walked five in his masterpiece while his mates finally got to Johnny Ayotte for two runs in the fifth and eight in the sixth. James was also big man with the willow in his first juvenile game with two hits..."

Another report described one of Gerry's performances this way: "The Greys, held a 4-2 lead with the bases loaded and only one out in the third frame when James relieved Tommy Hannesson. James proceeded to retire the side without any further damage and allowed only one run while his mates went on to rack up the verdict. James made sure of the victory himself by blasting out a two run triple to put the Dales in the drivers seat at 5-4."

The tributes continued but his baseball career was rapidly coming to an end. As one reporter had forecasted, Gerry would quickly become a gridiron star when he entered Kelvin. At sixteen, after a year at Kelvin, he transferred to Runnymede in Toronto to play hockey which, due to his age and a set of comedic circumstances, ironically resulted in his football rather than his hockey career rocketing.

Soon and not surprising to some, he was turning pro, in football. But during the summers, when he returned to Winnipeg, he continued to show his skill and versatility in baseball. He played for the junior Columbus Club which played its games in St. Boniface. However, with his new commitment to football and a rigorous practice schedule, baseball had become essentially a recreational activity. Terry Hind, Mr. Baseball in Winnipeg, and Manager of the Columbus team, a man Gerry liked and respected very much, remarked that Gerry could have gone pro in baseball had he not had other commitments. Unfortunately, baseball provided him with no incentives. His play was outstanding, but the sport existed in a vacuum. Beyond the local level, there seemed to be little or no future. Besides, in addition to playing all of these sports for the pleasure it gave him, Gerry was beginning to realize that he might have enough skill to earn a living as a professional athlete.

In an article entitled "May Exceed Famous Father" by Al Vickery, from the Canadian Press, the author noted that while Gerry was already an accomplished football and hockey player, at sixteen, with a decision to make about which of the two would become his career sport, he remarked in his last paragraph, almost as an afterthought, "He also is at home on a baseball diamond or a cinder track." While at Runnymede, Gerry competed at the provincial and then the inter-provincial level in the shot put and the 100 and 200 yard races. He won both dashes and set a new record in the 100 yard race in a time of 10.3 seconds. Significantly, he did this without ever having run in spikes before and with a minimum of professional coaching.

Gerry laughed about his efforts to throw the shot put.

"I should have been disqualified," he said, "but I managed to place third. I had no idea how to put so I threw the sixteen pound metal ball, as if I were throwing a baseball. I should have dislocated my elbow or pulled my arm out of its socket. The turn and glide motion you see expert shot putters employing was beyond me, but I did manage to stay within the circle. That was an achievement." In one of his characteristic understatements, he added, "I know now that putting the shot would have been far more successful than trying to throw it. When you see world-class shot-putters, you realize that technique is just as important as strength."

When we talked about his baseball career winding down, he recounted what he saw as one of the funnier and more ironic stories to come out of his dual career.

"Do you know how I lost my two front teeth," he asked, the Christmas song immediately leaping to mind? I shook my head and resisted the temptation to speculate. "Strangely enough it didn't happen in hockey or football. No stick or puck in the face, no piling on after a tackle. Nothing so dramatic!

"This was how it happened," a mixture of pride and self-mockery entering his voice. "I was called up to play baseball with Columbus, a senior team in St. Boniface — I was fifteen and suddenly playing with and against grown men — and a scuffle broke out at first base between our team and our opponents. I don't even remember who they were now, although I think we were playing at Stony Mountain, near the penitentiary. We were at bat. Several players charged the bag and I sauntered out from the dugout where I had been watching the game and minding my own business to see what was going on. I wanted to have a peek. I stuck my head in, jaw first, and suddenly I saw a fist coming towards my face delivered by a very large first baseman from the opposing team. I suppose he was looking for anyone in a Columbus uniform and I was closest. He caught me square and knocked out both of my front teeth. I couldn't even get back at him. That was it! That was probably the shortest fight I was ever in. For two days I kept quiet and hid my mouth because I knew my mother would be upset and I knew she couldn't afford the additional financial burden of replacing them. I never did find the teeth."

Gerry's ruminations about baseball and track have an edge of nostalgia to them. In an ideal world and if possible, I think Gerry would have continued to play every sport. His desire and passion to compete, to prove himself, is still palpable. This is when he seems most animated, when he guides you inside his view of the world to a vantage point where you might just begin to grasp his own intense passion for something he has done or is thinking about doing.

It's becoming apparent to me that in Gerry's view no matter what the activity, to do it well you need to find a way to get to its core. In other words, you need to get inside the game. Or you need to embody the game. Only then will you have a chance to excel. This has been Gerry's life-long credo and challenge. You can't "just do it", as the Nike ad urges.

Gerry has the dedication of a principal dancer or a world-class concert cellist, coupled with an equally keen fear of his possible limitations. That's what drives him. Today when Gerry bends over a new grass, one strategically placed in his garden, he is not simply sticking it in the ground. He surveys the garden, his composition, and knows where it belongs, as if he is conversing with and situating an old friend.

5 / Squib's Promise

When the muggy prairie summer on the Great Plain, rich with the scent of grasses and willows, clover and aspen, abruptly ended, the falling temperatures heralded the beginning of the hockey season. Young Gerry couldn't wait to tie on his skates. He didn't yet have football in his repertoire, so there was no transitional sport between the seasons.

Once the yearly harvest was in, the old question persisted. How do you grow a hockey player? In Canada this is both a mystical and scientific question. The process of actually developing a player, the scientific side of the equation, is fairly clear and detailed. We have developed very sophisticated skills tests, conditioning regimens, and game theories that indicate to us whether or not a kid has "the potential" to play on the grand stage, the NHL. And at the beginning of each new season, even the established players are required to pass a fitness test to see if they are in playing condition. Numbers will tell that side of the story.

What we don't understand quite so well, or perhaps not at all, is that "special" quality, that inexplicable something, that creates a Rocket Richard, Gordie Howe, Bobby Orr, Wayne Gretzky, Steve Yzerman or Sidney Crosby. There's a host of other names I could mention here but everyone knows the players I mean.

We know when emerging ice hockey players have that intangible quality. We see it in their skating, in the way they

glide over the ice, in the way they move into space or anticipate what's going to happen before it happens. Or perhaps
more so, in the way they make things happen. I don't think
there is a particular age at which it occurs, but occur it does.
Pop! A bud explodes into bloom. Just like that. Those of us
watching in the stands sense it happening or unfolding, as
if by magic, and intuitively we understand that what we're
beholding is special and immeasurable.

Bill Russell, the great Celtic's basketball player, once
commented on how he was able to out-rebound taller men
and take control of a game. He simplified his explanation
by suggesting it was his timing. When he had won the rebound, he went on to say, he would slow the game down,
in his mind, and it was almost as if the other players on the
floor did his bidding, did as he wished or predicted. I think
this is a combination of instinct and the ability to control
the pace of a game. In other words, he orchestrated the play.
I think all great players in whatever sport they play can affect
the game this way.

Gretzky and Crosby are the most recent masters of this
in hockey and Steve Nash and Kobi Bryant do it in basketball. I think the jury is still out on LeBron James—he has
a busload of talent, that's undeniable, but there is a difference between talent and this mysterious other sense. Pelé,
Maradona, David Beckham, Paolo Maldini, Zinedine Zi-
dane, Ryan Giggs, Dennis Bergkamp and Lionel Messi most
recently have demonstrated this wizardry in soccer. It would
be folly to overlook Mia Hamm and Cheryl Miller on this
list. Team recognition and commitment, I believe, are definite prerequisites if an individual is to produce this alchemy
in team sports. Michael Jordan, Magic Johnson, Larry Bird
and Charles Barkley each had varying degrees of talent but
all four had this transcendent genius. As do Tim Duncan
and Paul Pierce out of the current crop of court magicians.

Then there is the Nike triumvirate of Tiger Woods, Roger Federer and Thierry Henri. We can all add to this list but the sporting manufacturer knew what it was doing and who it was selecting when it put those three together to sell its products.

Now, I'm certainly not suggesting that Gerry had this mysterious, indescribable quality in hockey. Quite the contrary. According to his own assessment, he was a bit of a slug on skates. Thug on skates might be more apt, although on both counts I think he is a bit hard on himself. Often he was simply doing the bidding of his masters or doing what he did best. He was not one for deking someone out; he always took the shortest route to his goal. If that meant over or through someone, that's what he did.

Billy Reay, coach with the Leafs in the mid 1950s and later with Chicago, once commented to Marg that Gerry was deceptively fast on skates and probably would have been faster if he had quit football. But in football, there is little doubt in my mind that Gerry did have this additional sense. Like Parker, Jacobs and Flutie, for example, or in American ball, Lawrence Taylor, Jim Brown, Jerry Rice or Joe Montana, he could take control of a game with a sudden flash of brilliance. Instinct kicked in and he knew where space would open up. I'm not trying to compare him to Moses here but there is no question that defenses parted like the Red Sea before him, with the help of his offensive line of course — either that or defenses took an hypnotically induced nap. Some of his touchdowns were scored off runs that were nothing short of astonishing.

Yet, in spite of his considerable athletic ability, coupled with his strength, speed and size, these attributes did not translate into the same kind of success in hockey. Without doubt he was good, often very good, but he wasn't exceptional. He once told me that the two motions, running and skating, are totally different from each other. Each requires a distinct set of muscles. They are the antithesis of each other and practising one does not build up or develop the other. This may explain why he was merely a good journeyman in hockey and begs the question, How do you grow a hockey player? — especially when you are so accomplished in other sports?

The one personal trait or inner strength that Gerry brings to everything he does is perseverance. He will repeat an exercise or action *ad nauseam*, until he has perfected it. I've watched him repeat a chipping stroke around the practice green until it hurts just to watch. In the fall and early spring, his fingers turn red with the damp and cold and rub of the grip. A light mist or rain simply adds to the atmosphere. If anyone else is about, he'll challenge them to a chip off.

Old man, I have often wanted to say to him, you can throttle back, you can relax, but he persists.

The question is: where does this combination of perfection and quest for perfection come from? We know his mother championed her son and challenged him to be and do his best. We know the constant ribbing he took from friends and relations about measuring up to his father. "If you're ever half as good as your father" became a mantra for him and was a huge motivation to compete and succeed. But equally important to his development were the time and place.

The depression and war years challenged the entire population to be mindful of others and to be self-sufficient. There was a generosity of spirit in the air. In Winnipeg, someone in municipal government decided that neighbourhood community parks and centres would provide an excellent antidote to complacency, laziness and self-pity. Someone recognized that community centres were the perfect places for kids to hang out, play and socialize.

They were also ideal venues for encouraging and developing aspiring young athletes. According to Gerry, one idea in particular was critical for all of the kids in his era playing hockey in Winnipeg. Sixty or seventy years before Malcolm Gladwell advanced his theory about the effects of age on the development of athletes in his book *Outliers: The Story of Success*, someone in the Winnipeg system proposed the wise idea that no kid be allowed to advance into a higher division in hockey until they got better; until they demonstrated a certain level of hockey proficiency. What a simple and obvious concept! Skill rather than age would determine who you played against and at which level. How radical was that in a world where one's date of birth seemed to determine so much?

In school, a kid born in December was asked to compete with a child born the previous January. One youngster got an eleven month head start on the other; and the kid born late in the year suffered the ignominy of being smaller, shorter and slower, physically and mentally. Imagine, under this new system, you played with and competed against kids who had the same skills, not necessarily with kids born in the same year. No one was allowed to flounder and freeze on the bench because they lacked skating and stick-handling skills. Happily someone had seen that kids could cope with being competitive but not with humiliation.

While not very structured, the Community League was the perfect place for Gerry and most of his friends to learn to play the game. He played in this informal league for three years, from the age of seven to ten. He learned to skate and he learned the basic rules and formations of hockey. This was the practical application of what he was hearing directly from Foster Hewitt in Toronto via CBC radio broadcasts.

By the time he was ready to move up to Play Ground, aged eleven and twelve, he was acting out what he imagined

"Wild Bill" Ezinicki would do during a sequence of plays. "Wild Bill", who had a reputation for handing out some of the most punishing body checks in the game, was from Winnipeg and was Gerry's hero. Someone from Winnipeg had made it into the big league, into the NHL, and with the Toronto Maple Leafs. That was something to celebrate.

In the early days Gerry also learned a lot about how to play hockey over the winter months from shinny games. This was a variation of pond hockey. There were no positions and no goalies. Usually there was no body checking and no lifting of the puck. No one was wearing any sort of protective gear. Every day, after school, he would faithfully turn up at the local Sir John Franklin community club rink, in essence a lacrosse box, with boards three to four feet in height, which had been turned into a rink for the winter, and play shinny until last light. He had strict instructions to be home for dinner before dark.

Laughing, he said, "It took almost three years before I learned how to get the puck. Our shinny games were totally unorganized, as I suspect they were everywhere else in the country. They were chaos on ice. There were no nets, and as many players squeezed between the boards as possibly could. Often there would be twenty to thirty players on the surface at one time. And even though sides were picked, no one passed the puck. Essentially it was a game of keep away. If you got the puck, you'd have it for a few seconds at the most. What I eventually learned, although I have to admit it took me time, is not to join the swarm. If you kept skating and you picked your place on the ice, eventually the puck would come to you. And then you'd have your few seconds of glory before the pack relieved you of the puck. I would spend hours at the rink and never touch the puck, but again, as I say, I learned how to skate and where to position myself on the ice. From playing shinny I learned what is often the most difficult strategy to teach in hockey — to stay wide."

I told him the same is true of soccer. When you widen the field, you give yourself much more room in which to move. It's about space, but trying to get a young player to stand up against the sideline, heels on the chalk, is almost impossible.

Gerry nodded. "They all want to stray into the play. They want to follow the ball or puck rather than let it come to them. That's also true for hockey, for most team sports. We all want to be at the centre of the action. Moving without the puck into space is the hardest concept to pick up. The temptation to move towards the puck, or in your case the ball, rather than let the puck move to you, obviously at a much faster speed than you can skate, is incredibly difficult to grasp. Shinny taught me that."

By the age of eleven, Gerry had moved up to the Playground League run by the Winnipeg Parks Board. Here he enjoyed his baptism into fully-organized hockey, playing against teams from his own district before moving on to a city-wide playoff tournament between the winners from each district. For the first time, hockey had all the structure of baseball. The final was played between Queenston, Gerry's team, and Perth. After a closely fought contest, Perth won the game three to one.

This was when Gerry received his first mention in a newspaper hockey summary, first for the goal he scored in the semi final against Wolseley and second as the "son of the old football star." Initially he must have felt proud when his name was mentioned alongside his father's, yet I can't help feel that the constant repetition by reporters of the connection between the two, between father and son, must have become vexing, if not dispiriting. Perhaps even a cause for resentment? Didn't he eventually question whether he was getting this attention because of his "famous father" or in recognition of his own achievements? Was he annoyed? Gerry was quick to answer, quite emphatically, No! His father wasn't around enough for Gerry to form an image of him, either as a fine athlete or as a father. "And," he said, "I figured if I worked my butt off, I would be successful. On my own terms. My mother drilled this into me."

Still, having a famous father was a mixed blessing. Comparisons were inevitable and Gerry was tugged from admiration and respect on the one hand to annoyance and intense competition on the other. He would prove himself worthy in his own right. Playing in the Playground League was the beginning of a lifetime love for hockey.

A couple of notable facts emerged out of Gerry's somewhat foggy memory about this period. The rinks were outdoors — an obvious bit of information it seemed to me, since they were on the prairies — and, as if his next point will make clear why he's telling me this, "They were surrounded by twelve inch boards. For kids our age this was a perfect height. They demarcated the rink but they also made it easy to clean the ice, which the players and parents did before games and practices. The snow was shoveled into banks that surrounded the rink and provided a sort of grandstand for spectators who could carve their own bleacher or seat into the snow. For the players, when someone body checked you, you flew over the short boards, ending up either in someone's lap or in a mound of snow. The harder the check the deeper the impression. But the landing was always soft. No one got hurt."

Another interesting anecdote, one that should qualify as epic material in hockey mythology, was the story Gerry told of the spliced stick he used in the Parks Board Playground final. This was not unlike David stepping up against Goliath's shield and sword with a sling and five stones. Before the game, Gerry broke the only stick he had. Reluctant to ask if he could borrow a stick and afraid that he might not be allowed to play, he literally nailed the two halves of his stick together and then wrapped his repair job with tape he had collected by unraveling the knobs of discarded sticks from other players. He had been doing his blade this way all season — wrapping it with black tape he'd collected from other player's rejects. Even though his team lost the game, the repair job somewhat unexpectedly stood the test of three periods of "courageous and plucky" action.

For all players, graduation to the Bantam level was not only a relief but a symbol of success. For Gerry, Bantam hockey had all the trappings of the big leagues. Now the boards were between three and four feet high which made body checks meaningful. Moreover, the rinks were lit for early morning and night play. He no longer had to be home for dinner, and, with his mother's blessing, he could play until ten in the evening.

There is no question that Bantam hockey was much more serious and intense than the hockey he had played up till then. Predictably, Gerry's game took a leap forward; he loved the pace and spirited action. Bantam was a brand-new experience. He was excited by the travel to other rinks and by the attention the games received. Quickly he realized that if he did something "bad", if the supporters for the opposing team booed him, whether it was for what they thought was a dirty check or for getting into a fight, he was being noticed. Boos were as good as cheers. They meant that someone was watching and mindful of what he was doing, and that was what he coveted. From newspaper accounts, people were obviously noticing. At the end of the season he was rewarded with an all-star selection as a defenseman.

In response to his seasonal play, there were reports that noted: "Outstanding player of the game was Gerry James,

Franklin rear-guard, who made the plays for two Explorer goals." The inevitable comparisons were repeated: "Like Fathers; Like Sons: Gerry James and Jimmy Grant, bantam hockey league Free Press all-stars, appear to be following in the illustrious foot-steps of their athletic fathers. Gerry's dad was none other than the great 'dynamiter' of western football, the immortal Eddie...."

Comparisons aside, by this time Gerry had established himself as a notable hockey talent. "Importantly," he said, "hockey was a great equalizer. If I was disadvantaged, I never knew it. Every rink throughout the city was the same and everyone treated me as an equal. I didn't care where and how they lived. Bungalow or mansion made no difference. I believed I had all I needed. For the first time I felt like I had the run of the city. And I realized how lucky I was. Everyone clapped and cheered, booed and whistled."

This was the sort of pandemonium he was hearing in the broadcasts from Maple Leaf Gardens, and was exactly what he hungered for.

When the Parks Board Playground and Bantam seasons drew to a close at the end of March, there was an additional bonus. As the five to six feet snow banks that surrounded the rinks began to melt, pucks that had whizzed over the boards and tunneled into the snow during winter play started to become visible. "They were like small pieces of coal," Gerry said, "hidden in a field of white. For me, they were gold." Throughout his career in Parks Board and Bantam hockey, Gerry was always one of the first to dig through the melting snow for pucks. He learned quickly that he would find more than enough pucks to last him through the next season.

As the decade was rounding out of the 1940s, Gerry was as determined as ever to be self-sufficient and independent. One powerful lesson he had learned as a young man, one that sticks with him even today, was to help others, to share, to work cooperatively but never be indebted. Having a trove of pucks set aside for the following season had become a ritual not unlike his mother putting up preserves for the winter months.

Gerry's hockey skills flourished even more at the midget level. From all reports he tore up the league but there was an edge beginning to show up in his play that hadn't been there before. At fifteen he was playing entire games, a full sixty minutes on defense, a tribute not only to his endurance but also to his toughness. Laurie Artiss writes: "A rugged individual named Gerry James who goes by the moniker 'Jesse', was the only fellow on the ice in three midget games at the Amphitheatre Thursday night, as far as 75 spectators were concerned.

"The Monarchs defeated Norwood 2-0 and all James did was score both goals and play 60 minutes on the blue line. And this whole story could be donated to James."

This refrain was repeated when Ted Bowles wrote, "James played the entire game on the Monarch's blue line..." and an unknown reporter noted, "Monarch midget's one-man band, Gerry James again struck the loudest note for the blueshirts Monday night as he scored the solitary goal in his team's 1-0 victory over Tobans. James performed the complete game on defence..."

Because the Monarchs were a Toronto Maple Leaf franchise, all of the players were under constant scrutiny by scouts. In 1949, at Christmas, shortly after Gerry had turned fifteen, he met "Squib" Walker from the Lakehead, whose scouting territory for the Leafs was Northern Ontario and Manitoba. "Squib" had signed up many of the Leaf greats over his career and he was impressed by the young James.

Dressed in a suit and wearing a fedora, looking every bit the stereotypical hockey agent, he walked up to Gerry at the end of a game, complimented him on his play and, with a handshake, left a twenty dollar bill in Gerry's palm. Gerry put it simply: "I was hooked for life. First of all, twenty dollars in 1949 was a lot of money, but second, and far more important, he treated me as though I were a member of his family." Gerry went on to say, "'Squib' passed away before I had any success in Toronto. I never did get to thank him. The money was symbolic but his words, his encouragement, well, those I treasured. What he told me made a future in hockey actually seem possible. It was as though he had bequeathed me something special; all I had to do was prove myself worthy of his support."

As a result of his encounter with "Squib", Gerry would later sign a "C" contract with the Leafs which essentially indentured him to the team for the remainder of his career. While his mother conducted all negotiations, at sixteen Gerry happily signed away his future in hockey.

When we're as young as Gerry was when he met "Squib", I imagine most of us would give anything to know at least a little of what lies ahead, especially if our genie could guarantee us a future that fulfilled all of our personal wishes and dreams. I'm not thinking here of the seventy-two virgins of Islam. Or of a Hefner daydream. For many, I suppose, having some sense of the reality that awaits them is a comfort. Unquestionably most of us are reassured by the known. We've probably experienced enough of life to expect the occasional surprise or derailment that will inevitably come our way. Generally speaking, though, we're impatient to get on with living the life of an adult which we interpret with confidence as having control over our own destiny.

All of the assurances that accompany a contract to play hockey for a certain number of years, up to ten say, are pretty attractive. Beyond that, when the pact is made with an individual who is only sixteen, they're not likely to be too concerned about what's going to happen in the long term, whatever that might be. Why should they be? Ten years is a great leap into tomorrow. It seems an eternity. So much will happen, so many decisions will be made, that contemplating beyond a career in sports seems unreasonable, almost irrational.

To be honest, I don't have a quarrel with this, as long as the life being promised and lived is full and rich. Too often, though, it isn't. We hear too many stories of exploited or shipwrecked athletes, on drugs, broke, or simply living rudderless lives.

In retrospect, I don't think Gerry has been completely satisfied with his choices. Too much of life was left out of the equation. His new masters were only interested in purchasing a well-trained, productive hockey machine. Which they did! Ditto for football. His talent was exceptional and he was dedicated to a fault.

By the end of the season, in March of 1950, Gerry was pretty much a unanimous selection as an all-star. In the *Tribune* Laurie Artiss names his selections to the all-star team: "...while rugged Gerry James of the Monarchs teams up with Hoban on defense." He goes on to say, "One of the most colorful players to enter the league since Wally Stanowski and Jim Thomson, Gerry James' dashing rushes and rugged checks were one of the features of the loop the past season. On top of this, Gerry played close to 60 minutes every game and don't be too surprised if he is selected as the most valuable player in the league."

We can hear Artiss's excitement and enthusiasm in the breathlessness of his writing. So, too, in the *Free Press*. "The league had a host of hard working defensemen, but only two turned in steady, polished performances through the entire season, and both received the same number of votes....Both Hoban and James could be classed as full-time employees with their respective clubs. It was seldom either took a rest, and regardless of their long tours of duty on the ice, they were still battling at the end of every game. They are both big, hard-hitting boys and were the backbones of their teams. James stood out like a beacon on the Monarchs' defense. He was the only really solid player they had."

From Bantam all-star and most valuable player, the move up to Juvenile was an easy step for Gerry. By this time he felt he belonged. His tactical game was exceptional and he knew how to score.

Perhaps more significantly, the "rugged" side of his character emerged. Gerry remembered running the opposition goalie in a game against the West End Orioles and the goalie, Julian Klymkiw, chasing him all over the rink trying to hit him with his goal stick. "He never did catch me," Gerry said. "He was having a pretty good game against us and I figured we needed to get inside his head."

A report of the event in a local newspaper carries the headline: **Oriole Goalkeeeper Banned After Riot**. The article that follows gives a slightly different rendering of the event:

> The trouble started when Klymkiw came 15 feet out of his net to fall on a loose puck. Gerry James of the Monarchs slashed him over the hand and Klymkiw took after James, swinging his stick wildly. Wayne Starr jumped on Klymkiw's back and then everybody got into the act, including players, coaches, spectators and the youngsters snaffling the sticks dropped in the melee."

What I find interesting about this incident was that Gerry's name did not appear anywhere else in the report. He managed to stir the pot and yet he avoided the consequences.

At the end of the season, in the city playoffs, the Monarchs once again faced the Orioles and Klymkiw's dazzling goalkeeping. The two total-point games were tightly-fought battles.

At 6.55 of the third canto centre Tommy Rendall capped a big night with the winning goal on a sharp-angle shot with Bradley of the Orioles in the penalty box. Rendall had passed for both previous Monarch markers, while smooth-skating Jack Robertson scored them. Robertson also got help from line mate Wayne Starr on his second goal.

Their line, Rendall-Robertson-Starr, were Monarchs' scoring combination of the day with rugged Gerry James offering stern defensive work when he wasn't in the penalty box.

Two items from this article are notable. Once again we find Gerry and his good friend Jack Robertson paired together and, perhaps more prophetic as far as Gerry's future was concerned, his penalty minutes were significant enough to catch the eye of the reporter.

An interesting sideline to this playoff encounter was that a few years later, when Klymkiw was working in Winnipeg as a trainer for the Bombers, the two ex-competitors became good friends. As far as Gerry was concerned, what he did was part of the game. He was not trying to hurt Julian or anyone else he came up against.

Traditionally the city final would have meant the end of the season at the juvenile level but during those days, junior, juvenile and midget teams were often still connected organizationally and financially to one of the "big six" NHL teams. The Monarchs were a part of the Toronto Maple Leafs system, as were the Saskatoon Wesleys, and, with a little last minute manoeuvring, a regional playoff was arranged.

Originally there was to be no juvenile playdowns but it is rumored that Clarence (Happy) Day, business manager of the Toronto Maple Leafs, swung the deal since both teams are under the wing of the Leafs.

Monarchs will throw plenty of power at the Wesleys in the shape of a burly defence composed of Gerry James, Elton Taylor, Bill Riley and Ed Willems, while the forward line is led by the classy Tom Rendall.

The Wesleys have let little news leak out of their camp with regard to who are the big guns but when Happy Day last came through Winnipeg he was pleased with the caliber of hockey that the Saskatoon teams are dishing up.

Day saw the Monarchs perform early in the season and since he has coaxed the C.A.H.A. into giving the playdowns its blessing he must feel that the clubs are fairly evenly matched.

I'm not convinced that Day really cared whether or not the teams were fairly matched. He was undoubtedly on a scouting mission and used his considerable political influence to arrange a show for his benefit.

With the Monarchs' victory came a new challenge, this time on the road, in Edmonton, against the Oil Kings, for the Western Canadian Juvenile Hockey Championship. Again, this was not a sanctioned event but rather one organized "behind the scenes". Jack Robertson gives this account of the trip and competition:

Edmonton had a few notable hockey players namely Norm Ullman, Melinik and Johnny Bucyk. We travelled to Edmonton from Winnipeg on a train. It had bunk beds in every car where the whole team slept, or should I say, tried to. Gerry kept everyone up, jumping from bunk to bunk like a monkey. Finally the coach came in and shut him down.

In the game Gerry body-checked a player so hard that

he put him into the nickel seats. He wasn't a fan favourite
thereafter. Several fans were out to get him when we left the
arena. We were outnumbered. Our stick boy cut the bundle
of sticks and gave everyone a stick for protection.

We were runners up but it was very close series.

Gerry's version of the story is a little bit different. "We
got trounced," he says, "but we were a couple of bodies short
and not in the best of shape when we arrived in Edmonton.
I don't think we ever recovered enough to give them our
best shot."

A local reporter confirmed Gerry's rendition.

'Peg Juveniles Lose Opener 8 - 3:

Edmonton Maple Leafs Friday night whipped Winnipeg
Monarchs 8 – 3 to take a healthy lead in their two-game,
total goal series for the Western Juvenile Hockey Championship.

It was Leafs' 32nd win in 33 starts this season. Second
game of the series will be played here Saturday night.

More than 1000 fans saw a good, fast contest in which
superior finish around the net paid off for the winners. Edmonton held 2 - 1 and 5 - 2 period leads before salting the
game away by outscoring Monarchs 3 - 1 in the finale....

Gerry James of Winnipeg and Ed Zemrau of Edmonton,
both defencemen, were the best players on the ice.

"When the smoke had cleared at the end of the second
game," Gerry remarked, "I think we had lost again by an
equally one-sided margin. But we had a great time."

Gerry returned home to discover that he had been selected as one of the "first team" defenseman on the "Juvenile Dream Team". While he was not a unanimous choice of
the league's coaches, he was obviously good enough in the

eyes of the Monarchs' Junior coaching staff to bring up for the Memorial Cup final against the Barrie Flyers. He was a sixteen-year old thrust into a national final against nineteen and twenty-year olds. Can there be any question that Gerry's appearance in this competition was orchestrated, at least in part, by the brass in the Leafs' organization? They wanted to see how their future prospect would do against bigger, faster and more talented opponents.

Gerry felt he was the beneficiary of two major breaks when this decision to bring him up to play for the juniors was made. In addition to the exposure he received, the coaches moved him from defense to left wing. (Throughout the remainder of his career, when it was settled that he was destined for Toronto, he would play on right wing.)

"Probably if the coaches hadn't played me on the wing, I would never have been called up to Toronto. I couldn't skate backwards well enough to play defense. Smythe and Day would have noticed that right away."

I suspect Stafford Smythe and Hap Day already knew this about Gerry's game and had put in a request with the Monarchs' management that he be allowed to play on the wing.

Bob Moir in the *Winnipeg Free Press* noted that Gerry did more than prove himself equal to the task:

> However, if it hadn't been for a kid named Gerry James, his linemates Ron Barr and Ross Parke, right-winger Johnny Novak and Riley, Monarchs would probably still be trying to dig themselves out of the ice into which they were skated last night.
>
> James and Riley have definitely emerged as stars in the series, if stars can be picked out of a group of players which have been dominated so completely by a well-drilled and opportunist club like Barrie.

Vince Leah in the *Winnipeg Tribune* echoed these observations: "Johnny Novak, Ron Barr and James worked hard for Monarchs. James refused to be deterred by the rugged Flyers and Barr gave 'em bounce for bounce…"

Similarly, Maurice Smith in his column "Time Out" in the *Free Press* wrote:

And now we'd like to hand out a little praise to one unit of the Monarch team — we mean the Barr, Parke and James line. If the other Monarch forward units would show as much drive as this threesome, we know quite a few people who would be a lot happier. Young James, in particular, appears to relish the going, and give out more than he takes. James, who is the son of Eddie, once one of Canada's greatest football stars, was only three days too old for midget hockey this year, and thus still is eligible for juvenile next season. That is, of course, if he's still around Winnipeg, because Stafford Smythe thinks the kid is a pretty good pro prospect.

Most important, as far as Gerry's future was concerned, was the serious attention he was getting. In a short, anonymous clipping from one of the Winnipeg newspapers, the author wrote:

You have it straight from the junior partner of the famous hockey firm of Smythe and Smythe that it wasn't so much the Barrie flyers as the Eastern style of hockey that whipped the Monarchs, Wednesday night in the first game of the Memorial cup final.

Stafford Smythe, boss of Toronto junior Marlboros who gave Barrie a rare old battle in the OHA junior finals, points out the Monarchs were surprised by Barrie tactics which are commonplace in the East, where the 'amateur' teams follow the pro pattern.

"You will have to let your better players get out of Winnipeg if they are going to do anything in junior hockey," opined Staff. "We do a lot of things in the east that they don't do in the west."

"Did you see Leo Labine bodycheck a Monarch defenceman to score his goal? You don't see those things happen out here."

Labine did crash into a Regal rear-guard who was in the act of bringing the puck out. Labine picked up the rubber off the surprised Monarch and walked in to score on the lonely Don Collins.

Smythe also felt that Barrie can play "one hundred per cent better" than they did Wednesday...so can the Monarchs, who put on a dismal display for the customers and their Toronto sponsors who are represented by Smythe, Bob Davidson and chief scout Squib Walker.

Smythe liked Gerry James.

"But we'd have to move him out of here to make anything out of him. By the time he gets away it may be too late."

❧

There is a photograph of Gerry, different from all the other newspaper portraits taken around this time. I bypassed it completely the first time I was thumbing through the scrapbook his mother compiled.

He was fifteen and had just been selected as an all-star in high school football, after the 1950 season when he was playing for Kelvin. His hair was cropped much shorter than usual; not a brush cut common in those days, but sheered right down to the scalp, down to revealing the scars from hockey. His mother had given him money for a haircut but Gerry was particularly fond of apple turnovers. He spent his haircut money on one or more of those tasty treats. To help him out of his dilemma, his friends Bob Kirvan and Jack Robertson, agreed to cut his hair.

As they trimmed away, he ran his fingers through what curls were left to see how they were doing, and he kept telling them to cut it shorter, as if paying penance for the lie he might later have to tell his mother. He knew she would notice how close to his skull his hair had been shorn and wonder why. But she probably would not ask what had happened. She would accept his silence. He was certain she would know what he had done. When he later saw himself in a mirror, he was horrified. He knew, even at fifteen, what others know about us is revealed in our hearts and written and read on our faces. I'm confident that by this time he had a hunch there was nowhere to hide, not with his talent.

6 / Toronto: The Game Is On

When the end of summer rolled around, and the baseball season had ended, Gerry was on his way to Toronto.

As soon as Stafford Smythe extended him an invitation to come and play for the Toronto Marlboros, Gerry's mother took charge of negotiations. Smythe was quick to learn where Gerry got his genes; in particular those that defined his hard-nosed and competitive spirit.

Moira McLean — she had remarried by this time — was a very determined person. She made sure that her son was well taken care of. In addition to his accommodation and meals, Gerry was to receive a fifty dollar a week allowance. Then half-way through the summer she re-opened negotiations and insisted that Smythe also include a clothing allowance of two hundred dollars a year as part of the contract. She wanted her boy to look good; to look like he belonged. Smythe agreed to all of her demands. She also made sure Gerry was placed in a good school with a well-balanced and reputable academic and athletic programme. The year was 1951, the month August.

Gerry's most vivid memory of the move was his arrival at the fabled home of the Leafs and of Foster Hewitt's broadcasts, Maple Leaf Gardens. "I remember· taking the tram downtown and sauntering up to the Gardens' entrance, expecting some sort of fanfare — you know, a band, cheerleaders, that sort of thing — but when I announced I had arrived, no one knew who I was. There I was, in hockey central, home of my future teams, and no one knew me from Adam. I don't think I've ever felt quite so insignificant."

Quickly a dispute arose between the Ontario Hockey Association, the Manitoba Amateur Hockey Association, and the Canadian Amateur Hockey Association over Gerry's eligibility to play hockey for the Toronto Marlboros. He was only sixteen years old and the Association's rules made it clear that until he was eighteen, unless he lived with family, he was unable to relocate to Toronto just to play hockey. The Leaf organization was determined to contest a policy which they considered restrictive if not illegal. The debate spilled over onto radio and into the Winnipeg newspapers.

Conny Smythe, the Toronto Maple Leaf bossman, was telling Al (*Toronto Globe and Mail*) Nickleson that certain regulations of the Canadian Amateur Hockey association hamper the careers of budding young hockey stars, particularly those laddies with future NHL class.

Smythe wants to toss the agreements existing between the NHL and CAHA out of the nearest window and let the pros go back to a system of free enterprise.

The Leafian leader does not like the idea of the CAHA telling a lad who has not reached his 18th birthday he can't move out of his own backyard. Smythe, of course, has 16-year-old Gerry James in Toronto, not eligible to play for Marlboro juniors but playing great football for Runnymede Collegiate. If a lad moves with the folks or if he is working and gets transferred — that's different, otherwise he stays at home.

Says Smythe: "When these hockey moguls are saying that the kids can't move, it's like telling that 17-year-old golf champion, Marlene Stewart, that she shouldn't have gone near the pro at Fonthill," said Smythe.

"It's important that fellows get started young in hockey. They're paid on their ability, not their age. The rules are doing a disservice to the boys who want to become pros and to the teams which want them. When some kids are good enough to play junior or senior hockey, they still are of juvenile age and thus not allowed to move. That's poor legislation. I don't think the CAHA has any right to do it.

"The CAHA might have to go a long way down the age group to get to amateurs," he added. "Let pro hockey belong to the pros. None of this business of $150 a week to a player and still call him an amateur.

"The thing necessary to keep the game going is the supply of hockey players. There's nothing the matter with the game itself. I don't think the agreement with the CAHA and the changes made by it in rules during the last few years have done anything to produce players."

Originally, said Smythe, there was no age limit. He recalled that under that system the Leaf organization had brought the Metz brothers to Toronto from Wilcox, Sask., when they were in their early teens and had paid for their education while they went to school and played amateur hockey.

"They played their way up in hockey and they were on world championship Leaf teams. Now they're respected members of their community back in Saskatchewan with, as some of the sports writers say, 'a fair amount of lettuce.'"

"There were others too, whom we took at an early age. Fellows like Jim Thomson, Tod Sloan, Flem Mackell. Proof of the pudding is that the Leafs, as world champions, are a young club. All the fellows must have started pretty young and that's why they're good. Now the amateurs have stopped all that.

"In my opinion — and I learned this in horse racing — the great ones are born that way. They're not made. It's supposed to be bad to race a horse as a two-year-old. That statement probably originated with someone who wanted to lessen the competition while running his own two-year-old. Citation, the world's leading money winner, raced as a two-year-old and so did many other great horses."

"If a boy has a chance to make money as a proper pro, who's to tell him he shouldn't. As an example, let's say there's a kid of 17 who comes from a family of moderate means. He wants to turn pro to increase his earning power and is good enough to do it. Why should the CAHA prevent him from earning a good salary and thus helping better the living standards of his family?"

*   *   *

The rule was put in the book in the first place to try and prevent wholesale movement of young players away from their own fireside by the rich clubs, and to make it worthwhile for the poorer junior outfits to bring players along.

In any event, Monarchs will not have the benefit of the aggressive young James. However, being a member of the Leaf system, they can hardly tell the boss where their players shall play.

✥

Gerry agrees with Conn Smythe. For years he has been advising parents that the choice of where their children play any sport should be up to them. Associations and federations of sport should not be dictating where people play. Unfortunately, people think they might be jeopardizing their kid's futures if they don't do the bidding of a pro club.

"The reality is," Gerry argues, "if a kid is good enough to play at the pro level he will make a team somewhere. Talent is too rare. Too precious."

While the dispute between the federations raged, Gerry's mother stepped into the breach and offered to move to Toronto. She was also concerned that young Gerry was not being fed well enough, even though her son was living with Stafford Smythe's mother-in-law. Gerry's letters home might have exaggerated the status of the larder.

Eventually Gerry's mother took up residence in the city for a period of about three months, establishing a family presence, but in a curious plot twist, Gerry was not even practising and playing hockey with the Marlies. Until the eligibility dispute could be resolved, he was consigned to the Marlboros' farm team, the Weston "B" Dukes, a Tier 2 junior franchise located on the outskirts of the city.

On several occasions Gerry has remarked that, in retrospect, he probably was not good enough to play with the senior team. I think he was probably right. Some pundits at the time suggested that the Marlies already had a fixed roster and that Gerry was in need of additional coaching and conditioning before he would find a place on the senior team.

Even so, first accounts out of the Leaf organization, in particular those from Stafford Smythe, indicated that they expected Gerry in the senior ranks within two to three weeks.

For the next few weeks, 16-year-old Gerry will show his wares with the Weston Dukes. But Marlboro Manager Staff Smythe said last night that he'd likely be moved up within three weeks.

"We want him to get into shape with the B's." Smythe said. Besides, this is his first season as a defenseman and he still has lots to learn.

"Don't worry, James will be up there," he continued.

"I'm not just being pessimistic when I say there are bound to be injuries on a club and it's certainly nice to have somebody like Gerry waiting to get into action."

Whether or not Smythe was misquoted or simply did not know his own talent pool (the latter is most likely from what Gerry has told me), the fact was that except for his call-up the previous spring to the Monarchs for the Memorial Cup, he had played every game in his short career as a defenseman. He had lots to learn as a new Marlie, but now as a winger; in his case, on right wing.

As the 1951 - 52 season got off to a start, the expectations for Gerry were very high indeed. In fact, they were so high as to be unrealistic.

Gerry James, the sensational Winnipeg high school football star, has finally been cleared by the C.A.H.A. registration committee to play hockey for Reggie Hamilton's junior Dukes.

Clearance of the 16-year-old winger of last year's Memorial cup finalists, Winnipeg Monarchs, should enhance Marlies' chances of grabbing Canada's top junior honors.

A rugged type of player, James is expected to put back the bounce that the graduation of Ron Hurst cost the Dukes. Although he has been practicing hockey, James will play himself into shape with Weston's Junior B Dukes tonight.

In spite of this much-trumpeted optimism about his place on the senior team, fate conspired to slow his progress down. Gerry ended up playing a good part of his first season in Toronto with the Tier 2 Weston franchise. In October, during all of this turmoil about his status, Gerry turned seventeen.

Surprisingly, at such a young age he had also earned a

reputation as a fairly notorious character. He played hard and he played tough but what was often missed was that he was also assisting on and scoring his share of goals. While these successes were reported, it was comments such as the following that typified a good part of the ink Gerry attracted. "James supplied Dukes' off-color incident when he bashed Gordie Bruce into the sideboards, and the Lions' forward suffered a broken nose. The Jolter took a major as punishment." Or, "James was the game's bad boy with four penalties to his credit."

Of course, this rugged style of play was exactly what the Leaf brain-trust loved about Gerry's game and was what eventually earned him a spot in the Marlies' lineup as they entered the quarter finals of the OHA in the spring of 1952, but only after he helped the Weston Dukes to the Junior B championship against the Marlies' long-time rivals, the St. Michael's Buzzers.

※

Although Gerry had travelled east to play hockey in the Toronto Maple Leafs system, ironically it was in football that he truly excelled — at Runnymede Collegiate. As Gordon Campbell observed:

> Who has more trouble than Marlboros? After complying with all regulations in order to make Gerry James eligible to play in these parts, the Dukes now have to wait for a vote of the C.A.H.A. registration committee.
>
> When the mother of the 17-year-old Winnipeg grid and hockey star moved to Toronto this week (*he was actually only 16 at the time this article was written*), it looked like the last barrier to his branch-to-branch transfer had been cut down — but it wasn't so.

The Manitoba Hockey Association in a telegram to the O.H.A. refused the transfer on the grounds they weren't convinced Mrs. James had given up her Winnipeg residence.

"There'd be no doubt about the transfer, if it wasn't for the Marlboros," declared General Manager Stafford Smythe. "You can't force a person to sell all her holdings just because she moves."

Rules of the C.A. H. A. say that if a player's family moves to another branch, he can obtain a transfer despite the fact he's under 18 years of age.

Biggest problem facing Gerry, son of the great Winnipeg Blue Bomber, "Dynamite" Eddie James, is whether to choose hockey or the grid pastime for a career.

Since his arrival in the east in August, young James has been a terror of the grid for Runnymede Collegiate. In the Redmen's march to a first place tie in the T.D.I.A.A. football loop, Gerry has scored a touchdown or two in each of their games.

"For years I haven't had a boy any better than James," said Hal Brown, Runnymede coach, "and I doubt if you'll see many better in high school. They call us a one-man team."

Although the five-foot, 11-inch, 185-pounder has been compared to Argos' Ted Toogood after his 125-yard touchdown to defeat York Memorial a week ago, he plans to give up football for hockey.

"My first love is football," he admitted, "but I'd like to play pro hockey. I haven't made any money at it yet — but they pay three times as much here as in Winnipeg."

James said his mother didn't sell her home in Winnipeg because his older brother, Don is living there. Both Gerry and Mrs. James are staying with friends until they find an apartment.

Up to this point in his life, Gerry had played only one

year of organized football and while his career on the gridiron unfolded very differently from baseball, it replicated his hockey career. He learned a lot about the game from sandlot scrimmages; from kicking and passing the ball around with friends; from dodging between them on a field on a cool fall afternoon. Pick-up games, where everyone took turns snapping the ball, playing quarterback or going for a pass, were his early classroom. As with hockey, when he finally got into organized games, the coaching was excellent, often because his coaches were pros who lived in the area, and there were scouts galore. It wasn't long before he was tagged as a promising prospect.

From the beginning he was fanatical, partly in response to the challenges he had heard throughout his life, but also because he desperately wanted to please his father. At Kelvin he was an instant star, on both offence and defense. In high school, before he became known as Kid Dynamite, his nickname was Jesse, after the notorious American outlaw. This was an apt nickname as he burst on to this particular field of dreams. On offence, he gobbled up yards like a race horse and on defense intercepted passes with ease. Remaining true to form, in his first season he was named to the city all-star team.

At Runnymede he was also an immediate success. When his mother asked one of his ex-coaches in Winnipeg to send the school a letter reminding them of Gerry's potential as an athlete, the coach at Runnymede sent back this reply:

Dear Sir,
I am very grateful for your sending of clippings about Gerry James. I have seen already the truth of these; in fact, I recognized almost at once where Gerry's interests lie, and he has starred for me in our initial game (which we only tied, against the toughest team of the league).

Our school, though small, is known as the School for Athletes, and I only hope we can give this young fellow the best in training and in sports, as well as leadership.

I am having him out to the house tonight with some of the boys — we will try to look after him.

Thanks again —

Harold J. Brown

The Catch-22 for everyone concerned about Gerry's potential, in particular his dual calling, was summarized in a column from one of the major Winnipeg papers:

It seems that Toronto Maple Leafs are so determined to have young Gerry James playing hockey for their junior Marlboros this year, that they are also moving Gerry's mother east....Under the C.A.H.A. regulations, James, because of his age, does not qualify for a transfer to the "Dukes".... However, if his family takes up residence in the east then that would be a horse of another color....But even at that, the Manitoba Amateur Hockey association might fight the case, although we don't see where they would have much chance of winning....This is just a case in point to what extremes professional clubs will go to make sure they have a hockey player playing where they want him to play.... Had James been forced to stay out of hockey a full season, it might have retarded his development and the Leafs, who see "gold" in young Mr. James, just aren't going to take any chances....

*   *   *

Incidentally, here's a clipping from last Saturday's *Toronto Star* which concerns the same Gerry James:

*   *   *

For a 16-year-old youngster who wants to play hockey for a living, Runnymede's Gerry James is currently tearing apart the T.D.I.A.A.'s football record book, page by page.

Yesterday afternoon with less than two minutes left in the senior game, James took a York Memorial kick behind his own goal-line and ran it out. Not content with just taking the ball over the line, James turned on the steam and plunged right through the middle of the Memorial squad to cross York's goal-line 125 yards later.

Although sensational in its own right, James' effort broke a 6 – 6 deadlock and gave the Redmen a 12 – 6 victory to keep their undefeated status.

*   *   *

Looks like young Gerry is a real chip off the old block. At any rate, we know that his dad — Dynamite Eddie James — certainly gets a kick out of knowing that he has a son who bids fair to be a great football star, if hockey doesn't claim him.

Therein laid the dilemma; the powerful and influential Leaf organization, while battling to keep their hockey treasure in Toronto, could only stand by and watch their protégé surpass himself in another sport. He was doing this in a city league that was probably the most competitive in Canada. The accolades continued. This excerpt, for example, appeared in the *Toronto Telegram*:

Most spectacular game of the afternoon, however was at Runnymede where Gerry James made like the Montreal Flyer in Redmen's 26 – 3 win from Brampton. The Winnipeg scooter dashed 80 yards returning a kick for one touchdown, scored two others from small arms range and had a 120-yard sprint nullified when an official thought he had stepped out of touch. And it was while James was taking a five-minute breather on the bench that Brampton got close enough to kick into the end zone from whence Gerry started his 120-yard dash."

In short, Gerry's season with Runnymede was nothing short of sensational. He averaged over twelve points a game, played both offence and defense, and rewrote the record book.

One of the ironies of football then being played in Toronto is that although the league was superior to Winnipeg's, the coaching was definitely inferior.

"With all due respect to Mr. Brown, he was a teacher who had a passion for football," Gerry said. "But he had a limited knowledge of the game."

In Winnipeg, his coaches were pros doing their civic duty.

In Toronto they played on municipal fields in front of crowds of one or two hundred standing along the sidelines, while in Winnipeg they played at Osborne Stadium in front of five thousand seated yelling, cheering fans.

I suspect there was a downside to all of this success, in both cities. The physical and emotional demands on a young body had to be extraordinary. And how does a young ego cope with all of this attention?

Other athletes who have played in the top flight of their sport say that to compete at an élite level requires unqualified confidence.

"I hated to lose," Ferguson Jenkins said in a recent interview with Peter Mansbridge. "I had a will to win."

If such ambition is the norm for an élite athlete was it reasonable for people to expect someone like Gerry, who had the talent and the will of a seasoned veteran, to mature like any other young man? I think not. If at times he seemed unmanageable or socially awkward, who was to blame?

Jump ahead a few years and add to these questions already being posed in the spring of 1952 the fact that Gerry accidentally lost sight in his right eye at twenty (1955) while playing hockey and the fact that he suffered a severe leg fracture at age twenty-three (1958) while playing football, and you have the recipe for one broken human being. But Gerry did not break! I think he might have peaked much earlier than anticipated — the Bombers appeared to think so after the 1962 season — but he definitely did not break. In fact, he became what Tex Coulter, former Montreal Alouette tackle, called in a *Star Weekly* article, "Everybody's All-Star". The reality is that from the time he arrived in Toronto at the age of sixteen in 1951 to his career threatening injury at the age of twenty-three in September of 1958, he was being asked to grow up awfully quickly.

❧

After an exceptional season with his Tier 2 Weston team and his simultaneous success at Runnymede, Gerry was called up in February to play in the quarter-finals of the O.H.A. with the Toronto Marlboros. A *Globe and Mail* article from March 8, 1952 reported: "Husky Gerry James will replace Rod McElroy on the Marlboros' first forward line when the Dukes open their OHA Junior 'A' best-of-seven quarter-final series against Guelph Biltmores at the Gardens tomorrow." Another article noted: "As this will be James' fourth game, he's an 'A-er' from here on in." Gerry had finally graduated to the Marlies, a few months later than expected.

Back in Winnipeg, the press and presumably the fans were not as impressed.

It will interest Coach Walter Monson to learn that Toronto Marlboros are using Gerry James on the forward line "to give them more bodychecking." It's a fine thing when a forward is hired merely to knock other people down but that is what hockey has progressed to in this day and age.

Monarchs could have used James this season. Another lad that was whisked away to play for Marlboros is Chuck Lumsden. But the Dukes have not had his services in the playoffs. The big fellow has been ailing.

Lumsden and James on the Monarchs this term and you'd be awfully close to a Memorial Cup

The old debate about the violent side of hockey persisted. While complaining about the new, rugged style of play, largely advocated by Easterners we are led to believe, this reporter still wished Gerry were playing for the Winnipeg Monarchs. Presumably if the "belter" or "jolter" was on his team, that was okay. The point is, no matter where he played, Gerry would have been running at the opposition.

Gerry's session with the highly-touted senior team, picked to make the finals at least, turned out to be a short affair. The Marlies were eliminated 4 - 2 in a seven game series. Gerry, though, received accolades from the media. George Dulmage wrote: "Best goal of the game? Why by James, who scored the final Duke counter while Fontinato was serving time. Poland, who didn't get a point, passed back to Balfour from the corner, Balfour lateralled it to Lumsden, who slipped it ahead to James and Gerry hammered it in from eight feet." After the second to last game, Dulmage stated under the heading "Duke's Best": "In contrast to this the Dukes got maximum efforts only from Gerry James, who keeps improving each time out and was much their best player." After the elimination game, Dulmage made the following prediction: "Over the series Gerry James, Wally

Maxwell and Chuck Lumsden were the Marlies stars. James will someday be great."

While elimination from the playoffs was disappointing, Gerry had two causes for celebration. In the fall of 1951, he had made his first sighting of Marg Petrie.

One day, as he went to climb on the bus, he saw the lovely figure of a young woman descending the stairs. "I caught a glimpse of her face as we passed," he says, laughing, "and turned around to watch her as the bus crawled away from the curb. I decided then and there I wanted to know her."

For her part, Marg had already noticed Gerry on the football field. She was a cheerleader for the Weston school team and when they played Runnymede, Gerry, trying to get everyone's attention, had attempted to perform a cartwheel in front of all of the cheerleaders. "He looked like a spider climbing a wall and behaved like a complete jerk," Marg recalled, "but I still found him interesting. Perhaps odd is a better word."

By this time, in early 1952, Marg's parents, Bill and Lillian Petrie, had moved into their new home in the Conn Smythe sandpits, a development in the Runnymede catchment area of Toronto. But rather than switch schools in mid-term, Marg decided to complete her school year at Weston.

Even so, the romance was destined to happen. Marg's parents were big sports enthusiasts, especially of the Leafs, both hockey and baseball. Reluctantly they attended Weston games although they disliked the team because it was stacked with Marlie hopefuls who were usually bigger and more talented than their opposition. In particular they disliked Gerry, who they thought was a goon. He was far too rough — "the way he knocked around the smaller boys". Marg accompanied her parents to games and got her fill of watching Gerry. She also got an earful about his aggressive play.

During the Easter holidays, she went to visit a friend, Pat McGee, whose parents had also recently moved to the Runnymede area. Across the street from the McGee house was a school and field and, as if in accord with Cupid's plan, there was Gerry passing a ball around in a loose scrimmage with friends. Pat called Gerry over and introduced him to Marg. Soon the three walked off down the street, Gerry chatting up a storm. He was determined to impress Marg whom he remembered from the bus stop. During the walk he extracted her address and an invitation to come over to her house for a visit. He had little or no money so a formal date was out of the question.

When Marg told her mother who was coming over, perhaps for dinner, she was unimpressed.

"Surely not," Lillian Petrie said, "not that dirty player, James?"

Within a few weeks, though, Lillian and Gerry had become good buddies. Lillian was several months pregnant and as she grew bigger, Gerry called her jelly belly. "No one else," Marg insists, "would have gotten away with calling my mother jelly belly."

Faye, Marg's youngest sister, was born on May 3. Lynda, Marg's other sister, was already seven. Quickly Gerry had the quartet of Petrie women under his spell. Changing wee Faye's diapers particularly endeared him to Lillian. Off the ice, he could be a cheerful and affable young man, a side of his character he exhibited and exploited in his close relationship with his own mother. In a way, being in the company of women may have been the only chance he had to be completely himself.

Marg and Gerry were constant companions until school ended in June and he returned to Winnipeg, to pursue his dream of playing professional football. He would write to Marg weekly and in July return to Toronto, triumphant, as a member of the Winnipeg Blue Bombers.

⁊

Gerry's second stroke of good fortune that year came on February 28, 1952 when he received a letter from A. H. (Bert) Warwick — inducted into the Canadian Football Hall of Fame in 1964 as a builder — inviting Gerry to attend the Blue Bombers' spring practice which would start on May 15. Warwick went on to say that if this interfered with school Gerry could attend the senior practices starting around the first of July. He continued:

> You could even go right along with the team in practice & come east for the exhibition games and then decide, if you are through school if you'd finish the season. If you are not through your schooling & intend to return you could drop out after the exhibition games and so be eligible for High School football this season & then next year, as a result of the period with the club, be ready to go for the season.
>
> In either case spring or regular practice we will pay you for out and back, including berth & meals plus an equitable weekly payment, if you do not decide to stay and play with the Club all season & so go on a contract.
>
> For spring practice we would pay you $50.00 a week, for fall practice (July 1ˢᵗ on) the same, if you decided to go back to school, up to the end of the exhibition games. If you decided to stay for the full season that would be a different matter as we'd then like to give you a contract based on ability etc.
>
> Yours truly,
> Ald (Bert) Warwick
> V-P in charge of team

No doubt receiving this letter was a momentous event in Gerry's life. Because of school commitments, he showed up for the senior practice, expecting to gain some valuable experience but also assuming he would be cut. Training went well, especially under the guidance of Tom Casey who quickly became Gerry's principal mentor. After the Blue Bombers completed the exhibition schedule, management asked Gerry to stay on.

Once again, Gerry's mom stepped in and negotiated Gerry's contract. He would only be allowed to play during the regular season and the Bombers would have to arrange for him to receive some tutoring. The team would pay him two thousand dollars for the season, a pretty good reward for an under-aged rookie.

Used primarily for kickoff and punt returns, Gerry did manage to score a couple of touchdowns and maintain an average return on punts (at a time when there was no blocking) of 9.9 yards, only slightly behind Casey's impressive league leading average of 10.0 yards. They were an explosive duo.

Tom Casey would prove to be an invaluable mentor for Gerry as well as a life-long, close friend.

Dr. Tom Casey was the first Afro-American player to be inducted into the Canadian Football Hall of Fame. After a stint in the US navy and a year playing in an upstart US league in New York, he came north to play for the Hamilton Wild Cats (before they joined up with the Hamilton Tigers to become the Tiger-Cats). He had applied to McMaster's medical school but had been rejected. In 1950, he applied to the University of Manitoba, from which he would eventually get his medical degree, and offered his services to the Blue Bombers. What a happy marriage. Tom was a great two-way player, a superb running back and a fine defensive back. For six years, he was named an All-Star in the CFL and in 1950, two years before he met Gerry, he won the Eddie James Memorial Trophy. Ironically, when I told Gerry this recently, he was not aware that his good friend had won the trophy given out in his father's name.

This reticence was characteristic of Tom; he rarely spoke about himself and his accomplishments. "He was a lovely man — quiet, polite, well read. A brilliant man. Really classy," Marg said.

There was a wistful expression on her face, almost as if she were conjuring up an image of the man. I knew from my research that Tom had died in 2002.

"Close to Mother's Day in 1955," she added, "Tom phoned to invite me out for dinner. 'We will go out to a fine restaurant,' he told me. 'Mothers should never be alone on Mother's Day.'

"Moira and I had just returned from Regina where Gerry and the Marlies had won the Memorial Cup. Debbie, our baby daughter — who was about nine months by this time — and I had stayed on in Winnipeg with Moira while Gerry continued east to Toronto with the Marlies to turn in his gear, pack up our belongings and drive home to Winnipeg. Bomber training camp was only a few weeks away. I think Tom was doing his internship at the time.

"Anyway, when Tom showed up at the front door, dressed like a gentleman, he looked pensive, almost apologetic, and then asked if I would mind going to a friend's place for dinner instead of going out to the well-known restaurant he had mentioned. He said, 'I hope you won't be disappointed.' Of course I didn't mind but I must have looked puzzled because he then said that he did not want to embarrass me. He was afraid there might be repercussions if I were seen out in public with a black man. 'People will look down on you,' he said. I was shocked and embarrassed that he thought people, in Canada, would look at us that way. When Gerry got home I told him what had happened and he was furious. He couldn't believe that such a thing would happen in our city. But he knew it did. As did I, but it was one of those things I had put to the back of my mind. We like to feel superior to Americans when it comes to issues of tolerance. But we're guilty of the same ugliness."

After the following season, in 1956, Tom took up a two-year residency in England and eventually became a neurologist. He came back to Winnipeg where he wanted to practice medicine but was told by the other doctors and administrators from the city hospital that no one would want a black doctor. When he told Marg and Gerry this they both remember staring at him in disbelief. He liked Canada because it was less racist than the US, but, sadly, the country was racist all the same. Leaving behind the city where he had been named "Citizen of the Year" and had been honoured with a "Tom Casey" night at Winnipeg Stadium at the end of his football career, Tom returned to the States where he had a very successful medical career.

As we talked, Marg remembered other incidents of racism but Gerry stated emphatically that there was no racial tension between members of the team, not that he observed. I'm inclined to think this is wishful thinking, and, deep down, not likely to stand up to scrutiny. Gerry was, under that rough, gruff veneer, an idealist and an optimist.

In 1993, when the couple stayed with Tom at his home in Fairfield, Connecticut, he had become much more militant on the subject of race. He had attempted to take out a membership in the local golf club but was turned away, repeatedly. There was anger and sorrow in his voice. Not much had changed for the gentle man from Ohio.

Gerry and Marg named their first son, Kelly Charles, born in 1959, KC for short, not only to acknowledge Gerry's grandfather, but to celebrate their close friend Tom Casey.

To this day they refer to their eldest son as KC.

A short article describing a game against Ottawa characterized Gerry and his play during his first season with the Bombers.

> There was no doubt about the hard-hitting. At half-time as the players headed for the dressing rooms, Tom O'Malley said to Joe Zaleski, 'What have you guys been eating, raw meat?'
>
> Probably the most vicious collision of the day came when Gerry James roared in from nowhere to smash Baldwin into the 'top row of the bleachers.' The lanky Ottawa veteran end was out cold for a while and missed quite a few plays. More than one Bomber said afterwards, 'When Baldwin finds out it was only a 17-year-old kid that hit him he'll probably want to quit the game.

As if to put an exclamation mark on Gerry's first season in pro ball, he and Lorne Benson were the stars of the final regular season game against Regina. Gorde Hunter wrote: "Regina — Led by a pair of brilliant rookie backfielders, Winnipeg Blue bombers clinched first place in the W.I.F.U. Monday afternoon at Taylor Field, swamping the last place Regina Roughriders by a 37 to 1 count. Lorne Benson and Gerry James, a pair of hard running backs, playing their first season in senior company, stole the show with two touchdowns apiece. Gerry Palmer and Tom Casey counted the other Winnipeg majors on passes from Jack Jacobs. Jacobs also passed to James for one of his five pointers, kicked a pair of singles and converted five of the six touchdowns."

Gerry had announced rather emphatically his arrival in the big leagues. In an interview, George Trafton, Bomber coach, didn't mince words on the subject of James. "He's the best football prospect I've seen in Canada. He can be a star for at least 10 years."

❧

With the Bombers destined for the playoffs, Gerry left the team at the end of the regular season and headed for Toronto. He was now a full-fledged member of the Marlies and was looking forward to his hockey season. Frantically, Winnipeg would put in one more request for his services, for the third and final game of the western finals against Edmonton, a game which they would lose. But his focus now, from December 1952 to the end of the season in the spring of 1953, was hockey.

A few noteworthy developments occurred during this partial year back in Toronto. His relationship with Marg got back on track, he returned to school for his senior year and, with assistance from his mother, he managed to learn how to play one pro sport off against the other. With a few blips along the way, Gerry discovered he could coordinate his playing time in each sport quite handily. The major challenge to his playing in two sports came in 1956 when the Leafs insisted he play only hockey. But for the time being, he was on a roll. Once he finished his season with the Marlies, he would return to Winnipeg and play with the Bombers. What a life!

A lot of debate still swirled around his future in two sports. In an article by Alan Ryder Thomas for a major Toronto daily, his headline read:

Which will he choose?
hockey Gerry James football
He plays pro football, heads for pro hockey and he's only 17.

Gerry was actually 18 when this piece was written and he had made his decision: He was going to succeed in both sports.

His first weeks back with the Marlies proved quite controversial. Immediately he was grabbing headlines such as "*Enraged Father Throttles James in Mad Melee.*" Gordon Campbell went on to write:

A stick-wielding attack by Marlboros' Gerry James precipitated the biggest hockey rhubarb seen at the Gardens in two seasons as Dukes downed Oshawa Generals, 5 – 2., to run their undefeated string to 13 games in the nightcap of yesterday afternoon's OHA junior "A" double bill before 6,015 fans....

Everything was going along copacetic in the windup contest with Dukes leading 4 – 2 and just eight minutes of play remaining when the fireworks opened up. James boarded Oshawa's Phil Chapman on a sortie into the Generals' end and then the fugitive from Winnipeg's gridiron Blue Bombers slashed his stick over Chapman's head for a seven-stitch cut.

That did it. Before you could say "Frank Tunney" everybody was into it. Dukes' Tom McCarthy and George Stoyan squared off with Oshawa's Fred Etcher and Bud Hillman respectively while Chapman skated around trying to get at James.

Referee Hugh Barlow got James off the ice without incident but Phil Chapman Sr., the Oshawa player's spectator father, roared down out of his seat and grabbed Gerry around the throat as he sat on the Marlboro bench.

The next few seconds was confusion unlimited. Coach Reg Hamilton tore into Chapman senior while gendarmes and fans mixed in a mad melee.

Because Gerry and Chapman had been teammates the previous year, another journalist from Toronto wrote:

A family feud developed during an Ontario Hockey Association Junior A game here. The battle Sunday involved the James and Chapman clans. Toronto Marlboros' lusty Gerry James — the youngster who played for the Winnipeg Blue bombers during the football season — drew the wrath of the Chapmans when he boarded Philip of Oshawa Gernerals, then high-sticked him for seven stitches. Philip Chapman Sr. was so incensed that he jumped to the ice and tried to throttle young James. He had to be restrained and ejected from Maple Leaf Gardens. The injury to young Chapman was ruled deliberate and James received a match misconduct and an automatic suspension.

The language of these pieces is interesting. Perhaps "robust" would be more accurate than "lusty" in the context of his hockey game, but the incident, coupled with the emotive language, stirred the pot. More was to come. By implication it seemed Gerry's playing pro football almost automatically made him a hooligan. Maurice Smith, back in Winnipeg, tried to be more neutral and supportive when he published a letter from Gerry's mother, appealing for calm.

Another controversial confrontation followed quickly on the heals of the Chapman incident when Gerry threw a punch that knocked out Paul Megaffin, a player from St. Mikes. George Dulmage provided the following description:

From the vantage point of a box seat directly across from the fracas, here's what happened:

As the play swished behind the St. Michael's goal, Louis Bendo, the Marlboro wingman, belted Megaffin into the end boards and referee Percy Allen blew the whistle on him for a major penalty. Ten days ago it would have been a minor, but the OHA's "get tough" policy has changed that.

As Bendo skated for the penalty bench behind Allen, Marc Reaume, the St. Michael's captain, shouldered him.

Bendo turned and tied into him. As they tangled, Megaffin, having risen to his skates, also moved in. From the other side came Gerry James. He changed direction slightly as he saw Megaffin, dropped his stick and landed a whistling right with his bare fist into Megaffin's face.

Megaffin fell like a sack of flour, his head striking the ice, James on top of him. James continued to pummel him in the face while sitting astride him. Then he ceased, got up and started into the other fight as referee, Ken Holmeshaw, cradled Megaffin's head in his knees. "As I did so," said Holmeshaw, 'he started to quiver and shake and I yelled for a stretcher."

Fans were outraged by this display and the reports that followed. A sample of letters written to newspapers of the day read as follows:

How bad can a person get? Of course we are referring to Gerry James. Any player who hits an injured man should be barred from hockey. That is the worst kind of sportsmanship. As coach Charlie Cerre said, it was cruel. What kind of a man is Stafford Smythe to allow a player on his team like Gerry James? Why doesn't he take action? We think the OHA should stop this sort of thing. It is just about time someone gave Mr. James a lesson. We beg you to print this in your paper. Truly yours, Doug Totyke and Mike Gehl, Kitchener, Ontario PS — Former Marlie fans, but now Barrie fans.

Dear Sir: I am writing you at this time in regard to a letter which appeared in the column, "The Readers Also Write." This letter refers to a certain Gerry James. In Junior OHA games which I have witnessed this year, James has stood out mainly because of the "butchery" which he carries out on players of opposing teams. If James wants to "wrestle" why doesn't he turn up at the Gardens Thursday nights (*Presumably for pro wrestling*) and not Sunday afternoons? The Marlboros' coach, Reg Hamilton, remarked that "It made him sick to his stomach" to see James slugging the injured player McGaffen, but I have not heard of either Hamilton or Staff Smythe taking any action against James. Yours truly, B. Granton.

When I asked Gerry about both of these incidents, this was what he recalled.

"No question I checked Chapman into the boards. Then I lost my balance and as I tried to regain it, my stick was flying about as my arms flailed away. I did not mean to hit him. He was an old teammate, for God's sake. And seven stitches was barely a scratch. The fact that he chased after me and wanted to fight should have told people something. As far as I was concerned, I should not have even received the suspension. The cut was an accident.

"With respect to the Megaffin fight, I hit him and he went down. And, yes, I sat on top of him and might have thrown one or two punches, as you do in the heat of action. Then I realized something was wrong. As it turned out, he was having an epileptic fit. They discovered after the game that he should not have been playing hockey.

"I never set out to injure anyone. Hit hard, check hard, fight hard, yes, but there is no joy in doing bodily harm. You play tough, that is what the game is about. Or used to be."

Reg Hamilton, the Marlies' coach, also never uttered the words that the incident had made him "sick to his stomach." The reporter who made this statement was forced to print a retraction.

At eighteen, Gerry had defined himself as one tough hombre. He would not and did not back down from anyone. He loved the rough side of the game. Rumours and reports of that side of his play were true, and would remain so throughout his career, in both football and hockey.

Some fans recognized, accepted and enjoyed the fact that Gerry was willing to sacrifice his body and took exception to the Pollyannas who proposed that contact should be removed from the game. One fan wrote:

> Dear Sir, One of the letters that appeared in *The Star* pleaded with you to try and rid hockey of a certain Mr. Gerry James, presently employed by the Toronto Marlboros, for "brutality" and intent to injure rival hockey players. Gerry James has helped to put one player in hospital this year, Paul Megaffin of St. Mikes, and if it had been any player but James, not a word would have been said. James is rugged, and plays the game that way, but he is not dirty. I have seen every Marlboro home game this year, and a few out-of-town games. Not once have I seen James deliberately try to injure a player. Eric Smith

What was missing from these responses to Gerry's play were comments that recognized his considerable offensive skills. Yes, he had a reputation for being an aggressive player, but he had also impressed some people with his overall talent: "James and Reid combined for a slick one as Reid took the face-off after Burn's goal, went down and passed to James at the defense. The Winnipegger skirted the defender and sailed in for a deke."

"A trio of Marlboros, Parker MacDonald, Gerry James and Wally Maxwell contributed two goals each…James grabbed a looping rebound in the goal mouth with his hand, set it on the ice, took aim and fired backhand for his first; his second was a beautiful finish, deking Roy after Dave Reid sent him in."

Gradually the reports grew more favourable. "Gerry

James, the right winger who hasn't been half as spectacular on the ice as he was in the Winnipeg backfield, produced the winner with 36 seconds to go in the overtime, a glittering dash as Parker MacDonald set him free in centre ice. He swooshed around the Barrie defense and faked the brilliant Harrington in a manner that was more than vaguely reminiscent of Nesterenko himself." Gerry was finally finding a sympathetic audience. "Gerry James who keeps improving every time out and Bill Harris, who could be the best centre in the league, and isn't far from it now. James had a pair of goals and Harris four assists."

In a game summary that appeared in the *Toronto Telegram* towards the end of January, 1953, George Dulmage had this to say:

> James, who may have been playing hockey and thinking what a wonderful thing it is to be a Winnipeg football star, with the added load of having everybody in the league save up their best shots for him (including the referees) is the kid who came down here because he was such a hot pigeon against Barrie in the Memorial Cup final in the spring of '51. He was barely 16 at the time. Now that he's paying attention to business, the goals are coming — and some of them right fancy, too.

But perhaps the greatest tribute paid to Gerry and his growth as a player was acknowledged by Gordon Campbell in two articles, one in response to the season finale and the other during the playoffs between the Marlboros and Barrie. "Besides scoring a goal, James played a standout game for the winners and acted like a big-leaguer when he refused to be drawn into a penalty-box fight with Greenshirts' John Ford late in the contest."

The second of Campbell's articles carried the headline:

Gerry James Finds
Restraint Pays off
Proves Big leaguer.

At least two conclusions can be drawn from the controversial Barrie-Marlie contest at the Gardens.

First, the Dukes seem at last to have regained the form that made them league-leaders for most of the regular campaign and secondly, Gerry James is showing more self-control than most people gave him credit for having.

Acting captain of Dukes, since Wally Maxwell was sidelined with a broken foot, James has been exhibiting marvelous restraint in the face of the "let's punch James society."

The way he let Barrie's Jack Higgins slug him behind the Barrie net early in the second period stamped Gerry as a big leaguer. Higgins socked himself into a five-minute major — and Marlies started their victory march while he rested As hockey games are won on the ice, James' self-control could mean the difference in the series.

Barrie, Don Cherry's old team, would eventually defeat the Marlies and continue on to win the 1953 Memorial Cup. What stood out with respect to Gerry's career at this time was his maturity. He had started to play smart although he still could not resist a good hard hit. At eighteen, in addition to playing pro football, he was playing at the highest level of hockey in the world for young, talented, future NHL prospects.

7 / Learning the Ropes

At the end of the hockey season Gerry finished off his school term, said goodbye to Marg and returned to Winnipeg. Shortly after arriving home, Moira drove Gerry and Tom Casey to Crooked Lake in the Qu'appelle Valley where they could do some cross-country training. The two friends were once again determined to have an impact on the league, both in the backfield and as kickoff and punt return specialists.

"Tom ran up and down those hills like a gazelle," Gerry told me one sunny, spring afternoon after he had finished climbing the Notch, a part of his current fitness regimen. He was particularly proud of being back at his playing weight. "By contrast," he continued, "I felt like I had weights tied around my legs. I thought my lungs were going to burst, but in the end it did both of us a lot of good. We were in great form when we arrived at training camp and our conditioning carried over into games. From those days forward I was a conditioning freak. If you don't keep your body in shape, nothing else works. This is how you reduce risks as an athlete and it is how you fulfill all those promises you make to yourself — while you are grinding out the miles — about the forthcoming season."

Recruited as he was straight out of high school, Gerry's first year in pro football was magical. In a way, his first year was also to be a transitional year for both Winnipeg and the league. It was almost as if Gerry's arrival were the final piece of some complex puzzle, or the catalyst for a new beginning for the league. He was doubly rewarded. He got to play with many of the players he had admired from his perch atop the stadium wall and he got to play pro ball at the old Osborne Field complex in its final year. The old stadium was simply no longer large enough for the crowds who wanted to watch Indian Jack Jacobs run his show. What a show it was!

Winnipeg Stadium, the House that Jack Built, became the new home of the Bombers in 1953, when they moved from the old Osborne Stadium.

Jack was so popular that fans from all over the league wanted to see him play.

He came up to Canada because the money was better, which is hard to believe when you compare salaries in the CFL and NFL these days, but apart from the money he came north largely because they wouldn't let Jack play quarterback in the States. And that's what he wanted to do most in football.

"While he had the smallest hands you can imagine, he threw hard and straight. It was unbelievable. He gripped the ball at the end, not in the middle, and flicked it. You had to see it to believe it," Gerry recalled, in a way that contained the excitement he must have felt when he joined the team. "Talk about a rope. He could do everything. Kick, play defense, and so on."

Marilyn Bowering and Michael Elcock who once owned a pair of Indian Jack's trademark cowboy boots remarked how small his feet were for such a tall man. Not only was he graceful when he ran the ball but his punting was legendary. Jacobs had overcome what some considered major handicaps for a player wanting to throw and kick the ball.

"Once," Gerry continued, "in Edmonton, Jack was tossed out of a game, I think because he kicked an Edmonton player who was lying on the ground. The fans booed the penalty not because of what he had done to one of their players but because the refs banished Indian Jack to the dressing room. They wanted to see Jack play; and play he could, as no one else could. Until Parker came along.

"The league was going through a revival. More fans meant more seating and better fields. What astonished me about the new stadium is that when you stood on one sideline you could barely make out the players on the opposite side of the field. For drainage purposes, it had that much of a camber on it. Of course, when you were out there playing, you didn't notice it but what an optical wonder it was from the sidelines."

Undoubtedly all the time Gerry and Tom spent getting into shape contributed to the team's success throughout the season. In addition to running back kicks and punts, Gerry finally got an opportunity to carry the ball, maintaining a five-yard-per-carry average. Winnipeg won the West and the right to meet the Tiger-Cats in the 1953 Grey Cup.

There is a photograph from that final game against Hamilton which shows Gerry in full flight, his tongue sticking out where his two front teeth should have been. The caption reads: "Gerry James Great in defeat" and part of the game summary states: "In the backfield, Gerry James, playing fullback in place of the injured Lorne Benson, was a one-man gang for Winnipeg. The 19-year-old star got Winnipeg's lone touchdown and gained 167 yards during the game, which was more than that registered by any other player."

In fact, these were great statistics for a kid who had turned nineteen only a month earlier. His play was explosive, perhaps even unexpected by the Bombers' coaching staff, but it was no surprise to Gerry. His work with Tom had definitely helped and he had an extraordinary desire to prove himself and to win. To inspire further his confidence and performance, Marg was amongst the over 27,000 fans in attendance at Varsity Stadium in Toronto on November 28, 1953.

Gerry's participation in a national championship was rare, especially for someone his age, so the couple decided to party that evening to celebrate the occasion. Liquor is definitely quicker, Gerry quipped. Today they laugh and say they might have gone over the top, an expression open to multiple interpretations, but almost sixty years later, they have no regrets. As young as they were they knew the path they wanted to follow. With impeccable timing, Marg would give birth to their first child on August 28, 1954. There is something primal and honest about this story, something that communicates happiness and needs no explanation.

⚜

Even though the debate about his future continued to heat up, Gerry was simply looking forward to getting back on the ice with his Marlie teammates. As a winter chill descended on the city, Gerry was pretty clear about his intentions. While his play in the recent Grey Cup signaled his star potential in football, he was still living his dream of being a two-sport pro athlete.

On December 8, only ten days after he had performed in the Grey Cup and with only a few days of practice in the colours of the senior Leaf team under his belt, Gerry was playing in his first Marlie game. Immediately he was greeted with the same old derision from the fans and mixed reviews from writers: "Gerry James, a star halfback in football, is back to his old tricks in hockey. The big bruising defenseman who joined Toronto Marlboros of the OHA Junior "A" League last weekend after a great football season with Winnipeg Blue Bombers, scored two overtime goals last night as Marlboros beat the league-leaders, St. Catharines Teepees 6 – 4."

In response to the same game another writer stated: "Dukes emerged victors by 6 – 4 and held Teepees from boosting their loop leadership. James took his usual rough ride from the fans and did nothing spectacular in the regular periods, but he was Johnny-on-the-spot in the extra time, with a snap goal in 27 seconds and a repeater later, when he stole a loose rubber from a TP defenseman."

When I tell Gerry about these two articles he replies, "I never played defense when I went to the Marlies. Where did these guys get their information? Were they at the game?" What I notice is that Gerry was reported to have played an unspectacular game although prior to scoring his two goals he had two assists. I always thought four points in one night indicated a pretty damn good effort in any hockey game!

Don Hunt's report was a little more accurate: "Rugged Gerry James, a confirmed football star, is a hockey coach's dream. A 19-year-old kid who has suffered abuse for his rough, tough style of hockey since joining Marlboros, James moved from defense to forward in St. Catharines Tuesday night when Dave Reid was sidelined. All he did was score two over-time goals, pick up two assists and lead Toronto to a 6 – 4 win over the leading Teeps…. Conn Smythe is high in his praise of James for his rugged play. 'He doesn't back away from anyone. He can dish it out as well as take it,' the Leaf owner said."

A fan letter from the same period had this to say: "Instead of sending the Leafs to Russia, send Gerry James alone. Put him on skates, point him in the right direction, and the Russians will never know what hit them. He won't need a stick, and as for the puck, most of the time he doesn't know where it is anyway." Mrs. F. Scott.

One thing was certain; there was no neutral ground when it came to Gerry the hockey player. What was clear was the improvement in his play. He was racking up points as well as "taking care" of his teammates.

Then suddenly, as one headline announced, he had taken on a new line mate. In the middle of the Marlie season, between a home stand and a road trip, Marg and Gerry announced their plans to get married — which they did on January, 23, 1954. He played a game the night after the wedding and left for Quebec the following week.

But just as Gerry appeared to be turning the press in his favour — "In five minutes the Dukes rapped home four goals, ignited by a rink-long rush by James that set up the first goal…" — he was embroiled in yet another controversy.

James Returns to Hockey: Did Gerry Hurl Stick
Cat's Coach Says 'Yes
But Ref Doesn't Agree:

Notification that the OHA junior "A" puck circuit is officially launched, was given here yesterday as the first "we wuz robbed" scream by a coach vented the air following completion of the Gardens' Sunday twin bill.

And guess who was robbed? Hamilton Tigers, who played the first 0 – 0 standoff of the season with Marboros in the nightcap of the doubleheader that saw St. Michael's College Majors slay Quebec Citadels, 12 – 2 before 4,314 fans in the opener.

Not Jesse! Gerry

And guess who did the robbing? Referee Jack Shropshire and Marlies' Gerry James. Shropshire got into the act because he didn't reward the Tigers a goal when Hamilton coach Jimmy Skinner figured the gridiron star threw his stick. Brian Kilrea had broken away in the third chapter and Jamesie, attempting to stop him, fell backwards on the ice. His stick skittered out of his hand and across the ice. Kilrea went in and "blew his scoring chance.

From other accounts, it is evident that Gerry did not throw his stick. Even if he had, it was nowhere near the play and did not interfere with Kilrea's chance on goal.

No matter what he did, though, Gerry could not keep his name out of the headlines. In fact, from the evidence, it would appear that he favoured the limelight.

"Gerry James beat the crowd, Marlies beat the hypnotist and Reg Hamilton's team moved to within one point of first place in junior hockey's biggest week end. Booed every time he stepped on the ice by most of the 8,012 fans at Sunday's twin bill, James intercepted a Three Rivers pass and blasted home the winner with only 31 seconds left...Ignoring the 'Hate James Fan Club' who gave him a rough time in the first two periods, Gerry banged in the rebound from Hinky Harris' shot to tie the score."

Once again we see Gerry excelling when the fans were most derisive. He clearly thrived on insults and abuse.

As the season came to a conclusion and the Marlies were in the thick of the league race for first place, Gerry added to his notoriety when he squared off against one of the other supposedly tough guys from the league, Marc Reaume. Gord Walker covered this game between the Marlies and St. Mike's, won by the Marlies 4 – 0 and wrote:

Gerry James, always a controversial figure, and rugged Marc Reaume opened the riot tape with less than three minutes to go. There was no disputing the winner. James landed the most effective punch of the affair. It broke Reaume's nose.

While James was being escorted to the penalty box, another fight broke out between St. Michael's goaler Gerry

McNamara and Marlboro defenseman Al MacNeil. When this threatened to turn into a mass free-for-all, James jumped over the boards and was almost intercepted by a Reaume punch.

James swerved away from that, then halted his movement toward the fight centre. Reaume made for him and they joined battle again. This one quickly deteriorated into a wrestling match, with James winding up on top and staying there....

One obviously incensed young lady so far forgot propriety to the extent of whacking James over the head with her purse, which was slight punishment for one who has run head-on into such as Vince Mazza. (*Mazza played offensive and defensive lineman for the Tigercats*)

Even in the playoffs, Gerry continued to get his fill of condemnation.

CROWD CAME TO JEER BUT IT MATTERED NOT TO DUKE GERRY JAMES

To Gerry James, one of the most versatile young men on the Canadian athletic scene, it doesn't seem to make much difference whether they jeer or cheer. As a footballer in the uniform of the Winnipeg Blue bombers, James is a knight in shining armor and the recipient of the cheers of the crowd. But as a hockey player, in a Marlboro sweater, Mr. James is a villain of proportions exceeded only by the Mills brothers.

Slim Crowd On Hand

Last night at the Gardens, judging by the commotion, the voluble section of the slim crowd of 1,217 must have come to jeer at James. And jeer they did — and Gerry jeered right back by scoring two goals and coming up with his best game in a long time as Marlboros shaded Kitchener 4 – 2 in the first game of their OHA junior "A" playoff series.

Back in Winnipeg, Maurice Smith attempted to apply a little perspective to the many flawed characterizations of Gerry that now floated about in the press and amongst opposing fans.

> We see where young Gerry James is in the news again with one of the Reverend Fathers at Toronto St. Michael's college being quoted as saying that St. Mike's may consider withdrawing from hockey if James' attacks on his players do not cease…Gerry has been in hot water on a couple of other occasions this season because of his rough play… Or so it has been reported anyway…All of which makes us wonder whether James is too mature physically for the Ontario junior "A" circuit…Having played football all season for the Blue Bombers before joining the Marlboros, it may be that James, used to competing against players much older than himself, is just a little too "hard" for those he is competing against in junior hockey…Hence, when he hits an opponent — they really stay hit…Gerry is 180 pounds of solid muscle…Perhaps, if he's good enough, it would be the best thing if the Maple Leafs were to turn Gerry out-and-out professional…Certainly the kid wouldn't have to take a back seat to any of the big league pros in the intestinal fortitude department…

Jack Matheson also came to Gerry's defense, in a somewhat backhanded fashion:

> Reaume plays defence for Toronto St. Mike's. At least he did until young Mr. James took pains to clean his clock one night recently. Someone should have informed Reaume that James plays football for the Winnipeg Blue Bombers when

the frost is on the pumpkin and there's no evidence of his backing down from anyone.

If there were ever any uncertainty within the Leaf organization about what they were getting with Gerry, that ambiguity had been cleared up by his physical play in the 1953 - 54 season. He was exactly the sort of player Conn Smythe was looking for to fill the roster of the senior team. The kid from Winnipeg provided an ideal balance between scoring and enforcement. In spite of Father Faught's complaints about Gerry, most of the other coaches in the league supported Gerry's style of play and even went so far as to select him as an all-star.

The two top teams battled their way through early playoff rounds to face each other in what would become one of the most memorable if not, as Don Hunt described it, weirdest OHA Junior "A" finals in history. The Marlies were all but counted out when they went down 3 – 0 in the series and then fought their way back to force a seventh and final game against the St. Catharines TeePees. Again Don Hunt wrote: "Rugged Gerry James, special target of St. Catharines Teepees all series, pulled Marlboros back into the OHA Junior "A" hockey picture. Dukes, outplayed and behind 1 – 0 going into the second period, finally found the range and, led by James, downed Teeps 5 – 3 at the Gardens last night. Thus they stalled St. Catharines' bid for their first OHA title."

A comeback win and a place in the Memorial Cup would have been a great upset, if not miracle, for the Marlies but unfortunately both Gerry — he had a hip pointer and bad leg — and the Marlies outstanding goalie, Johnny Albani, were sidelined with injuries and the team lost the final game, rather decidedly.

When Gerry and I discussed this penultimate season

in his junior hockey career he wondered if he and Albani would have made enough of a difference to go on and win the cup. I have the feeling that he thinks St. Catharines might have been the better team but then he hums and haws, and reconsiders. This sort of speculation is a little like catching rain in a net.

Shortly after the loss to St. Catharines, the debate about Gerry's future was ramped up a notch or two and kept people guessing and talking until the new football season began. Almost simultaneously, reports had him signing contracts to play in both sports. Once again, George Dulmage got the facts and reasoning correct.

Just as everyone knew it had to happen, the crisis arrived today for Gerry James and the Toronto Maple Leaf Hockey Club.

James, the senior football star of Winnipeg Blue Bombers, Western Canada champions, and James the junior hotshot right winger of the Toronto Marlboros, OHA junior "A" team, clashed. The Bombers won the round. Temporarily. James today signed a football contract to play with the Bombers.

Conn Smythe, Maple Leaf president and general manager, said less than a month ago that the Leafs, which own the Marlboro team, would not let money stand in the way of James' advancement in pro hockey. "We aren't going to bid competitively against football (The Bombers)," he said, "but we can offer him more than football can hope to offer."

"TOUCHY" SUBJECT

Yesterday Hap Day, Leaf assistant general manager offered James a professional contract to play with Pittsburg. He didn't sign.

"I want," James told *The Telegram*, "to play football this fall and junior hockey next winter. I still have a year of junior.

"The Leafs want me to play pro with Pittsburg. I know, and they know that I'm not ready for the Leafs. So that's the way things stand. I think I should make up my mind next year, not this. The Leafs think I should make up my mind this year.

"It is a very touchy subject."

Touchy indeed.

James, the star of the Grey Cup last autumn, has been, according to Staff Smythe, the Marlboro manager, a rugged character to deal with in matters of finance. "He knows what he wants, and he wants both football and hockey as long as he can make both pay," Smythe has said.

Jack Meeks asserted that Gerry had signed with the Bombers and had discussed his plans to take Marg on a trip to Florida. Meeks also mentioned the price Gerry had paid to play in both sports: "James has been attending college in Toronto while playing for the Toronto Marlboros...However, he missed two months of college last fall while playing for the Bombers and missed a further 10 days this year due to junior hockey schedules, and has been forced to drop his schooling for the present term."

In part, this may explain why Gerry later placed such an emphasis on education with the players he eventually coached.

Stafford Smythe was soon on side with Gerry's decision when he remarked: "With me, that is fine. Maybe now we'll be able to go for the Memorial Cup next year." As it turned out, this was a fortuitous prediction by the junior Smythe. "If James wants to play football for the first part of the hockey season and get maybe five or six thousand bucks for it, then come and play hockey for us at say three thousand, I think he's smart. That's what I would do. I agree with him 100 per cent."

While Gerry had signed to play with Winnipeg for the 1954 season, it was a one-year contract. He wanted to know who the new Bomber coach was going to be and he wanted to keep his options open.

Smythe was quick to restate his position when he suggested to Walter Gray, another reporter, that Gerry would have to decide between football, hockey and his education.

But for now, football was a go. What a season Gerry was about to have. Clearly none of this on-going debate was a distraction. If his performance in the Grey Cup had not alerted football fans to his potential, certainly his award-winning season of 1954 would.

Even during the exhibition session, the team was once again being touted as a contender for the western title. Bob Moir of the *Free Press* wrote from Ottawa: "Winnipeg's football team is not to be taken lightly. The Blue Bombers displayed a marked superiority over the Rough Riders of Clem Crowe here Friday night, piling up a 29 – 6 decision without using up too much energy."

When the regular season got under way, Gerry was immediately inserted into the backfield as one of Jacobs' running options. He was usually used wide although as the season progressed he became an equally reliable inside choice.

In August, shortly after the Commonwealth Games had ended, in a contest the Bombers were supposed to win hands down, Gerry scored Winnipeg's only touchdown in an 8 to 6 victory over the B.C. Lions that was anything but a cakewalk. As Bob Moir saw it: "Jacobs tossed a 13-yard pass to Grant. As he was being tackled, Bud threw the ball at Gerry James, steaming up alongside him. Gerry was in full flight as he caught the ball and out raced every Lion in the vicinity during a 55-yard touchdown run. The Vancouver threat was over."

While the Lions hadn't exactly roared, both the offensive

and defensive lines gave the highly-rated Winnipeg pillars an unexpected battle. Gerry's touchdown was the first by a visiting player to Empire Stadium, with thanks to a well-executed assist from his future coach, Bud Grant. Many fans of football do not realize that before becoming a highly successful coach for twenty-eight years, first with Winnipeg and then with the Minnesota Vikings, Grant played both football and basketball in the pro ranks. For two years he was with the Minnesota Lakers of the NBA, before switching to football, first with Philadelphia and then Winnipeg.

Gerry's touchdown at Empire Stadium was particularly memorable for him because it marked the birth of his and Marg's first child. With dad on the road, Debbie was born on August 28, 1954.

Over the next few weeks the team would experience both highs and lows. A 46 – 0 drubbing by Calgary probably stood out as the lowest of the lows, while appearances in front of record crowds and wins over Saskatchewan, all epic struggles, thrilled everyone connected with the Blue and Gold. With the exception of the Lions, the five-team Western Conference was a tight race, especially with only three playoff spots available and home-field advantage a huge asset. Second and third got to beat up on each other to earn the honour of playing three games against the team that finished first which had the benefit of resting and healing for a couple of weeks.

Throughout the print media, Gerry's name began to appear on a regular basis, often alongside Bud Grant and Byron Townsend, Gerry's running partner. A caption beside a photograph read: "At the left, Gerry James could be sleeping with the ball but it's actually the second Winnipeg touchdown." In a 12 – 12 tie against Saskatchewan, Jack Matheson wrote: "Bombers, who liked to keep things on the melodramatic side, evened the count on the last play of the third quarter, Gerry James barreling over from the Saskatchewan 10 after a spirited land march all the way from their own 36." Another chronicler wrote: "How to score touchdowns — by James: There are several ways of scoring touchdowns, but when it comes to brute force, Winnipeg's Gerry James is a master." In response to Gerry's play in that same game Bob Moir wrote the caption to accompany the article: "Cutting the corners, Winnipeg's outstanding halfback, Gerry James opens his mouth and heads for open field as the Saskatchewan Roughriders close in on him during the first quarter of last night's WIFU game."

Meanwhile, mid-way through the season, another reporter was keeping sports' fans up to date on the hockey front. "Down east they hold little if any regard whatsoever for our junior hockey...Recently it was said Gerry James would line up with Medicine Hat Tigers" for the 1954 – 55 schedule. In addition to the uncertainty surrounding his hockey future, the lease ran out on Marg's and Gerry's Winnipeg apartment and Marg and Debbie returned to Toronto to live with Marg's parents. Gerry found this separation difficult although it did focus his attention and perhaps accounted for his determination, especially if he were going to support his family on the proceeds of sports.

As the season was entering its final weeks, Gerry's play gained more attention and further eulogizing. Many of the doubts that fans had about Al Sherman's choice of backs had been eased if not erased. The new coach had scoured the pictures of the Bombers' 1953 games and had seen what he was looking for. Like everyone else, he was impressed with Gerry's performance in the 1953 Grey Cup final. With Townsend as fullback and Gerry as halfback, he figured he had a winning combination. One old-time Bomber, Andy Currie, compared Gerry to his dad. He said: "Most people knew Eddie James only as a powerful plunger. Actually he was one of the best men to run the outside Canadian football has ever known. His son, Gerry, seems to follow the same pattern."

Once again, Bob Moir wrote: "Powerful Gerry James burst 72-yards down the touchlines on the second play of the game last night and ignited a powder keg labeled Blue Bombers which roared on to a 28 – 7 victory over the Saskatchewan Roughriders before 16, 418 uncomfortable, but joyous customers. Cheers rocked the Winnipeg stadium as James made his thrilling dash."

Ultimately this would be one of a few crucial touchdowns and wins for the Bombers as the season grew towards a climax. With only a few weeks remaining the Bombers and Roughriders were not only close in the standings, they were, statistically speaking, as close as pages in a book.

Around this time the public also heard the first predictions about who would form the all-star team, especially at the hotly-disputed position of half back. One writer listed his selection of backs which included Macon and Bottoms of Calgary, Parker and Miles of Edmonton, Carpenter and Williams of Regina, Pollard of B.C. and James of Winnipeg. Even though he appeared to favour Gerry, he wrote: "James can be ruled out because he erred 19 years ago by being born in Canada." He went on to suggest the selection process always leaned in the direction of the imports.

As the battle for playoff positions continued, Don Hunt reported on Gerry's hockey future.

James Signs With Dukes
But Not As Career — Yet.

Gerry James, still undecided on his future in sports, will play hockey with Marboros again this winter.

James, via telephone, agreed to terms with Stafford Smythe after suggesting he would like to play in Moose

Jaw. Smythe turned him down and the star Winnipeg half quickly agreed to come to Toronto after the Grey Cup.

The controversial right winger thus delayed the football or hockey decision for another year. The Maple Leaf organization tried to pin him down last year, but he headed west for the football season without any definite answer. He still hasn't given one but has said privately that he likes football better, money being the only thing that could make him prefer hockey. And MLG has the money.

Jim Hunt, another of the great Canadian sports writers, wrote in the *Toronto Daily Star* (several years before he moved over to the *Sun*) about Gerry's dilemma: "There's only one thing that seems likely to keep Gerry James from being one of the great stars in Canadian football. That's hockey. And there's only one thing that seems likely to keep the same Gerry James from being a star in the National Hockey league. That's football." Again, quoting Jim Hunt at length is worthwhile, for his insight, which was considerable, and the clarity of his writing:

This 19-year-old Winnipegger could be great in both sports. Football men can't say enough good things about him. Already they rate him as one of the best backs in the game, and he's still three or four years away from his peak.

And Conn Smythe, president of the Toronto Maple Leafs' vast hockey system thought enough of James as a junior to move his mother to Toronto and put Gerry in school here so he could play with one of the Leaf-sponsored junior clubs. The Leafs feel Gerry is an NHL player if he decides to stick with the game.

This is the year of decision. The day is past when an athlete can star in several sports. Gerry has to decide between pro hockey and pro football. And it won't be an easy decision.

Until last season it appeared football would win the battle. James had improved tremendously as a football player. He was rated as one of the most promising backs in the west and won himself a spot in the Winnipeg Blue Bombers' starting backfield. But Gerry the hockey player (with Toronto Marlboros) also improved last season. The improvement was startling enough for the Leafs to offer him a contract with their Pittsburgh farm club in the American Hockey League. He turned it down because he's still eligible for another year of junior hockey. And playing as a junior he can still play football.

If Gerry were still single, you'd have to rate his chances of picking football as a career pretty highly. He plays in his own home town, where he's popular. He plays hockey in Toronto, where he's booed more often than he gets a cheer. And he likes to play football better than hockey.

But Gerry was married early this year. And with a family to support, he has to consider where he can earn the best money. On past experience, hockey has always outbid football for anyone it really wanted. A hockey player can also outlast a football player.

But James is different from most of the others who have had a choice. He's as good as or better than most import halfbacks. And the Bombers are willing to pay him accordingly. If they do, they could win the scramble for the youngster with so much athletic talent.

If he sticks to football Gerry seems certain to be one of the game's great players. He has speed, heart and tremendous drive; in fact, everything a coach could want in a backfielder.

Bob Snyder, who coached Calgary last season, made a list of Canadian players he felt were good enough to make the National Football League in the U.S. And one of the players was Gerry James. George Trafton, coach of the Bombers last season, shared that opinion.

"He's one of the finest young halfbacks I've ever seen,"

Trafton said. "If he keeps improving he'll be one of the best in football and that includes the National league."

Gerry was receiving high praise from many quarters. Jack Matheson, in drawing up his unofficial all-star list, included Gerry along with Jackie Parker and Ken Carpenter as one of his choices for the three halfback slots. Edmonton fans, he suggested, would be shocked to see Gerry placed ahead of Rollie Miles in the running but in his first year as a full-time running back Gerry had scored some critical touchdowns and carried the ball 106 times for 576 yards, a respectable 5.4 yards per carry. Gerry's performance in the playoffs would further affirm Matheson's argument.

After tying the first game in a two-game, total points competition, the Bombers beat Saskatchewan on November 1, 1954 to earn the right to face Edmonton for the third year in a row for the Western Conference title and a place in the Grey Cup. The hero of the game was none other than the "Kid" himself. As Bob Moir wrote:

REGINA (Special) — Winnipeg Blue Bombers' homebrew haymaker, Gerry James, pulled his team off the floor in startling fashion here last night as the W.I.F.U. champions kayoed the Saskatchewan Roughriders, 13 – 11, to win the total-points semi-final, 27 -25.

James roared 87 yards right through the centre of the entire Roughrider team to score the first Bomber major and continually lifted the Winnipeggers out of trouble in a rugged battle which threatened at times to be a runaway for the eventual winners.

Jack Matheson riding a favourite hobby-horse observed that "In the final analysis, the Bombers won The Big One through the diligent efforts of their Canadian talent. Gerry

James, who didn't rate all-star nomination, ran a kick off back 87 yards for one touchdown and Lorne Benson, who Haunts the Roughriders annually, scored the other touchdown on a burst through the line." In what was described as a "gem" of a run, Gerry had made the first kickoff runback of 1954 and silenced the Taylor field crowd.

Coach Al Sherman had nothing but praise for his young half back. "He did that like a seasoned professional," he said. But lost in the discussion of the touchdown run was another 32-yard romp that set up a further potential score. In *Pigskin Parade* the author noted that "James, it seems, is destined for even greater stardom than most athletes of his tremendous ability. He has that infallible touch of being able to turn it on during the playoffs. It was his blue-chip goals for the Toronto Marlboros which kept that junior hockey team in the national playdowns for so long last spring."

After their loss to Edmonton in the first of three final games, Jack Meek in *The Winnipeg Tribune* suggested: "James stood out particularly and should be a top candidate this year for the award of most outstanding Canadian player in both the Western Conference and the Big Four." Before a record crowd of 20,933, the Bombers evened the series at one apiece, largely spurred on by Gerry and Tom Casey, behind a formidable Bomber line.

Winnipeg lost the final game, and while Edmonton headed to the Grey Cup, Gerry packed up his bags and rendezvoused with his family in Toronto. He had been looking forward to the reunion for some time.

To add more confusion to his life, midway through the 1954 season, on September 15, Marg had reluctantly packed up and moved with Debbie back to Toronto. She stayed with her parents and sisters while looking for a furnished apartment that she, Debbie and Gerry could live in when the football season ended.

Her mom and dad had bought a house in a new development known as the Conn Smythe sandpits, a low area in Toronto carved out of the landscape by the Smythe family's sand and gravel business. Marg's parents were less than a mile from the Humber River.

One evening in October, when her parents were out with friends, she was at home with her baby and two sisters, nine and two, when a storm blew up. As she sat reading, the rains pounded the roof and the winds swirled and howled around the house, unlike anything she had ever heard before. When her parents arrived home early they reported that cars were unable to get through underpasses and that the roads were flooding. Gerry phoned to see if they were okay. He had heard news reports in Winnipeg that Hurricane Hazel was passing through Toronto. Over one hundred people died that night. The Humber River swelled its banks, taking dozens of homes down river into Lake Ontario. Con Smythe's sandpit, though, just drained all the water away and remained dry as a bone.

"It's strange what you remember," Marg says, "what remains vivid out of all of your memories. I remember the relief in Gerry's voice when he heard that Debbie and I were safe."

This incident became a focal point in Gerry's thinking. He told me that from then on he was determined to minimize his time away from his family. He knew the grief this sort of separation could cause. All future decisions, whether football, hockey or further education, would place his family first.

Gerry went on to win the 1954 inaugural Schenley Award for the Most Valuable Canadian in the league. The only other award given out at this time was for the most outstanding player in the league.

James and Etcheverry Gain Cash Awards

TORONTO — Gerry James, Winnipeg's favorite football son, stepped up Friday and happily accepted a cheque for $500 as the best native-born in Canadian football. General consensus around the Royal York, where experts meet to expert, was that it couldn't happen to a better guy.

Kid Dynamite was only a step or two behind Sam (The Rifle) Etcheverry, who was voted the country's outstanding football player. For his trouble, Etcheverry picked up $1,000 which may or may not have an effect on today's Grey Cup final.

Awards were presented at the posh Granite Club, and everybody who's anybody in Canadian football was present. There wasn't a dissenting vote as the winners stepped to the platform.

In his acceptance speech, Gerry made a point of thanking his linemen. This was not a token acknowledgement. He knew the importance of his teammates. Buddy Tinsley, in turn, pointed out to a writer in Edmonton that Gerry's football capabilities were equal to those of the Bombers' best imports. Gerry would have been, he remarked to a reporter, everybody's All-American if he had happened to play football for Notre Dame, Michigan, Duke or Alabama.

❦

After a brief break from his football season, Gerry was back on the ice with the Marlies. He was determined to prove that he could play hockey at the highest level and the best way to do that was to be on the junior team that went on to win the Memorial Cup. By this time he realized that a season of football did not prepare him to play hockey. Running motions in football and the pushing stride of skating used entirely different sets of muscles. He desperately needed the sort of conditioning one gets from practice scrimmages and game situations. Whenever it could be arranged, he practiced with the Leafs as well as the Marlies.

Even though it was the opinion of knowledgeable hockey people that the Marlies were the *crème de la crème* of the 1954 – 55 version of the O.H.A., their play was disappointing. They were inconsistent, often bordering on lazy, and struggled in mid-table, especially when Gerry went down with a very serious injury. Just as he was rounding into shape after the football season, in early January, he took a puck to the face, below and very close to his right eye.

Dave Finn, another island neighbour at Fairwinds, who was playing midget hockey in Toronto at the time, happened to be in the crowd at the Gardens with his teammates when Gerry was hit by a puck deflected off the stick of Ken Linseman Sr.

Dave witnessed the puck hit Gerry high on the cheekbone and remembers him going down to the ice like a sack of spuds.

"After a few minutes Gerry raised himself to his knees and eventually skated back to the Marlboro bench. I remember he stayed there until the end of the period, watching the game. The ice was covered in blood. My teammates and I couldn't believe that he stayed on the bench although I don't recall Gerry re-entering the game. I do remember him being there at the end of the game."

If Dave and his friends had looked behind where they sat, up into the stands, they would have seen Gerry sitting there cheering on his teammates through the second and third periods. The young midgets were impressed, mostly by Gerry's toughness, but also by his dedication to the team. What Dave and his teammates didn't know was that after the game Gerry was rushed to the hospital where he remained for three weeks. Doctors were concerned that Gerry was going to lose complete sight in his right eye. They wedged his head between sandbags to keep him from moving his head and to prevent the eye from hemorrhaging.

The outcome was that in 1955, while playing for the Marlies, Gerry did lose most of his sight in his right eye, an injury that would affect both his hockey and football play for the remainder of both of his careers. He simply couldn't see all of a ball or puck coming at him from that side.

After six weeks on the sidelines, doctors allowed Gerry to return to play, on the condition that he wear a specially designed mask. Headlines read: **"GERRY JAMES EXPECTED TO RETURN WEARING 'MAN FROM MARS' MASK."**

By this time the Marlies were toiling in the bottom half of the table. But with Gerry's return, "The power everyone knew was there, finally surfaced on Sunday. Toronto Marlboros, a disappointment most of the year, lived up to their pre-season billing. And if anyone gets credit for the Dukes' sudden dynamite display, it must be Gerry James. The hard-rock footballer, a broken cheekbone still healing, returned to action without a mask and his fire spread to the rest of the team." The team went on to beat the Teepees 7 – 2, which right away had Stafford Smythe boasting that this was the team that would bring the Memorial Cup to Toronto. John MacDonald also forecasting a positive result observed: "Another point in Marlies' favor is the expected return of Gerry James." In their next game, Don Hunt wrote: "Marlboros' sudden power, St. Mike's brakeless skid are making way for a repeat of last year's thrilling OHA Junior "A" semi-final."

Meanwhile, as the Marlies' play improved, the parent team was plotting a raid. Under a headline that read **Leafs May Form New 'Kid Line' From Juniors,** Hap Day had fashioned his new line with Gerry and Gary Aldcorn as wingers for Brian Cullen. "The line, with an average age of 19, was being tested as a possible Leaf 'kid line,' Day said. He plans to work them again tomorrow and then decide when they'll be used. But with Marlboros entering the junior playoffs next week, it probably would be this weekend when Toronto meets Boston here Saturday and Hawks in Chicago Sunday."

As the final days of the regular season approached, everyone was back in a Marlie uniform. "The sizzling Marlboros have set the stage for a repetition of last year's thrilling OHA Junior "A" semi-final," wrote Don Hunt. "Gerry James brought the house down when Viger Gendron tried to pick a fight with him after drawing a penalty for tripping the Marlboro winger. James skated in circles, whistling, while Gendron did everything in an attempt to get at him." Then, on February 24, just as the playoffs were about to begin, Gerry got called up to the senior team to fill in for Eric Nesterenko against the Montreal Canadiens. His old childhood hero, Bill Ezinicki, by this time playing for the Rangers, had done the damage to Nesterenko with a heavy bodycheck. Once again, a peculiar twist of fate had a role in shaping Gerry's future.

Back with the Marlies, Gerry and the team rolled to a quick decision over the Galt Black Hawks.

In the next round, the team came up against the Guelph Biltmores...and the measles. But the fear of an epidemic seemed to inspire the team and they had soon taken a 2 – 0 lead in the series. In the third and final game, the players had to overcome a fan revolt against the referee, Hugh McLean. Here is how Gordon Campbell saw and described events:

Guelph, March 12 — They say the secret of success is being remembered. If that's the case, then referee Hugh McLean has to go down in hockey history as the game's most famous official. A few years ago, Rocket Richard couldn't forget McLean, despite a night's sleep and a ride to New York, and attacked the then NHL arbiter in a hotel lobby.

And here last night as Marlboros blanked Guelph Biltmores, 4 – 0, to sweep their best-of-five OHA junior "A" semi-final series, three games to nothing, it was another tough evening for McLean. The 4000-odd fans, who apparently were upset because of the rule which allowed Hamilton's Dennis Riggin to play goal for Marlies, decided to vent their spleen on the ambitious city whistle-tooter.

While this resulted in an assortment of fights off the ice, including an attack by fans on McLean and linesmen Jack Clancy of Hamilton and Murray Dunette of Brantford, the referee handled himself capably both on the playing surface and in the extra-curricular activities....

At the end of the second period, a group of rowdies waited for McLean and Co. as they came off the ice and a real battle-royal ensued.

McLean was struck but he managed to "plough" his adversary "but good". I mention this incident because it reveals how passionate Canadians have always been about their hockey. As an athlete Gerry loved this spirited response to the game, no matter where it was coming from.

Four days after winning their semi-final, the Marlies were once again playing for the OHA championship against the Memorial Cup defending champions, the St. Catherines Teepees. As Wilf Smith reported: "Toronto Marlboros maintained their prolific playoff pace here tonight by trimming St. Catharines Teepees, 4 – 1, in the opening game of the Ontario Hockey Association Junior "A" finals....Marlies required more than half the game to solve Teepees' tight defense, but when they did, they overwhelmed the defending Memorial Cup champs....For the Dukes it was merely a continuation of their domination over Teepees this season. In eight meetings, Marlboros have won six."

Then right in the middle of the hockey wars, Gerry's football future made the news. The timing for the Marlies could not have been worse, for morale and for Gerry's concentration. Under the headline **James Rejects Hockey For Football Career**, Don Hunt wrote:

Gerry James today decided to stick to football next fall and forget about a professional hockey career.

"It isn't fair to me or to the two sports to try both," the star Marlboro right winger and Winnipeg footballer said. "Next season I will play only football — no more hockey."

James said he wasn't shutting the door on hockey but won't play next season. "After that, if things change, I might decide to play hockey and not football. I certainly wouldn't try to do both."

Main reason for his decision, he said, was a desire to live up to the reputation of his father, Eddie (Dynamite) James, Winnipeg and Regina, star of the 30's. "Money also had something to do with it and I want to buy a home and settle down in Winnipeg."

Voted Canada's top homebrew footballer last season, he said he favored football over hockey because "I've always played the game, and enjoy it the most. I like hockey, too, but feel football offers better opportunities...."

James' decision, made at Christmas, was forced into the open at the request of the Winnipeg Football Club.

'PEG SALESMAN

"I wanted to wait until I was finished with junior hockey this season before making my decision public. But they phoned me this week and asked my permission to release the signing. They wanted to open season ticket sales so I agreed."

The three-year tug-of-war between the Blue bombers and Leafs over James' services was forced to a head this year — his last in junior hockey. Conn Smythe, Leaf president, said he would have to decide on one or the other.

James agreed, adding that "It's not a good idea to try both hockey and football. It's too hard on you and you can't give your best to two sports which overlap."

Game two of the series turned into a slug fest, a battle apparently touched off by Gerry. Perhaps in response to the announcement about his impending football future, the Teepees made a point of hunting Gerry down. While by this time he was considered one of junior hockey's top stars, Gerry could not resist retaliating, especially when repeatedly provoked. At the end of the game, two players were in hospital and the referee had handed out 413 minutes in penalties, an OHA record. Everyone but the goalies had entered the fray. If baiting and inciting Gerry was Coach Rudy Pilous's tactic to get at the heart of the Marlies, it backfired. The Marlies went on to win the best-of-seven series and the OHA championship 4 - 2. According to Don Hunt, by the end of the series the Teepees looked tired and deflated.

This was the Marlies first win of the championship in twenty-three years and Gerry had once again been a major part of the team's success. They would now go on to face and eliminate the Quebec Frontenacs in the Eastern Canada final before travelling to Regina to compete in the Memorial Cup. Gordon Campbell provided a brief anecdote from the trip west by train.

En route with the Marlboros to Regina, April 19 — The Eastern Canada Junior "A" hockey champions lost their youngest rooter this morning when eight-month-old Debbie James and her mother, Marg dropped off at Winnipeg, leaving "pop" Gerry on his own.

While Debbie and Mrs. James, both Toronto-born, plan to house-hunt in Winnipeg, Gerry will be busy trying to help Marlboros win the first Memorial Cup since 1929 in Regina.

After the series is over, James will return with the team to Toronto and then drive back to stay in the little grey home he expects his wife will have found in the west. Gerry recently announced his intention to give up hockey for a football career with Winnipeg Blue Bombers.

It will be the second Memorial Cup final for James in four years. This time he expects to be on the winning side.

Much to the surprise of the Marlies, the Regina Pats won the first game of the seven-game Memorial final rather handily by a score of 3 – 1. The Marlboros then won the next four games and won the national championship. When I asked Gerry why their win had been so decisive, he said: "They made the mistake of playing our game. We were bigger and hit harder. If they had stuck to their own game who knows what the outcome would have been. You always have to play to your own strengths."

For any kid growing up in Canada who plays hockey, the Memorial Cup is the Holy Grail. Gerry was about to leave the game on the highest of notes.

ع

At any given moment a person's life appears continuous, as if the completion of some fated pattern but when we review events we become aware of the randomness, the accidental nature of most actions. If we appear to have been favoured, we call it serendipity, if not we call it bad luck or misfortune. In Gerry's case, the planets seemed to be aligned.

To say that Gerry James's career as a professional athlete got off to a quick start would be a massive understatement. A snapshot of the early years looks like this. In 1952, after being invited to the Winnipeg Blue Bombers training camp, where he expected to be cut, he instead became a fully-fledged member of the squad, running back punts and playing halfback. At that moment, he became the youngest player ever to play in the CFL. He was seventeen. By the end of the 1953 season, he had played a significant role in the Bombers' drive to the Grey Cup final, where he scored the only Winnipeg touchdown. Then on August 28, at the beginning of the 1954 season, while scoring the first opposition touchdown in the new Empire Stadium against the newly minted BC Lions, in a game that Winnipeg went on to win by the score of 8 to 6, his first child was born. By the age of nineteen, he was a leading force in the developing stages of a Canadian football dynasty, he was still playing junior hockey for the Toronto Marlboros, although he would be called up to play one game with the parent Leafs, and he was married with a daughter. In 1955, he would win a Memorial Cup with the Marlies, the fulfillment of yet another dream. What a complicated and exciting life young Gerry had charted for himself.

8 / Football vs Hockey

Gerry's control over his own destiny was masterful. He played off football and hockey against each other with maturity and artfulness, and with no small debt to his mother. At the conclusion of the Memorial Cup, he declared his intentions in favour of football.

> Gerry James has signed a 1955 contract with the Blue Bombers, possibly ending all sorts of speculation about the future of one of Canada's outstanding athletes. James, selected the outstanding native-born player in the country last year, is a member of the Toronto Maple Leafs' hockey organization. He is presently playing with the Marlboros' juniors, engaged in the junior OHA final. Since joining the Bombers three years ago James has been playing both hockey and football. Last year the president of the Maple Leafs, Conny Smythe said James will have to make up his mind on which sport he would play professionally. It looks like football, seeing that he's signed for 1955. Gerry, although a three-year veteran of the WIFU wars, is only 20. A poised gridder from the first time he stepped on a pro field, he has since gained plenty of polish and is now one of the most feared runners in the nation.

❧

The question remained, How do you grow a football player?

What makes one individual a star amongst so many high achievers?

In amongst the memorabilia that Gerry kept was a program from the November 2, 1935 semi-final game between Winnipeg and Regina, a game in which his father, the "Dynamiter", played. Interspersed throughout the program, placed between the advertisements and photographs of the executive, were several sections entitled "Do You Know The Rules." One of the rules read as follows:

> Coaching from the side lines is prohibited in the rules because it is considered unfair practice. The game is to be played by the **players** using their own **muscle** and **brains.** If, for example, an onlooker, having seen all the hands in a game of cards, undertook to tell one of the players what card to play, the other players would have just cause to object. The sending in of substitutes for the purpose of giving information as to the following play is an **unfair evasion** of the spirit of true sportsmanship.
>
> When an official imposes a penalty or makes a decision, he is simply doing his duty as he sees it. He is on the field representing the integrity of the game of football, and his decision, even though he may have made a mistake in judgment, is final and conclusive, and should be so accepted.

This program had been inserted into an "Exercise Book" in which Gerry pasted photographs of players he admired: Fritz Hanson, Arnie Coulter, Cliff Roseborough, Russell Rebholz, Al Ritchie, Dick Lane, to name a few.

I suspect that reading through this program instilled in Gerry some of the values his father felt were important to the integrity of the game. This notebook coupled with an article about his father began to form a template for Gerry as a highly competitive athlete in hockey and football. We see what lessons Gerry learned from his father, what motivated him to excel in every sport in which he participated. He had much to prove and much for which he sought approval.

In an issue of *Touchdown: The All-Canadian Sports Magazine,* dated September 15, 1961, Al Ritchie, "probably Saskatchewan's best known and most respected sportsman," wrote:

> It's a little more than a year now since Eddie James passed on, but we old Roughriders still have fresh, green memories of the man who so rightly deserved that nickname of "Dynamite James."
>
> Eddie was not only the "Jim Thorpe", the "Bronko Nagurski", and "Red Grange" of his era but he was as popular as he was good.
>
> His opponents not only respected him but admired him because there was nothing dirty or vicious about the Dynamiter. He broke many a tackle with his great running and power but never resorted to any dirty work.
>
> You never heard Eddie, after a game, complain about some opponent using a knee or fist on him. He was so hard to stop that his opponents had to treat him pretty rough to get him under control but Eddie never noticed it. It was all good clean Canadian fun to him. His opponents admired him and his teammates loved him. He was an inspiration to every club he played with.
>
> In his day, "Eddie, Dynamite, James" was the king of the Western Canada grid iron and had no equal in Eastern Canada.
>
> Eddie was just as good on defence as he was on offence. He was the most symmetrically built man I ever saw. He had a perfect build. He was strong and fast. Eddie could figure out just how to stop those fast tricky runners. He had that instinct that goes with a good athlete.

Eddie was not a necktie tackler. He tackled below the hips, chiefly below the knees. He didn't need a gang to help him bring down a good ball carrier. Eddie was indeed the answer to a coach's dream or prayer.

Eddie James was a household word in Western Canada. The Babe Ruth, the Jack Dempsey kind of athlete. Eddie had the same kind of color. He did a lot for football. Fellows like "Eddie, Dynamite, James", Fritzie Hanson, Glen Dobbs, Jack Jacobs, Curt Schave are largely responsible for the great football consciousness and football enthusiasm we have in Western Canada today.

You can take your Allan Ameches, McDougalls, Brights Kwongs, Marlows and they are all great, but put them all in a line in their prime and ask me to pick the man I think had the best chance to take that ball over the goal line from the pay dirt area and I would pick Eddie James.

Eddie James played for practically nothing. Eddie didn't care about money. He loved football like no other human being ever did. To Eddie James it was a rare privilege to play football, to have men to play with, to have fellows to play against, to be part of a club with uniforms and a field.

Here was a diamond in the rough. A good, kind big-hearted man like Jim Thorpe and Babe Ruth, he didn't take life too seriously. He gave to sport and to Western Canada the same inspiration that Thorpe and Ruth gave in their respective fields; that combination of rare ability combined with color and pleasing personality.

"Eddie, Dynamite, James" will most assuredly be a prominent name in Canada's Football Hall of Fame.

I suppose one of his biggest thrills would be the acclaim he received from the Montreal fans after our Grey Cup game there in 1931. Despite the fact we were the losers, Eddie was the outstanding star of the game and the fans swarmed on the field immediately the final whistle blew to shake his hand and ask for his autograph. It was just another James' day. He was always great.

His biggest and most sustaining thrill, no doubt, was provided by his son Gerry, who is one of Canada's all time greats of the grid iron. Gerry is chip off the old block displaying, at all times, that tremendous James' competitive spirit.

Eddie James never started anything he couldn't finish. He finished by leaving us Gerry to carry on the great James' tradition. Gerry has already added much lustre to the James' name. I hope the James' line will be perpetuated for many years to come.

In Regina next year we are holding a Roughriders Reunion, a home coming for former Roughriders. We had planned to make Eddie James the centre of the big day. He was one of football's immortals.

The editor of *Touchdown*, Bill Good Sr., mentioned in his short preface that Ritchie "coached the Roughriders when Eddie James was a member of the team and the greatest plunging back of his day or, for that matter, any day. You're a skeptic? Read on, friend."

For Gerry, the challenge to live up to his father's accomplishments as well as to everyone else's expectations must have seemed intimidating. At once, I'm convinced, he could feel the promise that ached in his own bones, a promise that spread into his limbs when he was running downfield towards the goal line or the promise that surged into his hands when he was taking the puck onto his stick or handing out a body check, a promise he could feel from his father.

How to compete? That question would have gripped his gut whenever he thought about how much his father was admired.

The trick was not to look ahead. I sense Gerry knew

that. He knew he had to accept the challenge on his own terms and confront each game as a new beginning. In the moment. It was like picking and eating fruit. Squeeze gently before biting, remember the core or pit at the centre and let the sweet juices linger on your tongue.

As Gerry reflects back on the complicated relationship he had with his dad, what puzzles and bothers him is that nobody, out of all of those who spoke so highly of his dad during his career, seemed to be there for support at the end of his dad's life. Eddie and his second wife lived in relative isolation in a tiny one-bedroom suite.

"She was a lovely person," Gerry says, "small and frail with a great sense of humour. She made my dad happy. For that I was thankful. You would have thought, though, that someone could have helped them. They got by but that was about it."

Gerry pauses. We are talking on the phone. I can hear him fidgeting at the other end of the line, hesitating. He has something important to add but does not know quite how to say it.

"Half way through my career, probably around the time my dad died, I no longer felt I was challenging him. Whatever he had achieved and I was accomplishing, we were doing together. This is as close as I ever got to him. Do you understand?" he asks.

"Yes," I answer, "I think I do."

"Good. This realization meant a lot to me. A lot," he repeats.

❧

Gerry began his 1955 season in Winnipeg with great enthusiasm and anticipation; after all, at 20 he was a veteran. But what followed was a season of mixed blessings and a combination of team play and attitude that soon had Gerry questioning his decision to sign up for football full time.

The Blue Bombers got off to their worst season in club history, a 0 and 5 record. Yet despite five straight losses, fan support had not dwindled. Against the Lions in game six the team finally won, and suddenly everyone was optimistic. The season could be salvaged. This win, though, was followed a couple of games later by a rather listless effort against Saskatchewan. As Jack Matheson wrote:

> Totally unimpressed with the urgency of the moment, Winnipeg Blue Bombers rolled over and played dead for Saskatchewan Roughriders, Saturday night.
>
> The Bombers had expected to attend burial services for the Roughriders but merely dug a hole for themselves. In losing 12 – 7 on a deplorable display of absolutely nothing, the Bombers stopped a few paces short of the point of no return....
>
> The Winnipeg attack was commendable enough, matching the 'Riders nicely statistically, but the defensive unit spent most of the evening inspecting the Taylor Field turf from close range.

In Matheson's view a few players deserved attention, Gerry especially whom he called "a smoking pistol on the offence again."

In spite of the setback, Coach Al Sherman announced "This club will still make the playoffs....Gerry James will be the best halfback in the country from this game on. 'Quote me on that.'"

Sherman's comments and predictions would turn out to be surprisingly prophetic but what a load to place on a young player's shoulders, a young player whose role and successes in the league were always qualified by the best "Canadian" or "homebrew" halfback. Curiously, the same caveat never seemed to be applied to the China Clipper, Normie Kwong. I like to think that those reading and watching the game simply saw a great running back in action.

In another game against the Lions, Gerry hit his stride en route to one of the most outstanding performances in Canadian Football history.

Once again Jack Matheson provided the commentary:

Gerry James saved the greatest evening of his young football career for the one the Winnipeg Blue Bombers needed most, Saturday.

Kid Dynamite's pulverizing running, plus the canny field strategy of Buddy Leake and more swivel-hipping by speedball Leo Lewis, led the Big Blue to a pulsating 20 – 19 victory over BC Lions while 27,132 people registerd shock and dismay, in that order.

James provided the shock when he piled up an astounding 178 yards all alone…In winning the big one, Bombers moved right along in their desperate bid to pick off a playoff spot after their worst start in club history. They move on to Edmonton today and will take a crack at Pop Ivy's proud 7 – 0 record out of Clarke Stadium.

In his personal duel with glory, Gerry's 178 yards left him a mere six yards behind Howard Waugh, the great Tulsa Fullback who ripped large holes in enemy lines for Calgary last season. James ran the ball only twice in the last quarter and would have been a lead-pipe cinch for immortality with more work.

What was even more remarkable about Gerry's achievement was that he gained this yardage on only 16 attempts for an average run of 11yards per carry.

As Bob Moir noted about this team performance, they finally owned the spark.

One major question arose from this game. Why was Gerry not allowed to run more and shoot for the single-game rushing record? With a 6.2-yard rushing average, and a 6 yard difference between Gerry and Waugh, how many carries would it have taken for Gerry to Surpass Waugh's record? Again, Bob Moir observed: "James undoubtedly marked himself as one of the greatest Canadian players with his performance. It was thrilling to watch him every time he grabbed the ball...." Why didn't this sentence read one of the greatest players in Canadian football? Had he been used in the final quarter of that BC game there is a good chance he would have been the first CFL player to break the 200 yard barrier in a single game.

Gerry's example was infectious and in the next game against the league leading Eskimos, Leo Lewis, the Lincoln Locomotive, "was hitting harder than at any previous time this year," Bob Moir reported. "The blistering third quarter pace enlivened by the snappy running of Gerry James and Leo Lewis, plus the hard-hitting of the brilliant defensive crew which stopped the Eskimos in their tracks nearly all night, the Bombers thrilled a 1955 record crowd of 18,884 persons.

James bulled his way for 141 yards on 18 carries and Lewis scampered for 96 in 16 attempts."

As a duo, Gerry and Leo Lewis were closing in on the running totals for Kwong and Bright. The duel was on.

With four games left in the season, Winnipeg had moved from the cellar to sole possession of the third and last playoff spot in the WIFU.

Not since the days of Fritzie Hanson and Art Stevenson have the Blue Bombers had a pair of runners the calibre of the two, who today hold the second and third spots in the WIFU ground-gaining race.

Second-ranking Gerry James, the right halfback, and third-ranking Leo Lewis, the left halfback, have been two outstanding reasons why the Blue Bombers have moved steadily ahead in the WIFU race in recent weeks. Should this pair continue to tear asunder the opposing defences then the future could be exceedingly bright for Winnipeg.

Two games later, again against the hapless BC Lions, the headlines read, **James Romps Through Lions/Shatters Kwong's Record.** Not only were the Bombers destined for the playoffs, they were ending the year on a high note when they whipped BC 24 – 13.

The Bombers were led last night by Gerry James, home-brew halfback voted the outstanding Canadian-born player in football last year. A Winnipeg stadium crowd of 14,733 saw James carry for two touchdowns and burst overland to a conference ground-gaining record.

The 21-year-old James blasted 143 yards from scrimmage and also ran back a British Columbia kickoff 53 yards. Midway through the third quarter he bulled from the Lions' 37-yard line to the 11 and at that juncture surpassed the conference record of 1,058 yards set by fullback Normie Kwong of Edmonton last Saturday. He left the field with a total of 1,084 yards to his credit for the season thus far.

Jim Brooke wrote, "THE RUNAWAY…And now for another chapter of that current Western Conference best seller, 'What Makes Gerry Run?'

"Gerald James, the brash young Winnipeg Blue Bomber halfback, had the effrontery to shatter Norman Kowng's brand new WIFU ground-gaining record a mere 48 hours after the Kwonger had constructed same."

According to Bill Hawrylak, WIFU official statistician,

this was how the two backs stood, each with one game remaining to play. James had a net gain of 1,074 yards against 1,058 for Kwong. Both marks surpassed the league record of 1,043 yards established the year before by Howard Waugh of Calgary. James had carried the ball 174 times for an average gain of 6.2 yards a carry, and Kwong had carried the ball 211 times for an average of 5 yards a carry. A total of 16 yards separated the two men.

Strangely, as the football season was reaching its climax and the duel between Gerry and Kwong was front and centre, news was leaked that Gerry had signed a contract to play for the Maple Leafs at the end of the season. While there was nothing surprising about this news — Gerry had been flipping back and forth between the two sports for years — he would now be reporting to the senior hockey team. That was a significant departure from the old pattern. He would be entering the pro ranks of hockey, presumably on a permanent basis. No more football, at least that was the implication. What odd timing. Why did Toronto not wait until the end of the football season before releasing this news? Unless, of course, someone wanted to upset the football applecart!

What impact did this information have on Sherman's decision-making process in the final few weeks of the 1955 regular season? First of all, he had limited Gerry's play in the fourth quarter against BC when Gerry had an opportunity to beat the single game rushing record. As Jack Matheson had said, Gerry was a "lead pipe" cinch to break the single-game record. Then, with the season rushing title on the line, Sherman sat Gerry out for the entire fourth quarter of the last game. Sherman, of course, would have argued that he was saving Gerry for the playoffs.

To add substance to the conjecture that politics and a conspiracy were in the making, the Bomber game was played before the Edmonton game, so the Eskimos knew exactly how many yards Gerry had mustered in his few carries and added to his year's total. Kwong ran the ball over twenty times in a meaningless game and beat out Gerry for the title by around forty yards. The Eskimos did what they had to do for Kwong to win the rushing title.

Considering Gerry had a 16 yard advantage to begin with, it's not difficult to imagine that some sort of plot had been hatched to keep Gerry out of the record books. If he had won the rushing title and had set a single game rushing record, he would have been a shoo-in to win the Schenley as best Canadian for the second year in a row. The league could not reward someone who had deliberately betrayed them. I think they felt they needed to teach him a lesson. No individual was bigger than the league. If this is not the logic behind Sherman's decisions, then he comes across as a very mean-spirited man. Perhaps Gerry, too, is a victim of his own cleverness. He was certainly not innocent with his manipulation of the two sports.

Kwong was a great back. He would prove to be a consistent runner for many years and his rushing statistics are impressive. But was the 1955 competition for the rushing title fair? I think not. Two forces, one in Winnipeg and one in Toronto, were competing for Gerry's allegiance. I think Toronto released the information prematurely to embarrass Gerry, and Winnipeg took the bait. The Bombers were understandably annoyed and punished their young back accordingly. While this is pure conjecture, there is no reason to remove Gerry from the last quarters of two games in which he was performing in a way that Bob Moir described as follows: "Displaying his tremendous power on one of the finest nights of his brilliant and eventful football career, James ripped and snorted to a new WIFU ground-gaining record…"

Before the season-ending game, Jack Meek wrote an article that had to anger Winnipeg management. He began, "There is a possibility that this may be Gerry James' last year as a player with the Winnipeg Blue bombers. Gerry has reached the point where he must definitely decide whether to play hockey or football.... The great halfback, who at this writing holds the record for ground gaining in the Western Conference, is reported to have received an attractive offer from the Toronto Maple Leafs to play professional hockey. A two-year contract for James is said to be involved."

Meek goes on to confirm his information with Hap Day, who does nothing to dispel or delay the release of what can only be harmful to Gerry and Blue Bomber morale.

Bob Moir in "Pigskin Parade" wrote on October 24, 1955, only two days after Gerry's 21st birthday, the following:

> The night of October 24, 1955 will always belong to Gerry James.
>
> He has scored hat tricks in hockey, popped in the "big" goal in a playoff game, scored many touchdowns in the WIFU and been selected the outstanding Canadian player in the game.
>
> One night he battered his way for more than 170 yards, nearly eclipsing a single-game record.
>
> But last night he was Gerry James at his finest.
>
> The British Columbia Lions knew that James would be given a great percentage of the carries. They knew he was a few more than 100 yards behind Normie Kwong in the race for the ground-gaining championship in the WIFU and they knew the Bombers were going to go all out to try and square accounts for Gerry.
>
> Nevertheless he managed to pile up a convincing 142 yards and even had 25 yards called back because of an illegal interference penalty. He must have known how his team-

mates felt after that one, because it was he who patted the linemen on the seats of the britches, telling them with a small gesture that he knew they were trying for him.

And they were....

Gerry caught Kwong and passed him.

It is now a one-game battle between the pair for the league honors. The Bomber players feel it a personal vendetta. More than one inquired after the game about Gerry's progress. He is a popular player with his teammates.

He is a good humor man, always ready with the big gag.

As Moir pointed out, Gerry had several near breakaway runs where the last man barely managed to nudge him out of bounds. Just one of those close calls would have put him out of reach in the rushing race. When he was pulled from the game in the fourth quarter, he didn't complain to Sherman but simply remarked that it was a shame he had to leave the game on an effort as poor as his last. He had gained only three yards on a sweep.

Moir's article was glowing, was filled with admiration for Gerry's prowess as a football player. But curiously, he devoted the last four paragraphs of his piece to Gerry's signing with the Toronto Maple Leafs. Why? Why did Moir suddenly shift his focus to hockey. Sherman who did not want to discuss James's plans would only say to Moir: "If Gerry wants to stick to football, he has a most brilliant future. There's no reason why he can't if he wants to, get salaries reaching as high, if not higher, than the best-paid American backs. He'll be as good as them." Surprisingly, Sherman didn't realize that his young halfback was already as good as any one of them.

As Winnipeg cruised into the playoffs against the Roughriders, whom they beat in the two-game total point semi-final 24 – 16, the Leafs continued to broadcast to the four corners of the sporting universe their interest and signing of Gerry. As Hal Walker made clear, Hap Day was waiting on Gerry:

Let's see now, was it Omar Khayam who said it, or was it Hap Day?

Quote. You have to be great in adversity, end quote.

Mr. Day was recounting the horrible misfortune which befell the Leafs over the weekend, but he cautioned his listener that it wasn't the time for crepe-hanging....

"One of the things that displeased me at Detroit was that beyond Duff and Bionda none of our guys wanted any meat," Hap intoned unhappily. Wanting meat is hockeyese for wanting to play it rugged, of course....

"However," Hap warned, "I didn't place 'guts' at the first of that G and G and G slogan for nothing. That's our prime requisite. We know what we want. We don't know when we'll get it. But one thing I know, we'll get it. Whether it's this year, next year or the year after....

"Don't forget Bionda only played 10 games of senior hockey last year and yet he didn't look any more out of place than some of our more experienced hands," the GM said. "He doesn't back up from anybody, either."

That's why Day can hardly wait for Winnipeg Blue Bombers to conclude their footballing so he can get Gerry James out of his cleats and back on skates.

"Maybe Gerry isn't the smoothest guy in the world, but he doesn't skate away from anybody, either. We can stand some guys like that around here."

Day would soon get his wish. Winnipeg lost the western final in two straight games to the Eskimos who went on to win the Grey Cup against the Alouettes 34 – 19, much as Gerry predicted. Personally Gerry had to be pleased with the fact that he had been named to the West's All-star team, but I think he was disappointed that he did not have a fair crack at the rushing title.

Undoubtedly the highlight of the year for both Gerry and Marg was the birth of their second daughter, Tracy, on November 10, 1955, right in the middle of the Western playoffs. Gerry's role as a family man had been awakened once again and would continue to inform all of his decisions — family first.

ॐ

With Winnipeg unwilling to pay Gerry at least as well as the best imports, a two-year contract with the Leafs seemed to Gerry the wise choice. As Jim Hunt wrote:

> If Gerry James can find a Toronto Maple Leaf hockey sweater that fits, Canadian football may have seen the last of one of its greatest native-born stars...
>
> The NHL presents a challenge to James. He already has proved he is good enough for the big time in football. Now, he wants to show he can make it in hockey. If he does, Gerry realizes his football days are over.
>
> James believes football is a tougher game physically than hockey. You get beaten up in a tough hockey game, but nothing like you do in a football game such as we played Monday night," Gerry said.
>
> He also foresees a longer career in hockey than in football. James feels he can earn a good living from either sport. But as a big-league hockey player, he can hope to last a dozen years. The way he plays, his chances of lasting that long as a footballer are pretty slim.

In another interview, Hap Day and King Clancy had the following to say about Gerry's signing and prospects with the Leafs:

Day: This is another shot — a big shot — right on the bull's eye of our target to give Toronto fans the type of hockey they've been clamoring for and are used to seeing.

Coach King Clancy: He's my kind of hockey player. I'm tickled pink that he saw fit to turn pro with us. He's a rugged, hard-hitting right winger. From what I've seen of him he hates to lose. That's my man.

When Gerry walked through the doors of the Gardens in mid November, the Leaf season was well under way. Day and Clancy had phoned to suggest that Gerry take a few extra days off before reporting but the "Kid" was anxious to get started in his new role. As Stan Houston observed:

Don't look for Gerry James in a Maple Leaf hockey game for another month.

And don't look for Gerry James in a football game for at least another two years — if ever.

Now that the versatile 21-year-old athlete's NHL contract has been brought out of the secret Maple Leaf vaults for the first time since he signed it last March, football is forgone yet hockey is still distant.

James and the Leaf management both estimate it will take at least a month of practice before the Winnipeg Blue Bomber halfback is ready to play competitive hockey....

"There is a considerable difference between the financial terms of my hockey contract and my football contract," James says. "Hockey will pay me much more and that's why I chose it...."

It would be wrong to accuse Gerry of being a mercenary. Few if any athletes were paid excessive salaries in those early days of pro sport and a young man like Gerry had to look to the welfare of his family. As long as he remained healthy, hockey offered him the best and longest future.

In December he finally took to the ice as a member of the Toronto Maple Leafs. As one commentator observed, Gerry immediately got everyone's attention: "Gerry James made his first appearance of the season for Leafs and, as usual, managed to create excitement. First time out he flattened Real Chevrefils. On his next turn he crashed the Detroit net, knocked it off the moorings. He was inches short of a first down." Another scribbler noted, "There is, of course, some doubt if some of the Leafs are producing the 100 per cent demanded by Day. But players like Rudy Migay, Sid Smith and Gerry James have responded with some of their best hockey of the season." Yet another said, "Gerry James was just about the best Leaf in action..."

Even though Gerry's offensive contribution to the team was minimal, knowledgeable hockey people continued to praise him. When he was on the ice, he definitely got the attention of his opponents. In several newspapers, he is credited with scoring his first goal in early March against Detroit, but Gerry is adamant that he scored his first goal in Toronto in January against Boston.

"Sid Smith broke away down the wing and when I caught up to him he looked over, clearly saw me, sort of laughed and shot. The puck hit the post and squirted out, directly into my path. I wound up and shot, almost missing the puck and it went end over end into goal, over Terry Sawchuk's glove. I could read the puck as it flew through the air — NHL *Toronto* NHL *Toronto* — and fluttered into the net. I can see it as if it were yesterday. This was not the prettiest of goals but your first NHL goal is always magical."

Gerry also remembers another incident in Toronto that had a major impact on him. "A couple sat next to the bench, near to where I usually sat. Odd man out. They were at every

game. She was gorgeous, absolutely gorgeous. One night —
I don't remember who shot it or who we were playing — but
the puck rose over the boards and hit the woman in her face.
It was awful. She was very badly cut. The couple never returned to the arena at least not to those seats. The next year
protective glass was installed in every arena in the league. I
think that happened in 1956."

As the season progressed, Toronto climbed above Boston into the fourth and final playoff spot. In early March, a
place in the second season was looking like a certainty. On
March 8, the Leafs played the Canadiens in Montreal and
lost 4 – 3. "Despite the loss," Rex MacLeod wrote, "Leafs
preserved their margin in fourth place, three points ahead of
Boston....A crowd of 13,538, reputedly reduced by Montreal's worst blizzard of the year, saw Leafs give one of their
most impressive performances of the season....James scored
his at 18:55 in the third period, thereby setting the stage for
a last, desperate offensive by Leafs that failed to produce the
tying goal."

When I mentioned this game to Gerry and noted the
fact that Montreal had scored three of their four goals while
Toronto was short-handed, he muttered: "Typical. That was
typical. Montreal was the worst place to play in the league.
The heckling was fierce. And they were so avid, you felt like
you had no room to skate. They were right down there on the
ice with you. I would put my stick at head level, just above
the boards, then I'd skate the length of the ice, all the fans
ducking, except the guy at the end, who would hide behind
the glass at the last second. At that time they only had glass
along the end boards. Anyway, in the old days, when you got
a penalty you had to serve the full two minutes. You didn't get
out of the box if the opposition scored. It always seemed that
when we were ahead, we would get a penalty called against us
in the last five minutes or so and invariably Montreal would

score one or two goals while we were short-handed. I swear that's how they won so many close games. Sure they were a great team but I always figured Clarence Campbell and the head office wanted Montreal to win. At any cost."

Sports have always been rife with conspiracy theories and I suspect Gerry's was made only partially with tongue in cheek. Montreal was a hard "gig".

A few days later, the team travelled to Detroit and shamed all the doubters. As Bob Hesketh wrote: "Now it was after the game and the almost impossible had happened and the Leafs are in the playoffs. Not backing in because the Hawks had beaten Boston, but walking in as if they actually knew where they were going."

Ironically the Leafs would be meeting the Wings in the first round of the playoffs so they stayed on in the Motor City.

Hesketh went on to write:

You must rejoice if you are a Clancy fan, and there are few people who aren't. You must admire the tenacity of the Hawks who played out a meaningless string honestly. You must wonder that a club like the Leafs could win only five games on the road, two of them in Detroit, and still be good enough to finish in the playoffs.

Now they are young and vinegarish.

Saturday night they were as tight as a bull fiddle string. Sunday night they relaxed a bit.

Followers may be amazed to discover that they outshot the Wings by better than two to one. For 69 games they have been urged and staunchly refused to shoot the puck at the net.

Now there was a bus to take them back to the hotel and the Pullman that was on order to Toronto was cancelled. In the front seat Clancy sat down, his hat pulled down around his ears and his mouth a glitter of gold. This, you sense, is the most important night of his life and it is impossible to be cynical or discouraging. He has never had a present like this, he says, they have stunk out the joint on the road sometimes, he says, but they have made up for it now. They are spitting into a rainstorm, but don't count them out till it's over.

"We will move out to Dearborn Inn tomorrow," Clancy announces, and Gerry James, who gets $10 a day walking-around money with the Winnipeg Blue Bombers, asks the obvious.

"When do we get our expense money?" he says.

The playoffs commence officially.

The Leafs would lose the best-of-seven series against Detroit 4 – 1. In addition to Gordie Howe, Detroit was solid (although by no means great) through three lines, strong on defence and had one of the best goalies to ever play the game, Glenn Hall. Their win over the young and less talented Leafs was not a surprise.

For the first time in recent memory, as Gerry headed into summer, he did not have to concern himself with training. He actually had some time to himself, for rest and recreation, and ample time to spend with his family. Because of the demands of two sports, it had been years since he had idled away in the sun with his family. The less glamorous side of being a professional sportsman was that you got little time off to spend with your family. In addition to the games and practices, travel ate up the hours. As he joined his teammates on the golf links in the summer of 1956, he was relatively pleased with his performance and with what Maurice Smith wrote about Conn Smythe's response to his play:

"Gerry James is one of the greatest athletes I've ever seen. Our club was lying down dead until he joined us at the end of the football season."

That was the comment of Conny Smythe when questioned about how the former Blue Bomber star went with Toronto Maple Leafs this season.

Elaborating, Smythe said he ranked Gerry as one of the super-stars in the National Hockey League today. "I wouldn't trade him for any player who has come up into the NHL in the last two years," exclaimed the president of the Maple Leaf Gardens. "Why, James is one of the big reasons we were able to make the play-offs this year. I don't think the opposition scored more than two goals against him all season when we were short handed."

Smythe added he did not think there was much chance Gerry would return to football. "Under our present contract he certainly can't," said the man who has spent a lifetime in hockey and who has probably stirred up more controversies than any other figure in the game.

"We need players like James in hockey. You can get hundreds of good football players from the U.S. but you can't get too many hockey players of his calibre in Canada today."

Naturally Gerry was flattered by his bosses' compliments and unqualified support. One thing still puzzled him. No one had given him a physical so he had to assume that no-one knew that he had little vision in his right eye. He now knew that his loss of sight had far greater impact on his hockey game than it did on his football game, and yet no one seemed remotely concerned about his state of health. When he had reported for the past season, everyone seemed to accept that he was in great shape. His football stats were accepted as testimony to that. But when he inquired, he discovered that no one in hockey was given a physical examination. They were all athletes and consequently it was presumed that they had to be in shape. While Gerry looked forward to his next full season as a star on skates, he also knew his game needed a lot of work.

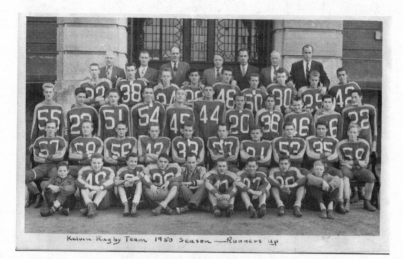

Kelvin High School, Winnipeg, team photo, 1950

Gerry wearing practice jersey.

Gerry on pitch out. Buddy Tinsley in background.
Told Gerry he would make him a star.

Gerry and Norm Hill on sidelines during game.

Gerry being tackled in Edmonton. Note third hand.

Gerry on bench, 1955, taken while he led league in rushing until
Normie Kwong broke the record on final day of season.

Gerry and Gordie Rowland in pre game warm-up,
Winnipeg Stadium, 1957.

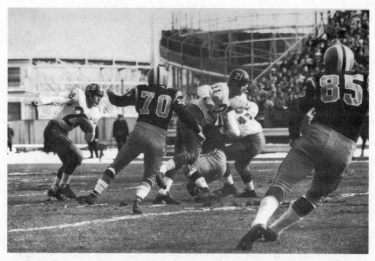

Grey Cup game against Hamilton. Gerry coming out of backfield
led by Charlie Shepard.

Gerry and his mother at Maple Leaf Gardens.

Gerry getting ready for Memorial Cup with Marlies.

King Clancy, Hap Day and Gerry, signing contract.
After they explained rules to Gerry.

Gerry with Dick Duff after Gerry scored his first goal.

Gerry with Johnny Bower in goal, Bobby Baun, Gary Aldecorn and Carl Brewer.

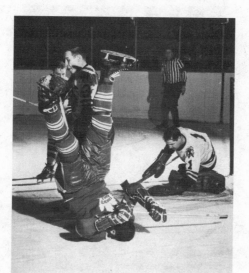

Gerry break dancing after Pierre Pilote check. Glen Hall in goal.

Gerry with Marg at home after Gerry injured shoulder in New York.

Gerry with Howie Meeker when he was coach in Toronto.

9 / The Glory Years

When Gerry walked into the Leaf training camp in the late summer of 1956 he was surprised to see a new coach, Howie Meeker, at the helm. Right away Gerry was concerned that the team's style of play would change; that his rough and tumble game would not sit well with the new crewcut coach. But in actual fact the season got off to a blistering start. Red Burnett noted that the play of the young team was "making coach Howie Meeker's pre-season statement that they are through being patsies on the road, stand up."

Gerry was so enthusiastic about what was happening on the ice he said in an interview that "It was relatively easy for me to forget football." He recalled as they retreated from Detroit, where he had scored one of three goals in a hard-fought tie, that "hockey was always uppermost in his mind." Hal Walker observed, "The young right winger, whose rapid improvement as a hockey player has confounded quite a few people, admitted that he was bitten by the ice bug a few years ago. 'Football was something I played just for something to do. Naturally I tried to play it well and I consider I did that.'"

It is interesting how a sense of exaltation and a feeling of joy can put a glow on everything.

In late October the team won its first game in two years at the Forum and they moved into a tie for third place. Red Burnett wrote: "Legs, fire and excellent goalkeeping last night gave Leafs their first win on Montreal Forum ice in two seasons." The team was euphoric. Howie Meeker's kids had taken play away from the mighty Habs in front of a crowd of over 14,000.

A week later, the team "smoked" the New York Rangers at home, 7 – 2. Gerry contributed in many ways. While his defensive work was outstanding, two witnesses boasted about his fisticuffs. Hal Walker described the battle this way. "**Jolted by James**: Evans was a loser on the night, clearly licked by Gerry James in a second period fight in which Gerry decked him with a startling bit of fistwork. A left uppercut and right cross to the obstreperous New York defenceman's face put him down and in need of six stitches of surgery in a post-game examination."

Red Burnett added his description of Gerry's play: "Gerry James showed the way in the muscles department with a one-punch decision over Jack Evans, Ranger defenseman who once had a fling as a boxer. Evans tried to comb James' hair with his stick in the second period and then made the mistake of going after the Leaf with his fists. Evans missed and James promptly decked him with a vicious right hook." Apparently Gerry's one assist and the fact that this game landed the Leafs in a tie with Detroit for first place in the standings was incidental to Gerry's fighting prowess. Although it was early in the season, it had been some time since a Leaf team had occupied such rarified air.

Even Meeker was confounded by his team's success. Hal Walker reported: "He couldn't put his finger on the answer but he suspects it's chiefly because this team is one that is dedicated to team effort." Curiously, Phil Watson, coach of the Rangers, wasn't at all puzzled: "What I liked about them was their skating. They kept coming back, checking much better than last year's team. And they never quit." Walker added: "Two other defensive stalwarts have been Rudy Migay and Gerry James, penalty killers par excellence."

Everyone seemed in awe. Yet the Leaf's fine, early-season play was a surprise to everyone except the players themselves. Even when a little reality had settled in, the team still held onto a playoff berth. Red Burnett wrote: "Most pleasing feature of the fourth-place Maple Leafs' 4 – 1 win over the tail-end Chicago Black Hawks was the continued goal production of the Gerry James – Billy Harris – Sid Smith line….In the past three games, this line has figured in five of the team's nine goals and picked up a total of 12 scoring points. James, the muscle man of the trio, has branched out as a playmaker, with five assists in three games."

The fact is, if all the skeptics had paid attention to Gerry's play in both sports over the past four years they would have known what a competitor he was; what an inspiration he could be to his teammates. Given a chance, he could be a significant role player in hockey.

Then in December the unthinkable happened. In a freak accident, Leapin' Lou Fontinato nailed Gerry into the boards and the young right winger was sidelined with a torn ligament in his right shoulder. He would be out for a minimum of four weeks. If there was ever any doubt about Gerry's impact on team play, his time on the injury list should have proved to the coaching staff how invaluable he was; how much he was missed by his linemates.

Instead, Meeker and his staff went on the attack. When the team started to lose on a regular basis, the players were blamed. I don't think there is any question that Gerry was asked to return to the lineup too early. Billy Harris was accused of not playing tough enough even though anyone familiar with the game knew that Gerry or someone like him was critical to the success of Harris's game. He was a goal scorer and play maker, not a fighter.

Even though Harris was an outstanding player, how he was treated indicated the uncompromising attitude of his employers. They had a style of play in mind and if a player failed to adapt to that style then he would be "sent down". Either Harris would learn under the tutelage of Billy Reay or he would be dropped. With only six teams in the league, the owners could dictate style and control quality. Everyone was replaceable. Essentially it was management's way or the highway. Such an attitude was demoralizing, especially when things started to go wrong. When the "fun" game Gerry and his teammates had been promised became a grim game, enthusiasm evaporated.

Unfortunately, as the second half of the season progressed, the Leaf ship never righted itself and sank to the bottom of the League, missing the playoffs, much to the dismay of management. What did they expect? They had an unhappy crew.

Meanwhile Gerry was receiving plenty of attention from the football circuits, both in Canada and the States. Under a headline that read, **Grid Giants Bait Exploratory Hook For Gerry James**, Rex MacLeod wrote: "New York Giants, champions of the National Football League confessed yesterday that they were interested in James if and when he decides to return to football....Raymond J Walsh, general manager of Giants, admitted yesterday that his club had written to James. But he stressed that no offer had been made."

The Leafs were quick to respond and pointed out that they were "quite statisfied with Gerry's progress as a hockey player. Until James was hurt a few weeks back I thought he was going ahead by leaps and bounds," said Hap Day, Leafs' GM yesterday. "And recently I thought he was starting to improve again Maybe his injury took more out of him than we suspected."

The Blue Bombers also let it be known that they were still interested in Gerry's services and that they felt they had a prior claim on him as a footballer. Gerry remained indecisive. Family would be his number one consideration in whatever decision he made. However, he is alleged to have said that "after such a disappointing hockey season I think I might be happy to come back to football and a lot of nice people." Bob Moir, paraphrasing Gerry, wrote under the sub headline **IT WASN'T FUN**:

> The Leafs have always played a defensive style of hockey. Recently they made a policy switch and Smythe said the Leafs were going to change the style of play completely. James was asked if he would have continued in hockey under a different system of play.
>
> "I think I would have," he replied. "I like playing a game because I enjoy it. It was no fun playing with the Leafs. At the start of the season Meeker (Leaf coach Howie Meeker) said we were going to have a lot of fun playing this year. After the first couple of games when we started losing, it wasn't fun any more. There were always threats of $500 fines hanging over our shoulders.
>
> "I had an exclusive membership in the $100 club along with about eight or nine others," said Gerry. "I got fined for missing a check on Fleming Mackell of Boston when we were killing off a penalty. They fined Ron Stewart $100 for indifferent play one night and he had scored two or three goals in the previous two games."
>
> A shoulder injury severely hampered Gerry's hockey after Christmas. "I think the shoulder is all right now," he said. "The Leafs' doctor said just to give the shoulder plenty of rest for a while."

As the 1956 – 1957 NHL season wound down, Gerry's two-year contract with the Leafs terminated. Coincidentally the Bombers and the Giants continued to express their interest in Gerry's services as a running back. The Giants finally presented an offer, when they thought it was legally and morally okay for them to do so. "It was a good offer," admitted Gerry, "so good, in fact, that I almost fell off my chair when Mr. Mara (Giants' president) made it. If I had been single I would have taken Mara's offer right away. It would have been worth the gamble."

In the meantime, Ralph Parliament, a member of the Winnipeg executive, travelled to Toronto on business and made a point of visiting with Gerry. While the two men did not sign a formal contract, Ralph, who Gerry liked a lot, agreed to take Gerry's two daughters back to Winnipeg on the plane on the condition that Gerry agree to sign with Winnipeg as soon as he got home. A deal was done with a handshake and formalized a short time later in President Jim Russell's office back in Winnipeg.

Gerry had made it clear that he would not have returned to football if Al Sherman remained as Winnipeg coach, so the appointment of Bud Grant as the new coach was a significant part of the signing. Contrary to what Gerry has said over the years about Grant's attitude to Canadian players, Bud Grant was elated to hear that Gerry planned to return to Winnipeg: "We've sort of been including him in our plans. We've always had one eye cocked for James. He's going to fit in nicely. We've definitely got a place for him."

When they were teammates, before Bud Grant became coach, Gerry carpooled with Grant to practices. The two would sit in the car and rarely talk Gerry told me. "Grant was very contemplative and disciplined. I thought if he coached as well as he played we were in for a wild and wonderful ride. He thought we should win. That was that!"

After sitting out the 1956 season to play hockey for the To-ronto Maple Leafs, Gerry was delighted to be back in the Blue Bomber fold at the start of the 1957 season. He be-came a part of one of the great CFL dynasties, winners of four Grey Cups in six years (1958, 1959, 1961 and 1962). At the outset, they would qualify for the Grey Cup in 1957 but lose decisively on the big stage to their perennial adver-saries, the Hamilton Tiger-Cats. A look at the roster of one of those cup-winning teams gives us a snapshot of the spirit, determination and talent of the company in which Gerry found himself.

Winnipeg Blue Bombers 1959 Grey Cup Champions:

Ed Kotowich, Bud Tinsley, Leo Lewis, Cec Luning, Wal-ter Bilicki, Ernie Pitts, Frank Rigney, Nick Miller, Ron La-tourelle. Bob Jones (Equipment), Ken Ploen, Gerry James, Norm Rauhaus, Steve Patrick, Herb Gray, Cornel Piper, Charlie Shepard, Gar Warren, Bud Grant (Head Coach). Ken Kovacs (Equipment), Rick Potter, Rae Ross, Tony Keh-rer, Ted Mikiliechuk. Jim Van Pelt, Dave Burkholder, Jack Delveaux, Roger Savoie, Carver Shanon, Joe Zaleski (As-sistant Coach), George Hills (Vice-President). Ralph Parlia-ment (President), Gord Mackie (Trainer), Gordie Rowland, Keith Webster, Ken Bochen, George Druxman, Henry Janzen, Farrell Funston, Ron Meadmore, Jack Bruzell, Pop Varnes (Equipment), John Michaels (Assistant Coach), Jim Ausley (Manager).

Much has been written and said about Gerry's return to football after his dramatic decision to leave the game for a year. Only one thing matters; he was pleased to be back. It also helped that 1957 was about to be one of his most successful years on the gridiron.

Tom Casey recounted in an article at the time a short anecdote about Gerry's pre-season physical. Apparently Gerry was going along well until he got to the eye room. "The doctor told him to face the far wall and read the third line from the bottom of the chart. 'What chart?' replied James. 'O.K.' said the eye specialist, 'Walk forward until you can read the letters.' So Gerry took off. About two feet from the wall, he got a startled look on his face and triumphantly shouted, 'E'…That boy isn't blind. He just can't see…"

Gerry passed the physical although he figured it was meaningless.

From the opening whistle there was something special about a Bud Grant-coached team. There was no doubt in anyone's mind that the team would be at the heart of every competition. Grant, Gerry said, spoke of destiny…and the players listened.

About Gerry, Grant had this to say: "What do I like about Gerry? He'll come up with the big play for you, that's what. He's an instinctive athlete, and you don't find many of them around, and he can be counted on to come up with the key play that most football players wouldn't think about."

Coaches and brass from the other four teams in the league argued that in their view, Gerry's play with the Leafs had been good enough for Smythe to re-sign him. To a man they felt hockey had dealt them an unkind blow by allowing James to escape the hockey wars and rejoin Winnipeg.

Stafford Smythe said: "I'm sorry Gerry is quitting hockey, but they'd made hockey so unattractive for him that he's gone back to football where he can enjoy himself."

"It's about time," Smythe told George Dulmage, "that we put a little enjoyment back in the game for the players."

This is an interesting admission from Smythe Jr. since he was definitely in a position to change Leaf policy.

Gerry in turn had this to say in a piece by Jim Hunt: "They made a defensive player out of me. I naturally wanted a chance to see what I could do as an offensive player. Maybe the Leafs will change their system. Everyone says they will. But I don't feel I'd fit in anyway." He went on to say that he felt that hockey players had too much wasted time and often developed bad habits. Perhaps Rex MacLeod got to the core of the matter when Gerry told him, "It was a tough decision to make. I still think I could play in the NHL...but I'd have to work at it. And I'm the type of guy that likes to be a winner." In this respect, his time with the Leafs had been a major letdown and miscalculation.

In the meantime he was looking forward to getting on with the new football season, with a coach who had declared that "he was elated to learn of James's decision." Grant understood the value of a little positive reinforcement.

In response to the first few practices and a couple of open scrimmages, John Brown made this assessment of Gerry's prospects for 57.

Gerry James is fighting off a slight ankle injury. However, he showed he is to be reckoned with in total yards gained in the W.I.F.C. again this year. Gerry is the swaggering, cocky type of player you like to have on a club. He reeks with confidence and to a person who meets him for the first time, may appear to be over confident. The fellows who have had the pleasure to play with or against him know the team spirit he possesses. Gerry certainly has a keen sense of humbleness toward the paying public. I would say he is headed for another top flight year.

After an exhibition game against Ottawa, Hal Sigurdson stated that "Gerry James proved you can play a couple of years in the National Hockey League and still be the best backfielder around on any given evening." Even though Gerry suffered a torn rib cartilage against Saskatchewan in his first game of the regular schedule, his play throughout the rest of the season would be stellar.

Once again Gerry was a favourite of the fans. Ronnie Tessler told me that she went to Winnipeg games in the 1950s with her father and what she recalls reflects the range of Gerry's fan base. The season ticket holders who sat directly behind her and her father were two elderly English ladies, who came to the games dressed in tweed suits, skirts and jackets and somewhat frumpish hats. You might have thought they were attending a garden party in the English countryside or taking the family pooch for a walk. They were delightful, Ronnie said, but hardly a couple you would expect to find sitting on a hard wooden bench in a Winnipeg fall watching and cheering on their boy idol. As soon as the team came onto the field these two would begin chanting "Gerry, Gerry", and when he was involved in the action they leapt to their feet urging him on.

By mid-season, Gerry had shown the league that he could still conjure up the old magic. In a drubbing by Edmonton, 41- 8, he scored the only Winnipeg touchdown on a 74-yard gallop. As one reporter acknowledged: "I have to admire the guy because he thinks he can beat Kwong's yard-rushing record if injuries don't sideline him too often. This isn't idle boastfulness or arrogance. It's quite a high aim for a fellow with pride in his work. I'll probably receive a verbal blast (from Gerry) for mentioning this." Hal Sigurdson noted that "Western Conference defences still haven't discovered a way of throwing Normie Kwong, Johnny Bright or Gerry James for a loss. James has carried more than 50 times and still hasn't been spilled behind the line of scrimmage. His average of 7.2 yards per carry is best in the west."

By mid-season, Gerry was a contender for the most yards title and he had pulled ahead of Parker in the scoring race. With the added responsibility of kicking field goals his chances of winning the scoring title improved.

On November 2, Jack Matheson summed up Gerry's history as a kicker in *The Star*:

> They laughed when Gerry James stood up to kick a field goal. In all probability they'll cease their chortling when he wins the WIFU scoring championship, tonight at about 11 bells.
>
> If James makes it, and he has 16 points going for him, as they line up for tonight's last fling of the regular league schedule, there will be a rather incredible success story to be written — all about James trying placements just for kicks, if you'll pardon the expression.
>
> Back last July, someone near the top of Winnipeg in the brains department noted the acute lack of an adept long place kicker. James tried kicking a few for laughs and suddenly found himself as a kickoff artist. One afternoon, against B.C. Lions, he found himself as field goal specialist, and it is doubtful if he will live to regret it....
>
> And so Kid Dynamite develops into a place-kicking threat, all of which makes him a decided lockup as far as the Schenley award for Canadians is concerned. If there's a better Canadian football player in the country, he hasn't presented himself to the jury.

Not only would Gerry win the scoring title, but he would do so with a total of 131 points, another WIFU record. In addition to that record, he set another with 19 touchdowns in one season, 18 of them by way of the run. To cap off this success story, he finished second in the rushing department with 1192 yards.

But perhaps the highlight of the year for Gerry came after a major win over Edmonton. Jim Hunt recounted the moment:

> Gerry James claimed he learned only one thing in two seasons as a serf of Toronto's hockey Leafs — he should have stuck to football.
>
> This bit of self-analysis came in the Winnipeg Blue Bomber dressing room as the club celebrated Monday Night's win over the Edmonton Eskimos — a feat well worthy of a party in this day and age.
>
> The well-wishers crowded around the 22-year-old Bomber back who had been one of the big cogs in the Winnipeg machine. His father, Dynamite Eddie James, was there to pound his son on the back and admit Gerry was maybe a little better than he was in his hey-day in Western football. Bud Grant, football's youngest and most handsome coach, moved in to shake the hand of his young star and tell the world here was a great halfback.
>
> "He's saved our bacon," Grant enthuses. "I don't know what we would have done if Gerry was still playing hockey."

The presence of Gerry's dad at a game was a rare occurrence but for him to congratulate his son in the way he did is something at which Gerry still marvels.

As Matheson had predicted, Gerry went on to win his second Schenley for Best Canadian Player. The native son had returned home triumphant and the long-awaited validation by his father had been passed on. Later he would be named Manitoba Athlete of the Year.

Undoubtedly Gerry was disappointed with the loss against the Ti-Cats in the Grey Cup, a loss for which he blamed himself — he fumbled four times — but he did have cause for celebration. On November 5, Marg gave birth to their third daughter, Tara. Whatever he did in the future would invariably consider the four women in his life. More and more, family took centre stage in Gerry's life.

At the end of the day, though, Gerry still asked himself this question: "How can I win the Schenley for Best Canadian in the league, be runner-up for the Lou Marsh Award and not win the Tommy Lumsden Award for best player on Winnipeg?" Sometimes, perhaps, we ask for too much. There can be no doubt that Gerry was blessed in 1957.

⚜

While there was considerable speculation about Gerry's return to hockey throughout the 1957 football season, he made it clear to everyone, including the Smythes, that he would only do so on his own terms. He had no intention of going to Rochester, at least not for the long-term, and the Leafs would have to make his return to the team financially worthwhile.

Gerry also had other plans. He hoped to open a service station in the Silver Heights neighborhood where he now lived.

Even though Billy Reay had replaced Howie Meeker as coach, the team was still spineless. They were the doormats of the league; they had occupied the cellar for most of the season and the other five teams viewed them as a pushover. Presumably Gerry would bring them some much needed muscle.

Between Christmas and New Year's Day of 1957, King Clancy phoned Gerry and brokered a deal for his services over the phone for the remaining few months of the 1957 – 1958 season. Even though Gerry was quick to point out that he had a broken hand, which had been evident from his play during the Grey Cup, the Leafs wanted him in Toronto immediately. Gerry insisted that he wanted $6,000 to turn up. Clancy almost gagged and pointed out that that was the sort of wage paid to a 20-goal-a-season player. Gerry made it clear that $6,000 was what he expected and Clancy finally agreed, saying "Get your ass down here right away."

Gerry flew into Toronto and was immediately discharged down to Rochester, to get in shape and to give the two broken bones in his hand time to heal. There was no doubt that Gerry would be called up to the Senior team as soon as he was ready. As Smythe Jr. put it: "I think our fancy Dans need another hard rock." As one scribe wrote: "James has proven without a doubt that he will never threaten Maurice Richard for most goals scored in a season but he has one asset that the Leafs need. He can lick anybody in the league on the ice or in the alley. The Leafs have won championships on such talent."

As he had proved in his previous stint with Toronto, Gerry was quite capable of being an offensive force in hockey. Prior to his shoulder injury during the 1956-57 season, he had been in the top twenty in league scoring. Once again, he quickly proved that he was more than simply muscle. In Rochester he was immediately scoring goals and tallying up assists.

When Gerry was finally called up to the senior team, he discovered a very demoralized group of hockey players. Billy Reay was positive enough; the team simply lacked the right balance of talent. Red Burnett had this to say about Gerry's arrival:

It would appear that the best cash outlay the Leafs have made this season was the cost of luring Gerry James back to hockey. In his two games against Chicago and New York, Gerry was one of the better Leafs.

Not only does the Winnipeg football great add muscles to Leafs' defensive set-up but his competitive fire makes him a valuable man for coach Billy Reay to have around.

"No one is taking liberties moving up and down our right side when James is in action," praised Reay. "In addition he surprised me with the way he handled the puck in the other team's defensive zone. He doesn't give it away with foolish passes but hangs on to it and tries to set up a play for a mate if he can't make a play on goal.

"His skating is better than I was led to believe and Gerry convinced me there is a place for him on our team."

While Gerry brought some much-needed energy and enthusiasm to the 1957 – 1958 version of the Leafs, it was not enough. With a month left in the season, no one could have resurrected that team. As one Toronto paper recorded:

When Toronto Maple Leafs sent a posse to flush a fellow named James out of the West they got more than they expected.

They're amazed. And frustrated.

The James wasn't Jesse. He was Gerry, alias the football fullback with Winnipeg Blue Bombers, who has developed into one of Leafs' few redeeming features in the current National Hockey League season.

Leafs figured James would help them in the brawn department but they didn't expect him to take a starring role as a skater and offensive man. He did just that, even though Leafs are still in fifth place and with little hope of making a Stanley cup playoff position.

Leafs are frustrated because Gerry still insists football is his future. Hockey, for the time being anyway, is a mere sideline for cash.

Unlike Howie Meeker, Billy Reay recognized immediately another James's virtue: "He works hard and checks hard and by making the opposition look for him, he has helped Billy Harris (James's centre) get untracked again."

But no amount of hard work by Gerry was going to alter the fortunes of Toronto.

The second to last game of the season, against Chicago, stands out in Gerry's mind and typifies the depths to which he felt Toronto had sunk in the hockey world.

First of all, a year earlier he had reached a personal low point in his career when he told a pregnant heckler, a woman who ragged on him and slammed him from the moment he sat down on the bench, that she looked like she had been putting out for the whole Black Hawks team. She had responded surprisingly quickly by saying at least she wouldn't put out for the whole Leaf team. Chicago management received complaints about the verbal battle and demanded that both parties meet at the end of the game and apologize to one another. This they did, somewhat more amicably than Gerry expected.

Now, at the end of yet another season, Gerry was involved in a game in Chicago in which he had received three minors, two fighting majors and a game misconduct — twenty-six penalty minutes in total. In his second fight, he was squared off against "Terrible" Ted Lindsay, who had a reputation for fighting and somewhat questionable tactics. Both players were being restrained by linesmen but the assistant who held Gerry stepped on Gerry's glove and slipped, momentarily releasing his grip. Gerry popped Lindsay with a good hard punch and "Terrible" Ted went down like a sack of coal. The fight was over and Gerry was shown the gate. He was out of the game.

Later, Gerry was out for dinner with Bob Pulford and Billy Harris at the Circle Bar, a well-known Chicago hangout for sportsmen, and Ted Lindsay and Jimmy Thomson came in with their wives. Lindsay was sporting a large shiner over one eye. Jimmy, who had played with Toronto until recently, walked over to Gerry's table and whispered to Gerry, "Ted didn't know you were left handed."

Gerry laughed when he told me the story then stopped and said, "Ted did a lot for the Players Association. He really got the whole thing rolling. Every player owes him a huge debt. He was a helluva hockey player to boot."

※

Six games into the 1958 CFL season, while leading the league in scoring, Gerry was hit with a clean, hard tackle in a game against Saskatchewan. On a perfectly innocent looking play, he broke his left leg in two places. He spent three weeks in hospital and several months in rehabilitation. Surprisingly, the team did little to assist him with recovery of any sort. Gerry himself set up a strict daily exercise schedule at his local YMCA and over time spent hours in the pool. The "Y" also assigned him a therapist who proved to be invaluable to Gerry's recovery. In particular, this man worked on Gerry's ankle flexibility through manipulation. "He twisted my feet in directions they'd never gone before. I think I actually came out of the therapy stronger."

During this time, Gerry felt quite alienated from the team. He had contact with a few teammates but for the most part was left on his own. When it came time for the team photo, the one celebrating Winnipeg's Grey Cup win of 1958, Gerry drove to the location of the shoot but stayed in his car, watched and then drove off. Even though he had made a major contribution to the team for half a season, he felt he did not belong. Yet he is listed as "missing" on the photo. Here is how Scott Young responded to the tackle and injury:

I don't suppose there is any real reason for a wake over Gerry James of the Winnipeg Blue Bombers. He'll be paid, and probably he'll do some scouting and some TV intermission-ing. He's only 23, and has a wife and a good young family, and in general there can't be many people better equipped mentally, physically and financially to endure a few months in a cast with a doubly fractured leg. All true. But it's us I'm thinking about; the watchers. We lose, the same way we souls lose if Glenn Gould broke a hand or Johnny Wayne got lockjaw.

All the same I wouldn't be surprised if the doctors are wrong when they say that James is out of hockey as well as football in the season coming up....

A few days ago Billy Reay was talking about him as a hockey player. The Leaf coach watched James closely last season, because he came to the team late and Reay may have had an idea that apart from the fact that James never backed up from anyone — a commodity Leafs needed — he couldn't be much of a hockey player.

"I've seldom been so surprised," Reay said. "He made moves out there naturally that other players who have been around the NHL for years never learned to make. Being such a good football player, I don't know if he'll ever give the time to hockey that he needs to correct the things he does do wrong. But if he did, he would become one of the best — and he'd be around a long time."

One mental picture I like of James: It was in Boston last spring, and a Bruin had just made the mistake of coming around his own net with his head down. James hit him. It was a clean check, but the Boston player went down as if pole-axed. A whistle blew, and Fern Flaman, the Boston captain, charged. I thought then, and think now, that Fla-man would have hit any Leaf player except James. He made all the moves. But James just stood there, his stick resting easily on the ice (rather than the defensive stick-waving some players employ) and talked back to Flaman with a sort of expectant half-grin. Full of assurance and poise. There was no fight.

A few months before that, you may remember, James — after one year away from football to devote full time to hockey — had reversed his decision and gone back to football.

Story was that a salary disagreement with Conn Smythe, Gardens' president, had been a deciding factor.

At the Granite Club last November, when James was accepting a cheque for $500 on being named the Canadian football player of the year, his acceptance speech, delivered with the same half-smile, was this: "In accepting," he said, "I want to thank all the many people who have made it possible for me to be named Canadian football player of the year...especially Conn Smythe."

Young's projection was wrong. Gerry would not return to professional sport until the fall of 1959 when he would help the Blue Bombers win their second straight Grey Cup. Even then his return to the team was difficult. Although he had added other exercises to his rehabilitation routine, such as running stairs at Winnipeg Stadium, Bud Grant figured it would be at least another two months before Gerry would be back to his old self. Naturally Gerry disagreed. Grant was right; game conditions demanded a much more intense response than Gerry was able to muster. Strength was one thing, instincts another. But in the last weeks of the season Gerry did start to perform at a peak level and the old Bomber backfield was back in service.

One incident from that season which struck Gerry as amusing occurred during a game against the BC Lions. His kicking skills were slow to return and his problems seemed to be amplified in this game.

"For the most part," he told me, "players did not much care about the convert, especially the lineman. Converts gave both sides of the line an opportunity to settle a score they might have with one of their opposites."

In a game against BC which the Bombers were leading by a score of 41 to 14 or so (Gerry doesn't remember the exact score), he missed the first convert attempt to the left but the Lions were offside. Intentionally. A penalty was given, the ball was moved closer to the goal posts, and the two teams lined up again for a second attempt at the convert. Various battles occurred along the line; Gerry kicked, and missed the convert again, this time to the right. Again the Lions were offside. When they regrouped back in the huddle, Farrell Funston looked at Kenny Ploen and Gerry and said, "I'm open for a pass if you two want to try that." When Gerry went to kick the ball for the third time, he was laughing so hard that he hit the ball square into George Druxman's (he was Winnipeg's centre) rear end.

Although he would place fourteenth in the scoring race, he felt his game was definitely on the mend.

Perhaps another reason for Gerry's improved performance in the latter part of the season was the birth of Marg's and his first son, Kelly Charles (KC) on October 30, 1959.

The Bombers went on to win the Grey Cup 21 – 7. Gerry says this may have been the most balanced of all the Grey Cup winning teams.

⁂

Sitting in front of me is a photograph of the 1959 – 1960 Toronto Maple Leafs, the Stanley Cup Finalists against the Montreal Canadiens that season. Gerry, who appeared in a

Grey Cup only five months earlier, is in the back row, third from the left. Others included in the lineup are:

Bert Olmstead, George Armstrong (Captain), Stafford Smythe (Chairman, Hockey Committee), Conn Smythe (President, Maple Leaf Gardens), George "Punch" Imlach (Gerneral Manager and Coach), King Clancy (Assistant General Manager and Coach), Allan Stanley, Dick Duff. Tim Horton, Carl Brewer, Billy Harris, Ed Babiuk, Johnny Bower, Bob Pulford, Bob Baun, Larry Regan, Tim Daly (Trainer). Bob Haggert (Trainer), Gerry Ehman, Ron Stewart, Red Kelly, Frank Mahovlich, Gary Edmundson, Johnny Wilson, Tom Nayler (Assistant Trainer).

This is an impressive collection of hockey talent and yet the Leafs went down to defeat to the Canadiens in four straight. The first two games in Montreal were close, but at home the Leafs were soundly defeated.

Conn Smythe once remarked to Gerry that if you can't beat them in the alley, you can't beat them on the ice. Undoubtedly this was one of the reasons why Gerry made the team and certainly explained why Conn Smythe liked him so much. If you look over the Toronto roster from this 1960 final, there was probably only one player who truly qualified as "tough," as a back alley boy, and that player was Gerry. Some would argue that the other two members of the "Puke" line — named after Boston's famous Uke line honouring players of Ukrainian heritage — Gary Edmundson and Johnny Wilson, were just as rollicking and just as tough as Gerry. The fans loved the trio. They stirred things up, but Punch Imlach wasn't prepared to risk a fourth line, not unless his stars were under-performing. Ironically, when he put the James-Edmundson-Wilson line on the ice, they often scored! If they didn't, the other team's players at least skated with their heads up.

The Canadiens, also loaded with talent, were tougher. This is something often overlooked when this great Canadiens' dynasty is discussed. Gerry laughs when he points out that Marcel Bonin, one of Montreal's wingers, was even reputed to wrestle bears and kangaroos with a circus to earn a living during the summer months. "Can you imagine any of our wingers taking on someone who wrestled bears?" Gerry asked.

A brief anecdote from that Stanley Cup season illustrates Gerry's point. "After a five aside brawl in a regular game against Montreal," he told me, "after I had returned from my broken leg and was reunited with the senior squad, Punch Imlach called me over to the bench and instructed me to start a fight in the penalty box. When I asked why, Punch countered, "That way we'll get all of their best players kicked out of the game.""

By the 1959-60 season, Gerry's role had been clearly defined, in spite of Reay's assessment of his hockey talent. Much to management's disgrace, Gerry was in the lineup merely for his muscle.

Gerry's sister-in-law, Lynda Ryrie, met Eddie Shack at a social function and during their conversation asked him if he remembered playing against Gerry James. Shack was with the New York Rangers at the time. Apparently Shack replied: "Do I ever, when he went into one corner, I went into the other. He was the meanest son-of-a-bitch I ever played against." Coming from Eddie Shack, notorious for his love of fisticuffs and his occasional questionable, if not dirty, tactics, head butts and spears, not to mention his fan-pleasing pirouettes at centre ice, this comment from one of the tough guys of hockey seems a tad ironic. All the same, when Gerry was told this story he laughed and said, "I always wondered why when we attended a fund raiser or something of that sort together he never talked to me."

It's difficult, though, for two foes to get close from the confines of two different penalty boxes and if these two were to celebrate a common achievement that's where they would have met. I suspect there is a little mutual admiration buried between the two somewhere.

In another game during his final season in the NHL, Gerry remembers hitting Red Kelly, just before he was traded over to the Leafs, with what Gerry considers the hardest check he ever dished out in his hockey career. After the check Kelly was made to sit out the rest of the game. It was obvious that his head was spinning because he couldn't stand up on his skates. The next night, in Detroit, Kelly, who had been a boxer in his youth, chased Gerry around the rink.

"I was fast," Gerry says, "when I had to be. He never did catch me and I suspect if he had he would have cooled off by then. You might say I was relying on his Christian sense of forgiveness. In reality, he was a kind and gentle man. When Red was traded to the Leafs, we were roomed together which had to be someone's perverse sense of humour. What a pair. As I say, Red was a devout Christian and often I would be coming in on a Sunday morning as he was heading off to church. He never said a thing, about the check or about my behaviour. I can tell you this, he was a very very good hockey player. Totally underestimated. He may have been the catalyst that finally led to Toronto winning the Stanley Cup over the next few years. I wish I had had another year to play with him."

At least Gerry had been a part of the squad that set the stage for the Cup winning teams of the 1960s.

❦

By the time the 1960 football season rolled around, Gerry was definitely his old self. He was once again a formidable runner and his talents as a kicker continued to improve. As Jack Matheson was quick to point out, "Conceding Davis and the rest of his defensive mates a satisfactory evening, I go with Gerry James as the man who made the champions tick Monday night. He ran the ball nine times for 63 yards and it looks from my seat as if the Bombers have the balance in the backfield they've lacked since one September night in 1958 when a young man named James ran into an open switch and came up with a broken leg."

Jim Kearney echoed these sentiments:

> The re-emergence Saturday (not from sleep) of Gerry James to the running form he consistently displayed before breaking his leg two years ago can only be bad news for the rest of the league.
>
> Until this win over the Lions James had never quite come back to the form that made him the boy wonder of the WIFU at the age of 17. In this one he was the top Winnipeg rusher (120 yards) and showed again the power, quickness and choppy elusiveness that makes him so effective.
>
> When he broke his leg he made a good job of if. A compound, complex fracture. He had his troubles getting over it.

Gerry scored 17 points in that game and went on to win the scoring title for the second time in his career. He had 114 points to beat out Willie Fleming and he managed to place fifth in rushing. Ironically, Winnipeg would have one of its best years as a franchise with a record of 14 – 2 and then lose in the Western finals to Edmonton. For the first time in three years, a Bud Grant team had missed the Grey Cup. That would be remedied.

The Blue Bombers continued their domination of the Western division of the CFL through 1961. On a personal level Gerry ended up second in scoring behind Jackie Parker and ninth in rushing.

Winnipeg's winning record was once again a decisive 13 – 3. Calgary, who had placed third over the season, squeaked by Edmonton in the semi-finals for the right to be trounced by Winnipeg. Grant was not going to allow a recurrence of the sort of losses they had suffered the previous year.

Once again the Bombers would face their old rivals, the Hamilton Tiger-Cats, in the Grey Cup final.

This was to be another epic struggle.

In the first overtime Grey Cup game in CFL history, Gerry scored 14 points with Kenny Ploen scoring the winning touchdown in overtime. Charlie Shepard punted for a critical single. Gerry had one touchdown, two field goals, and two converts. One newspaper suggested that James had won the game almost single-handedly although Gerry would never entertain such a notion. Bob Frewin wrote: "Three plays later Gerry James, the scoring star of the game, punched over the Hamilton goal line, then kicked the convert left-footed to tie the issue 14 – 14."

Kenny Ploen would eventually be named MVP of this Herculean struggle between two old combatants when he turned a broken play into a brilliant run down the sidelines. Even so, this is probably one of those instances when the entire team should have been acknowledged for their contribution although Ploen's run was both a dazzling and a magical conclusion to a great game.

At the end of the 1962 season, after participating on his fourth Grey Cup winning team, Gerry's careers in both football and hockey were in freefall. He was already out of the top level of hockey and now the Blue Bombers refused to sign him, at least at the salary he was demanding. Negotiations between Gerry and Jim Ausley, the club manager, became public and bitter. Bud Grant entered the debate when he argued that Gerry no longer contributed to the team as he once had. There was no doubt that after he broke his leg, Gerry's range as a runner diminished. But, in 1962, he had managed to finish second to Tommy Joe Coffey in the scoring race with 116 points — not a shabby total at all. Clearly he still had much to offer the team, not only in terms of his football prowess but also in terms of his character and his role as a motivator in the locker room.

Hal Sigurdson had this to say:

An era is over.

Edwin Fitzgerald James, the famous son of famous father, Sunday was handed his outright release by the Winnipeg Blue bombers, thus ending a relationship which had been both profitable and story for both sides.

Gerry James, whose father, the late Eddie (Dynamite) James, was one of the all-time greats of Canadian football, ranks as the leading scorer in Blue bomber history. In return the Big Blue made him the highest salaried Canadian player ever to wear Blue and Gold.

The release ended a bitter holdout siege between James and the club general manager Jim Ausley. It wasn't their first.

Ausley wanted James to take a cut from a 1962 salary peak of close to $13,000, to roughly $8,500. Gerry balked.

Sunday coach Bud Grant settled the issue when he announced the 34-man team he will take into the 1963 Western Football Conference opener Tuesday in Calgary. James was not included.

Also missing was the familiar name Cecil Roy Luining, a nine-year veteran at defensive end. The Selkirk Milkman, who gained equal renown as a team man, rugged competitor and practical joker, will go on waivers today.

When he made the announcement, Grant added a personal comment:

"This is the toughest thing I've had to do since becoming a coach. Guys like Gerry and Cec have helped me look good so often, releasing them is almost like..."

The words trailed away.

It didn't help matters during negotiations when a member of the club finance committee, a Scottish expat, compared Gerry to a used car. Gerry remembered that as a low point. To say that he was disappointed with the way he was released would be a huge understatement. When he had surgery on his leg, doctors told him he would have to work hard if he intended to play the game again. The fact that he travelled to Toronto to take care of his own rehab spoke volumes about his dedication to the game and the team. He had not only made a comeback, but he had been a key player in three Winnipeg Grey Cup wins. No one had mentioned or thanked him for his effort. Now that he had reached the ripe old age of 28, the Bombers were dumping him.

Midway through the following losing season, one fan, D. Ashmore, wrote to ask management to reconsider their position on Gerry:

I have just read...that 'Bombers cut all ties with Gerry James.' The club would not accept him even on its own terms.

Bud Grant doesn't think James can help the team....

With the Bombers' dismal showing so far this year, partly because of inexperience and injuries to some of the veterans, is Grant serious that James could not help the team now?

Nobody can dispute the great record Grant has as a coach....

However, anybody can make a mistake, and it looks as if Grant might be making one by closing the door on Gerry James.

Apparently James and the Bombers have parted company and not on very friendly terms. Whether this is really the final word or not, let's see if the club is big enough to forget present differences and remember just what Gerry has done for the Bombers for the past 11 years by giving him a night. Surely if any athlete in this city ever deserved to be recognized in this way, it's Gerry James.

Another fan, an acquaintance at the golf club, noted that Gerry was no longer playing golf due to a bad back. He went on to mention that he had just returned from Winnipeg where one of the premier radio stations was featuring and celebrating Gerry as their past player of the week. They were making much of the fact that Gerry was not only one of the greats to play in Blue and Gold but perhaps one of the all-time greats in the league.

Then he said, "You know, when I first met Gerry in person I was surprised to discover that he was shorter than me and not at all big through the shoulders and chest. I grew up in Winnipeg as a fan and thought Gerry James must be at least six foot four and weigh well over two hundred pounds. He was that big in my mind, a giant that linemen and linebackers found almost impossible to stop. I was amazed that he was as small as he is. No wonder his knees and back took such a beating." He said this with a sense of awe, surprise and a hint of regret. Too bad management didn't view Gerry's devotion to the team with such confidence. Reconciling our dreams with reality is often difficult, especially when those dreams spring out of our youth.

Gerry would never get his night and rather sadly an air of distrust and bitterness appeared to linger between the team and their once faithful and dedicated native son.

Ironically, at the end of the 1963 season, Winnipeg, reigning Grey Cup Champions, did not even make the play-offs in the West. How much of this was due to Gerry's absence as a kicker and potential threat in the backfield would be pure conjecture. But a study of Leo Lewis's running stats shows a dramatic drop. There is no question that Gerry was a formidable blocker and his presence in the backfield always got attention from defensive units. Perhaps the decision to release him was premature. Perhaps a player who had given his team so much positive service deserved better than Gerry received. Perhaps this was why Gerry felt Bud Grant did not support his Canadian players as much as he could and should have done.

※

In 1966, when Gerry had returned to the amateur ranks and was living in Yorkton, playing for the Yorkton Terrier Senior Men's team, Scott Young published his engaging and often humorous book, *The Leafs I Knew*. While the glamour of the game was history for Gerry, the thrill, the adrenaline fix, the camaraderie, the "competition", call it what you will, all of those old sensations still rushed through Gerry's blood when he stepped out onto the ice. Young captured Gerry in all his glory:

Gerry James is the right wing. He is known in hockey as The

Fullback and in football (where he is a fullback for Winnipeg) as Kid Dynamite, because his father was Dynamite Eddie James and they both hit the line without regard for danger and as hard as strong legs will carry a man. James is an affable and witty young man of twenty-five who looks like a model for a pro athlete; dark-haired, good-looking, with all the give of a steel bollard.

Johnny Wilson, thirty, is the left wing. He is the Iron Man of hockey, so called because as of this morning, in a sport that is hard on human bones, he has played eight hundred and twenty-eight consecutive league and playoff games. Hasn't missed a whistle since he became a professional in 1949.

It isn't a dirty line. But its forte is robust use of the body. This is a part of the game forgotten or largely ignored by many modern forwards. If you knock a man down, he can neither score on you, nor take a pass, nor check the man with the puck. These gents knock people down, dig all the time, and in general skate as if their pants are on fire.

They don't score many goals. Once recently Edmundson and James were at a public function, representing the Leafs, when one young chap in the audience piped up and asked James how many goals he had scored.

"Twice as many as Edmundson," James replied blandly. Which was correct: Two for James and one for Edmundson.

As Larry Robertson said and Scott Young implied, and in spite of what Gerry himself has said, Kid Dynamite was a very good hockey player. You simply didn't make it into the six-team NHL if you didn't have talent. As kids growing up, Gerry was like Gordie Howe, Larry told me. "We looked up to Gerry with the same degree of awe, not so much as a hockey player but because he played two sports so well. In our eyes they were both great."

Gerry will cringe when he hears this, but these words

are like a promise we make to ourselves when we are young and confident. Words we should hear and heed, if we are so lucky, when we are old men.

⁂

When Gerry was inducted into the Canadian Football Hall of Fame in 1981, everyone in attendance shared in one of football's most emotional moments. What they heard and saw was as visceral and as immediate as a human response can be. Rick Winston described the ceremony in the *Hamilton Spectator*:

> Gerry James proved he is still capable of capturing the hearts of Canadian football fans even though his tremendous rushing and kicking abilities have long since faded.
>
> James was just one of four past members of Canadian football who were inducted into the Canadian Football Hall of fame Saturday night. But it was James who stole the show.
>
> In a touching moment, James had the more than 900 dinner guests visibly moved when he asked that his bust be placed next to that of his late father in the hall of fame trophy room.
>
> Eddie "Dynamite" James, a great player of the 1920s and '30s, was an original member of the hall of fame. The entry of the younger James is the first father-son combination in the hall's history.
>
> "I never really got to know him until the late 1950's," James, a star running back — kicker with the Winnipeg Blue Bombers, told the audience. "And just when I did finally get to know him, he died.
>
> "Dad: I want you to know that you gave me the drive to succeed and match your accomplishments on the field. If the Hall of Fame puts our busts together, we will be two of the happiest people in the world."
>
> Hall of Fame director Bill McBride promised to fulfill

James' wish, much to the delight of the emotionally-moved audience.

To add to the occasion, Tom Casey made the long trek north to participate in this special moment with Gerry and Marg.

Of all the moments in Gerry's life, this event ranks up there alongside his marriage and the birth of his children. To share this time and this place with his dad was very special. Gerry could finally be at ease with who he was and with what he had achieved.

10 / Impressions of an Era

In an interview a few years ago with Rob Vanstone in *The Leader-Post* out of Regina, Gerry's responses to a series of questions were revealing. When asked who was the best hockey player he ever saw lace up skates, Gordie Howe's name popped immediately to mind.

"He could do everything," Gerry said. "He worked harder and had more raw talent than anyone I've ever seen on skates.He was also the most feared man on the ice. I remember a game in which Bobby Baun took Howe into the boards fairly heavily in the Detroit end, a good clean check. The puck was iced and Bobby went back to touch it. Howe took off after him and I remember standing at our bench, leaning out over the boards and yelling at Bobby to look out, Howe was on his tail. I was screaming at the top of my voice but Bobby couldn't or didn't hear me and just as he touched the puck Howe hit him hard, into the boards, his stick in Bobby's face. After the collision and after they parted, all of this taking only seconds, Bobby's forehead and face were cut up pretty badly. And no penalty call. Bobby was wrecked.

"Not only was Howe tough but when necessary he could cross-check and slash with the best of them. And get away with it. He was also fast and could play from his left or his right side with equal ease. His shot was just as hard right- or left-handed. The amazing thing, though, was that he could switch from one to the other so quickly. You were never sure which way he was going to come at you. And while you were making up your mind, he was around you and gone.

"For all-round skill, Gordie Howe was the best," Gerry reflected. "But, for sheer entertainment value, the Rocket would get my vote. He brought so much drama to the game with his speed and timing, his flair and grace. He could stick-handle and skate like a god and shoot from anywhere. When the fans got listless, when the game had turned into a real howler, as dull as dishwater, he could turn play around in a flash with one rush down the ice. He could be breathtaking, creating the most exhilarating exhibition, seemingly out of nothing. He had charisma, like no one else. Maurice Richard was the magician, the director, the conductor, all rolled into one. Talk about stage presence! He had more in his little pinky than the rest of us combined.

"But, and this is my final but, if I were starting a new franchise or creating my dream team, I would select Bobby Orr first. Good defensemen, and I played with a few of them, are as rare as hen's teeth. Orr had some of the Rocket's flair and a good measure of Howe's talent. I don't think anyone has ever read the game as well. His stats were phenomenal. What was it, for six straight seasons he put up over a hundred points on the board. That's amazing for any position but for a defenseman those are staggering numbers. He also had all the other qualities you want in a star player — an unbelievable work ethic, a great team man, competitiveness, toughness, the whole package."

Gerry could be describing his own work habits and devotion.

Perhaps an apocryphal little tale, Gerry remembered the night the Rocket (after his retirement of course) was alleged to have been asked to pick the three stars in a game between

Montreal and Detroit. The Rocket was alleged to have said, the first star I give to my brother Henri who skated fast and hard all night and scored a goal. He play well. The second star I give to Doug Harvey who patrolled the blue line and did all he could to stop the other team. And the third star I give to my old friend, Jean Béliveau who play with such class and grace and score a goal. When asked if there was anyone else he would like to mention, Richard apparently responded saying, Oh, and Gordie Howe, he play well, too, and score three goals for his team.

Hockey, of course, like all sports, is filled with such stories and, whether true or not, they add a lot to the lore that ultimately defines the sport. In addition to everything else, Richard had a delightful sense of irony.

Around Christmas in 1957, when Gerry was departing from an uncrowded Winnipeg airport, on his way to training camp in Rochester, he passed within a few feet of "The Rocket." Still a young man unaccustomed to the spotlight, Gerry felt too bashful, too intimidated, to say anything, so he ducked his head as if he had not seen the great man and continued on his way. Besides, what could he have possibly said? When Gerry got back to Toronto, word was out that he had snubbed Richard, who was upset and reportedly annoyed. "Who does that Gerry James think he is, brushing me off like that? Not talking to 'The Rocket?'"

Richard was to go on and win the Lou Marsh Award for 1957, and Gerry would be runner-up in the voting. The trophy is given to the best amateur or professional athlete in Canada each year, but Gerry felt "The Rocket" was in a league of his own and was far more deserving of winning the award than he would have been. In his mind, they didn't even belong on the same stage. He also did not think Richard would recognize him or know who he was. Wrong. To this day Gerry rues the moment he ignored a hockey giant for whom he had such great respect. "That's one moment I'd like to have back," he said, "although I still don't know what I would have said."

❦

The best football player Gerry ever witnessed play the sport is no surprise — old spaghetti legs himself, Jackie Parker. (In recent times, Gerry was left off a list of the top fifty CFL players of all time, which I believe is spawned of ignorance; and Flutie places ahead of Parker on the list at number one. Both decisions are ill-informed and demonstrate a prejudice for more contemporary players.)

"Jackie was something else," Gerry said.

What I recall other players saying and reporters remarking, I mentioned to Gerry, was that Parker was the sort of runner whose body was never quite where you expected it to be.

Gerry agreed. "Like all great athletes he had a change of pace that was remarkable. You thought he was slow, that there was no way he could beat you, but when you went to tackle him, he was gone. He was moving in a completely different direction. He had literally disappeared. It was like tackling a shadow. And when you combined that running ability with the freedom to pass, which Parker had, of course, as quarterback, well he was almost unbeatable. We were relieved when Don Getty was made quarterback in Edmonton and Parker was inserted as a running back. This took the passing option away from Parker and made it easier for us to control him. I've often wondered if we would have beaten them in those later years of Parker's career if he had remained at quarterback."

Rollie Miles, another member of the Edmonton Eskimos, from 1951 to 1962, also ranks up there on Gerry's tableau of "greats". "For one thing," Gerry said, "he played both ways, as a defensive back and as a halfback. Plus he ran back punts and kick-offs. Just assuming all those different roles is challenging enough but to be as accomplished as Miles was at all positions, well, that is rare and special."

Miles had come north from the States to Regina to play baseball but Annis Stukus, then a player and coach with the Eskimos, talked him into playing football in Edmonton. "I can see why," Gerry observed, "Rollie could do anything." Not particularly big, Miles was a natural; an all-round athlete.

"One game in particular stands out in my mind, from 1954 or 1955," Gerry continued. "I can remember the game like it was yesterday, but the year, well, that's like remembering your first kiss. We were scheduled to play against Edmonton and word got out that Parker was injured and the Eskimos were without a quarterback. In addition to all of his other responsibilities, Rollie offered to stand in as QB. We were elated. Obviously this was going to be a rout. Or so we thought. Well, Rollie made us look like a junior varsity team. He ran circles around us and had us chasing phantoms. We were puppets and he was the puppet master. It was like a sandlot game, every play worked out in the huddle. He was making it up as he went along.

"At the time we argued that he didn't know the play book and therefore was behaving unpredictably. Erratically. How were we to know what he was going to do next? The fact is he out-played us. One man out-played an entire team. We won the game but by the slimmest of margins. The final score was embarrassing. Something like 7 – 3."

At the end of the game, the Winnipeg fans gave Rollie Miles a standing ovation. A well-deserved ovation. He had played an incredible game. At quarterback!

Another player of equal stature as far as Gerry is concerned was Garney Henley of the Hamilton Tiger-Cats. He, too, was a player who seemed capable of doing anything and everything on the field. Like Parker, he had a change of pace that could leave you grabbing air. He started out playing defence but soon coaches and fans alike realized he was equally good on offence. He played flying wing or slot back, what most people would call a receiver. He also ran back kick-offs and punts.

"His stats are amazing, especially the game in which he caught four TD passes. That he won the Schenley for most outstanding player in the league only once, in 1972, is surprising. I think he was nominated six times," Gerry mused. "The strange thing about Henley was that when you looked at him you wouldn't have thought he was much of an athlete. He was so slight. But he soon put that notion out of your mind. He didn't tackle you with force, he used angles and your own momentum. And you went down. He was a great player. One of the best."

Perhaps the most influential player in Gerry's life, the player he most wanted to emulate, was Neill Armstrong. Armstrong, who had been drafted eighth overall by the Philadelphia Eagles, won two NFL championships with Philadelphia in 1948 and 1949 before he decided to move north to play with Winnipeg. As was the custom in those days, he was a two-way player, plying his trade as an offensive end and as a defensive back. But what impressed Gerry was his attitude. He was tough on the field, uncompromising and as hard as nails, but never played outside the rules. On and off the field he was a perfect gentleman. He never swore and he never got flustered. He was a family man. "What made him a total enigma as far as I was concerned," Gerry pointed out, "was the fact that he simply didn't behave like a typical football player. There was no ego to flaunt, there were none of the crude edges common to so many players. I know this may be hard to believe, but as a rookie for Winnipeg, I wanted to be like him. I probably would have had problems following his example when it came to the quiet, tactful and gentle side of his nature, though."

Neill Armstrong went on to assume head coaching jobs with the Edmonton Eskimos and the Chicago Bears and assistant coaching tenures with the Houston Oilers, Minnesota Vikings and Dallas Cowboys. He and Bud Grant hold the distinction of being the only two players to have played and been head coaches in both the CFL and the NFL.

Two other players, both Canadians, made it on to Gerry's list of notable players. Harvey Wylie was one of the best athletes ever to play the game at the free safety position. He was also one of the best at running back punts and kickoffs. His stats speak for themselves. His record of five touchdowns on kickoff returns still stands. He won the Schenley Award for Best Canadian in the League in 1963 and was inducted into the Canadian Football Hall of Fame in 1980. But what Gerry remembers was how unforgiving fans can be when a player makes a small mistake.

Playing in Winnipeg, in the third game of the Western final, with about ten seconds left on the game clock and Calgary with a one point lead, Gerry lined up for a field goal. His kick was partially blocked, skidded into the end zone, and Wylie attempted to kick the ball out of the end zone, back down field. Had he fallen on the ball, he would have conceded a single point and the game would have been tied. Or so he thought. In fact, Winnipeg would have been called for encroaching and therefore penalized. Unfortunately, Harvey didn't know this and went to kick the ball which was spinning like a top. He caught nothing but air, which is not hard to do given the shape of a football. A Winnipeg player fell on the ball and was awarded a touchdown. This was 1961 and the Bombers went on to win the Grey Cup.

"Had I been in Wylie's place," Gerry said, "I would have attempted to do the same thing. Probably his coaches had told him to catch the ball and kick it out if I missed the field goal. There was no way anyone could have anticipated the deflection and the spinning ball."

Sadly, in Gerry's view, the Calgary fans never forgave Harvey Wylie, one of their most celebrated players, for what he tried to do to win them the game.

Sport can be incredibly cruel to those who fail to live up to our expectations.

"Harvey was a great one," Gerry said, "no doubt about it."

The other Canadian he holds dear to his heart, largely for personal reasons, was Tommy Lumsden. Tommy lived in the same Winnipeg neighbourhood as Gerry and when Gerry was still a Rookie he would catch a ride to games with Tommy. A defensive end, Tommy was as tough as they come; he was as strong as an ox and 'big'. A lethal combination.

"In a game against Saskatchewan, I remember someone coming out of their backfield and Tommy simply sticking out his arm and the guy running into it and hitting the deck, like he'd been hit by a bolt of lightning. He went down like a brick. Not unconscious but certainly stunned. Tommy didn't hit him, just stuck out his arm.

"For some reason one of the geniuses on our coaching staff thought I should be paired against Tommy in practices. This meant I had to block him. Good luck. When Tommy played the game, whether in practice or actual game conditions, he knew only one gear. Full out. Even though we were friends, he gave me no quarter. I think he thought this was good for me, and perhaps it was. All I remember is the

bruises and bumps. We used to have an expression for players like Tommy: 'Meaner than dog crap.'"

In Gerry's mind, Tommy is the forgotten Blue Bomber,
even though the Bomber organization presents a trophy in
his name each year to the team's most valuable player. After
a freak illness and while still a young man, Tommy Lumsden died on the operating table in 1954. "His trophy is one
I wish I'd won in my career. Honouring a friend through
achievement has to be very special."

※

Back in the late 1960s, when I was at university in England,
I remember BBC announcers interviewing soccer players
who were about to retire. Many of them talked about buying into small businesses. One of the most frequent responses and the one that several comedic teams picked up on,
including Beyond the Fringe, was the often stated desire to
own a clothing boutique on King's Row. "I think I'll open
me a boutique," they would say, as if this were as easy as
slipping on a pair of boots or stabbing an opponent's ankle
with a set of raised cleats. Or, executing a ten for a beautifully landed swan dive inside the eighteen yard box. The
fantasy was a joke. These athletes, with no prospects at all
after their soccer careers, had had a small taste of glamour
and expected the same sort of treatment as rock stars of the
day. Their expectation may not have been unreasonable but
the only skill they possessed was dribbling a ball.

I'm not sure when North American athletes began to
feel this sense of entitlement but I'm certain it becomes a
"part of the game" at about the same time salaries skyrock-
eted into orbit. Suddenly everyone had an agent or manager
and the full commercialization of sport was underway. The

only person Gerry mentions with a similar idea from his day was Tim Horton who told all of his teammates repeatedly in the 1950s about his plans to open a doughnut shop. They all nodded and chuckled and said: Sure sure, Tim, whatever. The rest is history.

Gerry himself never thought much about a life beyond sports. Football and hockey were his preoccupation. If he wasn't playing football or hockey, he was coaching hockey and trying his hand out at curling. His passion for golf came a bit later.

⁂

When Vanstone from the *Leader-Post* asked Gerry who was the best hockey player he ever coached, Gerry answered quickly and unequivocally, "Brian Propp. He was such an exceptional talent. He was strong. He had natural ability and good instincts. He wasn't shy. He won the SJHL scoring title with Melville as a 16-year-old and went on to have one of the most successful careers in NHL history."

His sort of skill and dedication was rare.

"Coaching Brian Propp was one of the great pleasures of my career," Gerry concluded.

⁂

Gerry remains a big fan of Canadian football and hockey. He follows both sports avidly on television.

In football his loyalties shift back and forth between Winnipeg and Saskatchewan. "It's agonizing," he observes, "to be a loyal Winnipeg supporter these days." But when it comes to the team he loves to hate there is no doubt in his mind: the BC Lions win hands down even though he now lives on the west coast. "They are so arrogant At the end of every successful play, they act out some little drama; and when they fail, they pout and look for someone or something to blame. It's comical and annoying."

"Maybe my dislike of the Lions comes from a game we played against them in Winnipeg in 1955. As a running back you get used to opposing players using you to push themselves back to their feet. They lean on you, push down on your helmet and lift themselves back to a standing position. In this particular game, after every play, a huge lineman for the Lions, a recent reject from the NFL I think, kept grinding my face in the mud and gravel. Finally I jumped to my feet and challenged him to take off his helmet — even then helmets had a bar across the face — and I'd give him a good thrashing. The big oaf immediately took off his helmet and said, 'There. Give it a go.'

"He called my bluff. So I turned and ran back to the huddle and told Dick Huffman, who had played four seasons with the LA Rams and is the only player to have been named both an offensive and defensive all-star in the CFL in the same season, that the guy standing back on the line holding his helmet in his hands wanted a piece of him. From that point on I decided to make most of my runs to the other side of the line. Even so, I think Dick might have had a word with him."

Gerry finds it difficult to comment on individual players in today's game because the game has changed so much. "In my day you couldn't block downfield on any kind of return. That makes some of those stats from the old days quite impressive," he says. "Nor could anyone block for you once you were ten yards beyond the line of scrimmage. You were on your own. That makes a big difference when you tally up yards gained. Mind you, we could crawl along the ground after our knees hit the turf. Normie Kwong, who was built so low to the ground, was great at that. He often gained an additional three or four yards crawling. You actually had to be stopped.

"In my dad's day, he was known as a plunger because the object was to plunge into the line and scramble any way you could for yardage. On feet, knees, belly, didn't matter. Back then, the game was much closer to rugby.

"I remain faithful to my roots as a running back. In my view the use of running backs as an equal option has all but disappeared from the modern Canadian game.

"These days, most plays initiated out of the backfield are drawn up for a receiving core. In order to get a head start downfield for a pass, you get anywhere between four and six receivers lining up a few yards back of the line of scrimmage ready to go in motion before the ball is snapped. These players are not running backs, at least not in the traditional sense. There are fewer and fewer places for good running backs in the Canadian game; that part of our game has all but disappeared. Most great running backs are swallowed up by the NFL. However, there is an appeal to watching several players burst out of the backfield, running short and deep patterns, criss-crossing the field and so on, but it's an aerial game. The emphasis has shifted. An aerial attack exerts a lot more pressure on the offensive line and quarterback. The game has opened up somewhat but I'm not convinced it's better."

Gerry concedes that today's game is filled with great athletes. They are simply playing a different game from the one he played. From his own day a list of the greats would include (and this list is by no means exhaustive): Ken Ploen, Charlie Shepard, Frank Rigney, Cornell Piper, Leo Lewis, Herb Grey, Ken Carpenter, George Reed, Bob Marlow, Don Getty, Johnny Bright, Normie Kwong, Wayne Harris,

Earl Lunsford, Don Luzzi, Willie Fleming, Joe Kapp, Mike Brown, Russ Jackson, Ron Stewart, Whit Tucker, Bernie Faloney, Gerry McDougall, Sam Etcheverry, Red O'Quinn, Hal Patterson, Dick Shatto, Pat Abbruzzi.

One player he really enjoyed watching play from a slightly later era was Joe Theismann. But once we open that box, a flood of names begins to pour out. "Compiling lists is a mug's game," he argues, "but Parker will never be topped as the best to play in the CFL."

❧

Hockey has also changed but in Gerry's view less dramatically than football. Most of the rule changes have speeded up the game and for that reason have had a positive impact on the sport. What disturbs him is that some players seem to put themselves before the game. In his day, the game always came first. You owed your success to the game. He hasn't much use for the specialists, especially those who fulfill the role of bully or hitman or designated enforcer. This is ironic since Gerry's hockey career owes much to the fact that he was tough. But he makes this important distinction. "Yes," he will admit, "I was a sort of enforcer, but I was always a hockey player first. I loved playing the game.

"I would have no difficulty providing you with a long list of very talented players, from my day to the present. But I think anyone who follows the game can do that as well as I can. Perhaps this is also true of football. In fact, I'm sure it is. Both sports are blessed with talent."

From the old six-team league a list of some of the players Gerry admired would include: Jean Béliveau, Henri Richard, Bernie Geoffrion, Dickie Moore, Doug Harvey, Jacque Plante, Bill Gadsby, Ted Lindsay, Alex Delvecchio,

Terry Sawchuk, Andy Bathgate, Dean Prentice, Lou Fontinato, Harry Howell, Camille Henry, Real Chevrefils, Leo Boivin, John Bucyk, Jim Morrison, Jerry Toppazzini, Bobby Hull, Stan Mikita, Red Berenson, Elmer Vasko, Glen Hall, Frank Mahovlich, Tod Sloan, Tim Horton, Bill Harris, George Armstrong, Red Kelly, Allan Stanley.

From this list, the player Gerry most dreaded playing against was John Bucyk of Boston. This might seem an odd choice but a quick glance at Bucyk's statistics reveals a player of major talent. Even though he won the Lady Byng Trophy twice, a trophy awarded to the player who exhibited the best type of sportsmanship and gentlemanly conduct combined with a high standard of play, he never gave an inch. "He was one of those players who was all over you without drawing penalties. Tenacious and frustrating. You felt his body checks in every bone in your body. His hits were heavy and hard but never dirty. On top of all that, he was one of the top scorers in the league. He coupled his skills with great imagination and a work ethic second to none. As I recall, I was either chasing after him or being flattened by him."

❧

In December 1992, Gerry gave Rob Vanstone of the *Leader-Post* his impressions of some of the better-known sports celebrities he knew during his career.

Gordie Howe: Howe called me Football Head. I called him Blinky. He really couldn't get at me too much because I was usually sitting at the end of the bench. I was pretty hard to hit. He was vicious. One time, I saw him run a guy from centre ice into the end boards. He purposely ran him into the upright that holds up the glass. I personally have scars on my body because of him. He is the perfect example of somebody who would do anything to win. Even so, he was the greatest player to ever play the game.

Bud Grant: It's hard to explain how he motivated players, but he did, like no one I've ever known. That was his greatest tool. He would rerun plays until you got it right, even during games. He made it seem like it was our right to win the Grey Cup. He would tell us, "We should be there, we're going to be there." He made everyone strive to achieve that goal. It was his attitude that made us the teams that we were. He was very bright and a very talented athlete in his own right, at several sports. When I first started playing for the Bombers, I often caught a ride with him to practices. He was a man of few words, but you always knew his expectations.

Conn Smythe: He was a great person. He had a very high standard of excellence. He knew what he wanted. If he couldn't get it, it made him want it more. He was the type of person who wanted you to stand up to him. If you did that, he appreciated you more.

Howie Meeker: He was my coach with the Leafs in 1956 – 57. He was a different type of person. It seemed to me he was more interested in pleasing Conn Smythe and Hap Day than he was in the players. He ranted and raved, just like he does on TV. That's how he coached…He was really Mickey Mouse. I don't think I've ever disliked a coach more than I did him. In retrospect and to be fair to Howie, though, this was his first coaching job and I now think he probably had the same problems I had when I went to Davos. Playing the game and coaching require two very different sets of skills. I admire most of the coaches in the game today. Because I follow the Vancouver Canucks now that I live on the west coast, I'm always impressed with the job Alain Vigneault does.

Punch Imlach: Punch was the best hockey coach I ever had. He was very down to earth and he told it like it was. You always knew where you stood with Punch. Of course, some players didn't appreciate that sort of honesty.

Bob Shaw: He was a very intelligent guy but he did not handle people very well. Shaw, who had been coached by Paul Brown and Earl "Curly" Lambeau, was not always popular with his players, in particular Ron Lancaster and George Reed, two Saskatchewan greats. Unlike me, Gerry adds, Shaw sometimes found it difficult to be diplomatic. He made a couple of very wrong-headed comments about Lancaster and Reed. Shaw once caught five TD passes in one game in the NFL, a record tied by Kellen Winslow and Jerry Rice.

❧

I am trying to understand why Gerry is letting me into his story this way. I know in one sense he is flattered. But in a far more important way, we are paying homage to his family, to a way of life, and to all of those people who shared in this dream of sport. I think these may be the most important reasons for his letting me pry. Even so, I sense there are secrets he holds close to his chest, secrets which may be fraternal and that he feels must be left unstated.

It is during one of these moments when his story seems

to have come to a still point, when there is the feeling that we have been marooned in the eye of an internal storm, that he blurts out a new thought or detail that has been worrying him or that he thinks is critical to acknowledging him fully as a person.

"I've always thought that Canadians were under-appreciated in Canadian football. In their own game," Gerry observes. "We're always quick to celebrate American players first. When we discuss the issue of imports and home-grown bodies, we always wonder how we are going to maximize our use of imports. The question always seems to be where do we put the Canadian contingent so they will do the least damage to the squad. We use them on special teams or, if they are big enough, on the line. We rarely use them in critical offensive or defensive positions. Someone like Lui Passaglia is a blessing because not only was he a great kicker, he put points on the scoreboard. People took notice of him and he had a lengthy career.

"If given the opportunity, I think there would have been more outstanding Canadians in the league, but too often they remained hidden and unknown. This is Don Cherry's complaint about hockey, junior in particular. You never know when a kid is going to develop and shine. We need to give our home-grown talent more chance to develop and more credit when they do.

"When I look at the cover on Bob Irving's *Blue & Gold*, I see a whole host of American players suspended above the turf, alongside their American coach. Why? There is no doubt Bud Grant was a good, perhaps great, coach, but he favoured American players. I always felt he distrusted me and all the other Canadians on the team.

"The divide, the prejudice, was not racial; it was between Americans and Canadians. Even though I think it is fair to characterize me as a team player first and foremost, I felt we Canadians were considered second rate in our own country. We were the cannon fodder. The chaff."

❧

Perhaps the best place to conclude this chapter is with the subject himself. Former tackle for the Montreal Alouettes, Tex Coulter turned to writing, drawing and painting at the end of his football career. On September 27, 1958, he published an article in the *Star Weekly* entitled: **GERRY JAMES: Everybody's All-Star.** The piece included a subtitle that read: **"Here's an assessment of a young Canadian before injuries sidelined him."**

Coulter wrote from the inside, from the position of someone who knew the sport as a participant. His take on Gerry as a player was passionate and insightful. Gerry had completed his most inspired year as a football player, winning the Schenley as best Canadian for a second time, and had recently broken his leg in two places, potentially ending his career. Length prohibits me from reprinting Coulter's entire article but it is a gem. The portrait, which accompanied his narrative, gave the piece an added dimension, one that expresses youth, optimism and a hint of devil-may-care innocence.

Gerry James is one football player who commands an old pro's admiration. The Winnipeg Blue Bombers' fullback plays like a pro, acts like a pro, looks like a pro, thinks like a pro and talks like a pro.

His distinguishing characteristic on the field is determination. Honesty of expression is his trade-mark off the field. His unguarded manner of speech has earned him the reputation of smart aleck. Admittedly, he is a little flippant, but refreshingly so. This is a reflection of supreme confidence in himself as an athlete.

The football player is like the average citizen in the matter of confidence. If he has none, he'll never be worth shooting. Yet, if he has confidence, he's often frowned upon for showing it openly. James lets his show. He's tough, and obviously revels in this robust reputation.

Perhaps much of James' confidence...and independence...comes from his unique position in athletics with football and hockey offering him star pay.

Any football team would be happy to have the 23-year-old whiz. This includes National Football league teams. A look at James' record last season makes this point understandable.

The facts:

Set a new Western Interprovincial Football Union scoring record of 131 points. He scored 19 touchdowns, three converts, four field goals and two rouges.

Rushed for a net of 1192 yards on 197 attempts for an impressive six-yard average. His longest gain was 74 yards.

Caught 12 of 16 passes for 190 yards. Pass receiving is considered one of his few weaknesses. This is something he continually works on, but his eyesight will never allow him to be a great receiver. However, he's dangerous enough in this department to command respect of the opponent on short throws.

Impressive as the statistics are, they don't reveal James' true worth to the Blue Bombers. Statistics aren't kept of the amount of pain James endured in playing many minutes of last year's Grey Cup game against Hamilton Ticats with a broken hand. Nor do statistics reveal the moral value of such courage to a team...nor do they reflect the true worth of James' realistic faking on plays when he doesn't carry the ball.

Good faking is the real mark of an outstanding team back. If he hits the hole hard after a fake handoff, he'll often draw one or several defenders from the actual ball carrier.

Of course, the faker has to be willing to take the clobbering he'll get from those fooled.

George Druxman, all-star offensive centre for Winnipeg, says about James: "Gerry is a left-footed runner...a little unpredictable. He'll do anything to gain a few extra yards,...even run over a blocker if that's the only place to go. I thought Gerry an improved individual player last season over the 1955 season largely through natural development. However, his greatest improvement was as a team player.

"He's a great kibitzer and kids a lot...except when he's running with the ball. He does a lot to keep the team from getting too tight. He gets along exceptionally well with the other players. He hits his holes extremely fast so is easy to block for."

Later in his article, Coulter went on to provide the views of other knowledgeable football men on Gerry as a player.

In spite of Gerry's ambivalence about his Bomber coach, Bud Grant had this to say about Gerry: "Determination is the trade-mark of James. However, his outstanding attribute is his great sense of balance. He can change direction almost unbelievably without loss of speed. This lets him hit the smallest of holes and enables him to require less blocking than almost any other back. He can do almost anything well."

Clem Crowe, former coach of the BC Lions said: "Gerry James is one of the outstanding backs in Canadian football. He has tremendous power and speed. I would rate him with the all-time 'greats' of the game. He has hurt Vancouver more than any other back in the league."

Pop Ivy, ex-Edmonton Eskimo and Chicago Cardinal head coach added: "Gerry James is a strong, determined ball carrier, with enough speed to go all the way. He hurt the Eskimos most of the time on the quick pitch-out." Keith

Rolfe, Eskimo executive secretary-manager, added: "As was stated by a sage observer last season, James' best plays against our club seemed to be any time he carried the ball."

Otis Douglas, Calgary coach, made it simple: "Gerry James…if only we had him!"

George Terlep, Regina coach, agreed: "A really great player."

After scouting the previous season's playoff games between Edmonton and Winnipeg, Ray Cicia, Montreal Alouette assistant coach observed: "James is all football player. He is the one the Bombers go to when in tight situations. In other words, he's their bread-and-butter guy… James plays the game tough and looks tough…hard and lean. I understand he never kicked field goals or extra points before Buddy Leake was injured early last season. James put in extra practice hours and quickly developed as a top field-goal kicker."

Coulter continued his *Star Weekly* tribute with a few anecdotes from the inside:

> Before this season the Bombers handed out press questionnaires to their players. James filled out his with typical light comedy.
>
> He said his nickname was Jesse because he was a bandit and a bad hombre. When asked in what theatre he served during the war he stated it was the Uptown and he held the impressive rank of usher. Much of the war work was done in the secrecy of darkness, needless to say. He considered his outstanding football accomplishment was talking the Bombers into letting him play hockey last season.

On hockey Coulter rustled up a few choice and revealing comments and admissions.

While Gerry hasn't enjoyed the type of success in hockey he has attained in football, he has the Toronto Maple Leafs sold on his ability as a puck-chaser.

Last hockey season after James came to the Maple Leafs in late February and got off to a good start, Stafford Smythe, acting Maple Leaf manager, stated: "The biggest mistake this club ever made was in letting James get away to football for the sake of $2,000." The $2,000 was the difference between the Maple Leaf offer and James' asking price that brought James out of a one-year football retirement to the Bombers for the 1957 season. James will return to the Leafs for the 1958-59 season...after the football season.

"They told me he couldn't skate," said Billy Reay, new Maple Leaf coach, during the last hockey season. "But I couldn't see anything wrong with his skating. They said he couldn't score, but he can. He works hard and checks hard and makes the opposition look for him."

Reay's statement that James checks hard tallies with what Doug Harvey, Montreal Canadiens' great defenceman, told me last season: "James is a wild man on the ice. One game he came at me at full speed, yelling, 'Stay still, Harvey, and I'll knock you over the boards.' He's more interested in hitting people than getting the puck."

When James' hockey opponents want to insult him, they call him "football head."

Most hockey players are football enthusiasts, just as footballers are hockey fans. Camile Henry, slick little New York Ranger forward, told James prior to a face-off last season: "James, congratulations on being named, what you say, Canadian football player of the year."

11 / Davos & the Roughriders

In the autumn of 1963 the curtain appeared to have come down on both of Gerry's careers, at least as a player at the top level. Body parts no longer did his bidding and pain was a constant companion, especially in his knees. Although he would return in 1964 to play as a running back for half a season with the Saskatchewan Roughriders, a year earlier he had begun thinking about and searching for alternative careers. He still loved a stadium filled with people, the buzz he felt when their voices rose and ebbed from cheers to groans, but if he couldn't perform for them at his best then he felt he didn't deserve to be on the field.

For some time he had wanted to visit Europe, and when HC Davos, hosts of the Spengler Cup, came knocking on his door, the invitation to coach the famous Swiss club seemed perfect. As he saw it, they obviously knew enough about his credentials to take a chance on him, even though he had never coached before, and for him their offer presented an ideal opportunity to fulfill a dream. He could try his hand at coaching while escaping a world that had lost a great deal of its glitter and glamour. At this stage in his life, being dropped into a new culture was an incredibly exciting prospect. A different set of pleasures and experiences beckoned: new food, new friends, a new landscape, a different attitude to life, a wholly different world view. He hungered for a taste of the unknown.

Simply moving from the flatness of the prairie into the mountains would be a significant change. Also, for years he had wondered about the controversy that always seemed to surround international hockey tournaments, and living at the heart of the other side, squarely in the centre of Europe in its highest city, home to one of the major international competitions, might provide some answers to a few of the questions he had about the way the game is played.

He wanted to see how the European game differed from the Canadian brand. Up to this point, for him hockey was hockey. The rivalry between European and North American hockey had definitely stirred the imaginations of most Canadian hockey fans, especially after the victories of the Penticton Vees in 1955 and the Trail Smoke Eaters in 1961 at the World Championships. The Smoke Eaters would be the last amateur team from Canada to win the title and the last Canadian team to succeed at the championship for some time to come. The debate regarding styles of play, between what was described as the roughhouse, chippy, often brawling, tactics of the Canadians and the smooth-skating, synchronized, artful play of the Europeans, raged between fans of the sport on both sides of the Atlantic. To compound the issue, there was the debate about who was amateur and who professional.

Even though the birth of their fifth child was imminent — Brady was born on October 31, 1963 — both Marg and Gerry felt this was an opportunity that Gerry couldn't miss. With Marg's blessing — she also wanted him to "scratch his travel itch," to get this bug out of his brain — Gerry packed his bags and headed to Europe in mid October of 1963 to what he hoped would be a new life with new challenges. HC Davos, the celebrated club of the Swiss "A" League, had been founded in 1921 and had never dropped out of the top tier of Swiss hockey. Under Gerry's guidance, management hoped the team would not only thrive but would once again return to the winner's circle. They made Gerry two promises: he would have the best goalie in Swiss hockey — he was a member of the Swiss national team — whom Gerry knew would be critical to his success, and a team of local, exceptionally skilled players. Of this they were confident. Coupled with Gerry's magic wand, this would be a winning combination. Or so everyone thought.

Gerry arrived a couple of weeks before the season was to start only to discover that the highly-touted goalie had recently been charged with theft and had been suspended by the league for one year. His replacement was the team trainer, the only person available to play in goal. He had no experience at the position. No doubt he was brave but he definitely did not inspire confidence. Though he tried his best, he was the proverbial Swiss cheese of goalies. To compound problems, shortly after receiving this mind-boggling news, Gerry learned that at least half of the roster of the regular team had been called up for national service, for their obligatory stint in the military. Needless to say, this came as a shock. He couldn't believe that Switzerland had conscription. His introduction to Swiss culture, or at least to the sporting side of things, left him feeling abandoned. Like Wylie Coyote, he felt as though he were a few steps beyond the edge of the precipice. What need, he wondered, did this tiny neutral nation have for a national service? He was told the players would be available for games but not for practices.

In a report filed from Zurich with *The Tribune*, the author wrote:

Gerry James, the former Winnipeg Blue Bomber who is starting a brand new career as a Swiss hockey coach, is on thin ice already.

The day before Gerry arrived to officially take over as coach of the Davos team, Switzerland's best, the police put his goalkeeper, Walter Bassani in jail. Bassani, who impressed the Galt Terriers in 1962 at Colorado Springs while minding the net for the Swiss national team was found guilty of stealing money from another hockey player.

Bassani, whose talents as a goalkeeper far exceed those as a thief, has been suspended by the Swiss Hockey Association.

And that's not all. Two other key players have defected to other teams, which means that Davos will have to dig in to stay in Switzerland's top league, and Gerry's work is cut out for him.

Meanwhile, Gerry isn't saying much. Called to the phone during the first practice session of the Davos team, Gerry hedged a little: 'It's too early to give any impressions yet.'

Gerry left his wife and four children back home in St. James, but he hopes to have them with him in Davos next season 'if everything works out well here.' He has announced his formal retirement from football and plans to concentrate on coaching.

As Gerry was soon to discover, he had reason to hedge his comments and little reason for optimism.

Even though the hockey and coaching experience was a disappointment, some might argue a comedy of errors, Gerry's sojourn at the top of Europe, in amongst the lush valleys and sculpted mountains of Switzerland, was inspiring if not a bit perplexing. After taking a gondola to the top of the mountain where he could see from peak to peak, he got his bearings and no longer felt hemmed in. When he returned back down to the valley floor, the town no longer felt like a prison; after all, he had almost touched the sky. His prairie-boy claustrophobia vanished and he settled into village life like a man expecting to be surprised and happy to be entertained. In this respect, he was not disillusioned

The team arranged for him to stay in a small but very comfortable *pension*. From the day he moved in to the day he departed, he never met his landlords. His bed was soft, as he liked it, and his rooms were well furnished and cheerful. He had no complaints. Although he had a beer with his players on a couple of occasions, for the most part he was treated as an outsider. While there was a sense in which many things "European" converged in Switzerland, below the surface the Swiss protected a way of life that was absolutely unique and secretive. "They were cliquey," Gerry said. While he decided he had no choice but to honour their privacy, why should he ruin his own days?

He rose mid-morning and headed out to a local establishment for breakfast. Most of the time he selected an English breakfast, eggs and sausages, which were cooked in a frying pan and, to his amazement, served in the same frying pan. He loved it. He was looking for something different and this was different. The food was always hot, beautifully prepared and delicious. In mid-afternoon, an hour or two before practice, he would stroll down to a tavern where they served the local canton beer. Even though it was only three or four degrees centigrade outside, on sunny days he would sit at an outdoor table and watch the pedestrian traffic. Others gathered around him and lapped up the sun, their tans deepening. At that time sitting outdoors in any season was a novelty for most Canadians who were used to having their drinking restricted to a dark and dingy, smoky beer parlor. Here, out in plain view, he didn't feel as though he were breaking some inviolable taboo. With no phobias or prohibitions to nurse, he felt liberated. This freedom, different from the freedoms he knew, was what he had been seeking when he took the job in the first place.

For dinner he would have pasta. The team paid for his rooms and for his breakfast; dinner was at his own expense. After he had sent most of what he earned home to Marg, he had little left to spend on himself. But, he had to admit, life was good

"Even with a population of around 8 to10,000, Davos was so compact you could walk everywhere. Butcher, baker, chemist, restaurants, taverns, gift shops, all were near at hand. People seldom used cars to get about. What impressed me most, though, was how clean and tidy the streets were. The town was gorgeous."

Gerry was there during an Olympic year and many of the skaters, especially the speed skaters, who would later compete in Innsbruck, Austria, came to Davos to practice. He spent hours watching them. "The power they generated was awesome. This is where I first thought about using skaters from other disciplines to help train hockey players," he revealed. "Balance is so important when you're on skates and watching figure skaters taught me a lot. The outdoor rinks were fantastic, as were the ski hills. The place was a perfect winter paradise. Lots of snow, great food and drink. For visitors, Swiss civility and restraint added to the adventure; it was as though the Swiss were, by contrast, willing their guests to have a good time."

Amongst the many memorable things Gerry remembers about being in Switzerland was team travel through the mountains on electric trains. With hardly a sound, they snaked their way over trestles and through tunnels. On one of those trips, he remembers watching skiers racing down a mountain, between alpine trees and rock outcrops, towards the train, like James Bond on a mission, and then suddenly they disappeared from view only to land on the opposite side of the railway tracks where they continued their journey to the base of the mountain. "Right over the train," Gerry marvelled. "I loved the thrill of the jump, the risk those skiers were taking. Skis tucked up under their bodies, goggles protecting their eyes from the wind, scarves tracing a path behind. It was an aerial act I could only imagine."

Feeling inspired, he decided to try skiing himself. He enrolled for a lesson but once on skis he felt vulnerable and hopeless. "Even on a little bitty one degree slope," he said, "on land as close to flat as you can get, I thought I was going to lose control. My knees wobbled and I was certain my skis would shoot out from under me at any second. Nearby, a woman fell awkwardly and called over to me for help. I couldn't move. I was frozen to the spot, petrified. I can't imagine what she must have thought of me." Suddenly the tough guy was like a room without a window; he could only imagine mountains, music, dancing, birds in flight. "In my defense, he said, "I decided skiing was a bad idea. If I broke a leg, I would lose my job. And somewhat perversely I took heart from new people arriving in town, all smiles on their first day, only to see them three or four days later, all glum with downturned mouths and the inevitable plaster cast on one limb or another."

Over the next two months, November and December, the team didn't win a game and soon they were anchored at the bottom of the "A" League table, living with the unthinkable threat of demotion. "If the team didn't win the league," Gerry said, "they at least wanted to stay out of the bottom two places. Both of those teams would be relegated." Without practices and with much less talent than he had expected, the games were little more than sixty minutes of free skating. Chaos on ice. After two months, the dream of coaching a team to a league title was out of the question. Finally, at Christmas, Gerry had an opportunity to get involved in the action. To show the players, fans and management what he wanted and expected from everyone on the team, he suited up to participate in the Spengler Cup, held between Christmas and New Year. This was a competition that had been going on since 1923.

Every year, five teams were invited by HC Davos to play in the tournament. Some were club teams, others were national teams drawn from a pool of talent playing in Europe. Most of the teams bolstered their ranks with players from other teams and leagues. But apart from allowing Gerry to play, Davos stuck with their regulars. For Gerry it was like stone soup with nothing added. He could have used a few extra vegetables and a little meat added to the mix.

In the 1963 holiday competition Gerry would literally make a name for himself. After a couple of games, the local media and many of the fans had given him the nickname *König der Strafraum* or King of the Penalty Box. Every time Gerry entered the action, he cruised about the ice, throwing body checks haphazardly, and as quickly as he did so the referee blew his whistle and gestured towards the sin bin. His sort of impetuous play wasn't going to be tolerated. Yet the referees would ignore dives, some of them so comical that Gerry was left speechless. "You could literally knock most players over with a feather."

He was receiving his first lesson in European rules. While the team failed to win the cup, they did at least win a couple of games and finish respectably. On the brighter side for the new coach, as the season progressed the team began to win a few games; they actually rose to mid-standings. By the end of the season, though, management made it clear that mid-table wasn't a good enough result, in fact was an unexpected disappointment given all they had done to support him, and they let Gerry go, somewhat unceremoniously — business is business after all — but from Gerry's point of view the club at least retained its place in the "A" League. And it had managed to do so essentially without a trained goalie and with only a part-time team.

In February of 1964, with the season still in progress, Gerry organized a team of Canadians, made up of coaches and players from other League teams, to play a couple of pre-Olympic games against the Swiss National Team. This improvised team managed to knock off the National Team 10 – 2 and 9 – 1. At the time these two results reflected the quality of hockey being played in Switzerland. Interestingly, after these games, young fans didn't search out the goal scorers for autographs; they sought the players who had been more physical, those who exhibited the rough and tumble styles of play for which Canadians were renowned.

When I asked him about this first coaching experience, how he thought he benefitted, he waffled a little and then said, "To be honest, the whole thing was a bit of a bust. It wasn't great. Sadly, I learned very little about coaching; I spent most of my time teaching basic skills. But I had an adventure in a beautiful country. Perhaps if I had been more mature…

"These days the Swiss have definitely elevated their game. Whatever training methods they've implemented since I was there have helped the whole program. The coaching in the country is much better and they've seen the merits of sending young players to play in the Canadian Junior Hockey League and on North American university teams. Ironically they've embraced our style of game, throughout Europe. They have developed their skills even further and they now play tough. More importantly, the cultural exchange has brought a different attitude to the game on both sides. Perhaps the best part of the story is that we are genuinely interested in each other. Sports, hockey included, and cultural exchanges may be the best form of diplomacy we have. Everyone benefits."

With his coaching obligations completed, he made his way home via London. Although they had talked on the phone three or four times during his absence — the cost of trans-Atlantic phone calls at that time was prohibitive—and he had written letters home almost every day, Gerry was anxious to be back with Marg and the kids. Long distance communication combined with Swiss reticence, especially in the heart of a crowded town, heightened his feeling of solitude. At home when he wanted to be alone, he went out and sat under the expanse of a star-filled prairie sky. Even then, there was always a presence near at hand that he understood. But this hadn't been the case in Davos.

In London he discovered his luggage coupled with his hockey gear weighed too much and he was told there would be a surcharge. He didn't have a penny on him — a short anecdote explains this lack of cash. The night before his departure he went on a pub crawl with members of the team and the next morning, when he got up, the police appeared on his doorstep and asked him to surrender his passport. They accused him of kicking in the door of a car, presumably a random and thoughtless act of public mischief, and told him he would have to appear in court some time in the next few weeks. The only way he could avoid this, and make his flight, was to pay a hundred franc (about thirty dollars) fine. Even though Gerry knew this was a trumped-up charge, he emptied his pockets and secured his passport. He figured it was payback for having been footloose all those months. Everyone was happy. Well, everyone but Gerry, that is. He was flat broke!

The Hudson's Bay jacket he was wearing saved him. He'd been given the jacket by the Hudson's Bay Company while playing for the Bombers and it turned out to be similar to the one being worn by the Canadian Olympic athletes. When asked by the attendant in London if he was with the Canadian Olympic team he said yes — at the time he suspected the customs official didn't believe him but saw this as a way to send Gerry on his way — and with a little white lie Gerry was able to board his plane on the final leg back to Canada.

Once back with Marg and the family, he signed a contract to play for the Saskatchewan Roughriders for the 1964 season. The man who had been born in Regina was returning home.

In an article entitled *"Former bomber star joins Riders*: Mr. James makes it official," John Robertson wrote in the *Regina Leader Post*:

As little as two or three years ago, the news would have brought out the marching bands, green and white pennants and a motorcade escort to Taylor Field.

Today, therefore, it would seem rather incongruous that the Saskatchewan Roughriders should announce the signing of Gerry James, the highest scoring native player in the history of Canadian football, as a free agent — and an unknown quantity.

Nevertheless, that's what they did — and that's what he is.

Can Gerry once again attain the heights he scaled during his brilliant 10-year career with Winnipeg Blue Bombers? He thinks he can, coach Bob Shaw of the Riders hopes he can, and the Bombers will be sorely embarrassed if he does.

At 29, the son of former Roughrider great Eddie James could hang them up right now and take his place in football's hall of fame.

He vaulted right from the high school ranks into prominence with the Bombers at the age of 17, back in 1952. In the next decade he carried the ball a record 991 times for 5,541 yards and a gaudy 5.6 average. He has scored 63 touchdowns, kicked 35 field goals and 116 converts for a total of 601 scoring points, second only in Canadian football annals to the incomparable Jackie Parker, whose lifetime total is 667.

In his last active season, 1962, he was injured mid-way and lost his starting fullback job to import Roger Hagberg. Nevertheless he rushed for 345 yards, scored five touchdowns and amassed a total of 116 points, mostly as a result of his educated toe.

He has played on four Grey Cup championship teams, twice won the western scoring title, twice won the Schenley Award as the most valuable Canadian and twice made the WFC all-star team.

Last year he refused to accept a drastic salary cut from Winnipeg and was subsequently released after holding out through the first part of the season. Coach Shaw pondered picking him up last year, but decided it was too late in the season, and agreed to talk terms with him for 1964 instead.

Can he help the Riders this year?

"We obviously think he can," said Shaw. "You just can't pass up a boy with a record like his. If he's healthy — and he says he is — he could turn out to be a valuable addition to our football club."

Of course, the great George Reed had signed with the Riders the previous year and the likelihood of Gerry cutting into his playing time was nil. Reed would go on to have a remarkable career. You can see why fans were excited, though; what a one-two punch these two great athletes would have made.

Still, at the beginning of the season, headlines such as "James' Legs Undergo Acid Test Tonight" appeared in an Edmonton paper and similar headlines cropped up in other newspapers across the country.

The road back after a one-year layoff has been a long one

for Gerry James but the former Winnipeg blue Bomber ace gets a chance tonight to prove most of the journey has been completed.

James was named Thursday night to replace Dick Cohee as a starting halfback for Saskatchewan Roughriders, who meet Edmonton Eskimos in a Western Football Conference game as both clubs attempt to end three-game losing streaks.

Saskatchewan coach Bob Shaw said he was pleased with James' progress "but he isn't as young as he used to be and it's tough to tell how his legs will hold out."

Don Blanchard wrote in his "Pigskin Parade":

Forget about the wheel chair, fellas!

It's been established with some degree of certainty that Gerry James won't be needing it this fall.

The fullback-halfback a lot of people insist is over the hill was a lively-looking invalid Tuesday night at the Stadium as he pranced sprightly in the get-up of those redoubtable Roughriders from Saskatchewan.

Kid Dynamite didn't break any track records, or tear up much turf. But he showed enough ability to convince coach Bob Shaw he belongs in a Saskatchewan uniform.

If, as Shaw insists, this was James' moment of truth, he was equal to the challenge. Shaw said before the game Kid Dynamite's future hinged on his performance against his former mates.

"Gerry showed me all I want to know out there tonight," Shaw began. "He ran with the ball well, and blocked well. He's made our football team."

John Robertson, anticipating once again the Riders/Bombers first encounter of the season, wrote wonderfully about the forthcoming game:

It's still two weeks away, and already coach Bob Shaw is nervously dropping dishes in the kitchen as he whips up what he hopes will be a yummy recipe to take to Winnipeg on July 28 for the Salad Bowl game against Winnipeg Blue Bombers.

His spies tell him that the once-mighty Bombers are famished for some fresh greens. With this in mind, the head man has been going heavy on the limburger and garlic salt in workouts, hoping his entrée will repeat on the big bad 'Peggers to the extent that publicity man Hal (Horse-radish) Perry will be forced to declare a quick national indigestion week.

'This Salad bowl stuff is really old hat to us,' said Shaw, licking a spot of mayonnaise off his finger. 'The way I figure it, it's mainly for the women. It's a good excuse for those ripe tomatoes to take a handful of lettuce out of their old man's celery and try to top each other's dressing.'

…James who reported in excellent condition, has been hampered by a muscle tear in his thigh but Shaw is sure he'll be ready at least in time for the Winnipeg game, and he has gone on record saying he intends to start him in the Salad Bowl.

I'm not sure Robertson knew what he was mixing when he tossed his words onto the page, but there is a whimsy in his writing that is infectious. He clearly had a passion for the game and its players. He wore the game like an old vest.

Yet in spite of the support he received from all corners, as Gerry put pen to paper in the summer of 1964, as he signed this latest contract, he knew doing so was a last desperate attempt to see if he had any of the old pizzazz. Both the Riders and Gerry needed to know that he was still a viable running option. There is little doubt that Shaw wanted this comeback to happen as much as Gerry did. He said as much in an interview. "I hope he scores 128 points for us, half of them against Winnipeg.'"

Regrettably, Gerry's resurrection didn't happen. He had the muscular horsepower, but his knees were coming unhinged or seizing up — he wasn't sure which, he just knew that they wouldn't bend and that they hurt like hell. He couldn't move as he once had, not without his joints feeling like they were going to explode. Sudden cuts were out of the question. His body simply wouldn't follow the route he saw or imagined was there. He no longer ran like a gazelle as one reporter had said about him in his early days, but rather he plodded along like an old pack mule. If the fans hadn't noticed, he, at least, was aware of his limitations. His being cut mid-way through the season was amicable but heartbreaking.

Today Gerry still expresses his gratitude to the Roughriders for their support; for giving him another chance. He regrets failing them but acknowledges they did what they had to do. The young boy in the man doesn't like to feel indebted, so I sense this is an awkward but sincere admission.

As he reviewed his future, Gerry came to realize that in the short span of four years, his career as a pro athlete had been shutting down. At the end of the 1960 season, the Leafs had refused to renew his contract. Punch Imlach, whom Gerry characterizes as one of the good guys in hockey, had made it clear that the Leafs no longer wanted a part-time player on the squad. Gerry, who felt he was still at the pinnacle of both of his games, was unwilling to compromise on his career in either sport; besides, when he looked at the team Punch was assembling, Gerry wasn't confident that he had what the Leafs needed in their future lineup.

"A goon?" I ask.

"Yes," he answers. "Look at these hands. Blocks of stone. Not exactly the soft hands of a scorer."

I know these large hands from shaking one of them at the end of a round of golf. In addition to being as rough as a rasp, Gerry likes to apply a vice grip. This is his submission hold on the golf course. Or perhaps it's merely his way of stopping someone from picking his pocket to collect their winnings. In either case, these are hands meant for policing, not scoring.

"But the Winnipeg Warriors of the WHL were looking for someone with my particular skill set so I played with them, through 1960 – 1961, their final season in the league. No, I wasn't responsible for them going bankrupt. I think television was probably the principal culprit there. Once people could get their fill of NHL hockey on a weekly basis, watching the Leafs, Rangers, Canadiens, Hawks, Bruins and Redwings, they stopped going to their local rinks. In a way, I thought these second tier leagues were where you went on your way up to the NHL, or, equally likely, on your way down, and out.

"Mind you, there were a lot of fine players on these lower level teams, some of whom had made it up to the NHL and for whatever reasons were sent back down. Some had amazing skills and stats; Phil Maloney in Vancouver and Guyle Fielder in Seattle, for example, who had only short stints in the old six team league. And that's a shame, because they could play with the best. Sometimes it was an issue of size. They got hurt too easily. In other instances there seemed to be neither rhyme nor reason to someone's selection or demotion. In my case, there was no confusion. "Hard-headed" and "palooka" are words that come to mind. I thought my hockey career was finished."

To compound his grief, at the end of the 1962 season, Gerry was blind-sided when the Blue Bombers decided to dump him. For someone who felt he had been a loyal team player, he was dumbfounded. All team management would say was that he no longer fitted into their plans. They saw Leo Lewis as their best and most consistent running threat.

This assessment hurt and if one examines the stats, it's also untrue. Per carry, Gerry's and Leo Lewis's averages were almost identical, Gerry perhaps winning by a nose. He had the additional skill of being a kicker. Plus, and this makes his being axed puzzling, he had finished second in total scoring for the 1962 season with 116 points. Why Winnipeg decided to cut him at this time is a mystery, although there is no question Gerry was less versatile than he had been, especially as a running back. Perhaps Winnipeg knew what Saskatchewan was to learn two years later.

As he and his family looked ahead to 1963, prospects looked grim. Suddenly Gerry was unemployed and unwanted. It was difficult to go from being a part of a team which won two straight Grey Cups, four in five years, to the sidelines. Coincidentally, Winnipeg would not win another Grey Cup until 1984. I wonder if the team would have dropped from first in 1962 to fourth in 1963 in the West standings if Gerry had remained a part of the team? More dramatically, would the Bombers have fallen out of playoff contention altogether if Gerry had been in the lineup? Ageing and injuries aside, and I realize this is pure speculation, I think not; I believe there would have been too much fight in the team for that sort of collapse to happen. Some people are an inspiration to others no matter how limited their apparent contribution. Sometimes contract disputes interfere with good judgement. Sometimes it's better to consult a Ouija board. Sometimes, as the old cliché goes, it's best not to try to fix what ain't broke!

After the Saskatchewan experiment failed, Gerry was on his own. He knew that you either lived with hope or fell into despair. It was time for the "Kid" to move on.

12 / The Senior Circuit

When you look into Gerry's eyes, you can see he is a man who, when necessary, measures and calculates every word and thought within a hair's breadth. Off-hand and off-colour comments are sometimes spontaneous but just as often they've gone through a grinding kind of scrutiny. What he has to say about his career is carefully considered, and he won't offer an interpretation of events if he feels it's not his place to judge. Sometimes he gives the impression that he accepts his fate. But his emotions, depending on the circumstances, are sometimes a little less guarded. I think he feels he was short-changed by the Bombers. The facts, as I see them, confirm this interpretation.

Fortunately Davos came calling and while Davos was far from a success, in October of 1964, after he had been dropped by the Roughriders, the Yorkton Terriers of the Saskatchewan Senior Hockey League stepped into the picture. Miraculously they were looking for a player/coach. Gerry provided them with exactly what they wanted: dedication and toughness with the added bonus that people knew him by name and reputation.

Yorkton was not one of those places that evolved haphazardly; a place that seemed to spring out of the earth in response to a random act of chance or by coincidence. The town was not inhabited by drifters drawn to a particular geography for personal and unspecified reasons. Nor was it a town that grew out of some sort of spiritual connection; a site connected to the stars or the alignment of the heavenly bodies. Yorkton was a planned development, although in comparison to Davos, Gerry remarks, it sprawled out like oil spreading over a large puddle of water.

At the end of the nineteenth century a group of English settlers from York, Ontario, heard the area was prime farming land. Like-minded people, these early settlers moved to the area because they shared common goals, which they clung to, distrustful of newcomers bringing different dreams. Soon the town was the hub of a thriving agricultural community, most farms growing wheat and canola. "In my lifetime, I don't remember ever seeing crop failures," Gerry mentioned, "not in that area. It was exceptionally fertile land. Vast, flat and fertile."

In 1964, when Marg and Gerry moved to Yorkton, their home for the next ten years, the population was around 10,000 people. The city was a trading centre for those who lived in a one hundred mile radius. In typical prairie fashion, one of the two national railways ran plumb through the centre of town. The dominant architectural features, rising above the landscape, were the grain elevators, which stood at the nexus of farm life like cathedrals do at the centre of towns in the old world. Awkward wooden or concrete spires reaching like dominoes for the boundless blue sky.

"You know," Gerry reflected, "a grain elevator on its own, adrift on the prairie, beside steel rails running off the horizon in both directions, has always been a symbol of great loneliness for me. Yet, as well, the tracks signified something else. A yearning, perhaps. Possibilites. Endless possibilities."

Gerry used to walk across the tracks, much as he had as a kid in Winnipeg, to get to the town rink which was a converted aircraft hangar. What he remembered most about that relic from the war was that when it was twenty below freezing outside, it was thirty below in the building. For some reason the building constructed of heavy wooden timbers and tin, held the cold. Sometimes it almost hurt to breathe. "Surprisingly, these were great playing conditions for hockey, as long as you wore long johns.

"Even though Yorkton was laid out on a grid, a predictable design — as far as I know, no great revolutionary conspiracies were hatched in its boundaries — it was a great place to live and to raise a family of five kids. Soon after we arrived, we bought a three-storey house downtown, near the court-house. There was only one other house on the block. Otherwise, between us on one corner and the courthouse at the other end of the block, there was a beautiful grass field, open to the prairie sky year round. The park made the house feel like it was on an estate with its own private grounds. The sense of space and light was fantastic. On the corner behind us there was a Rotary Club playground, filled with swings, teeter totters and monkey bars. It was an ideal situation for a young family.

"The one drawback was that on warm summer evenings, teenagers congregated around the field. For a while it would be okay, but once they had soaked up a little liquor and the air was blue with the smell of grass, things got a bit rowdy. When I tired of playing policeman, I bought a Doberman, Brutus, and after a few patrols around the block, with Brutus on a leash, things quietened down. Brutus was a gentle animal but the kids didn't know that. Poor Brutus was killed by a car a few years later when we moved to Melville."

No longer in football, Gerry now gave all of his attention and energy to playing hockey for the Senior Yorkton Terriers, a semi-pro team. For two years he assumed the dual role of coach and player but when he felt that arrangement wasn't working he resigned as coach and happily continued to play for another six years as a member of the rank and file.

"When I didn't have to worry about who to dress (if enough guys showed up to play, that is), or who would play with whom, or whether or not management was happy, that's when the game was the most fun."

Mind you, after Gerry was replaced as coach, when it came to the playoffs every year, the team gathered in the dressing room and voted Gerry back in as coach because they totally lacked confidence in Jerry Bulitz, the man who had been hired to coach them through the season.

Bulitz, who would eventually join Gerry as co-owner of the Junior Terriers, was knowledgeable about hockey but his coaching style, consisting mainly of yelling and calling the team members names, left a lot to be desired. You dogs! You f...ing pigs, he would belt out at the players! His style was not inspiring. Once Bulitz posted a four frame Andy Capp cartoon of a coach giving a pep talk to his soccer team. First frame: They raped your women! No response. Second frame: They burned down your houses! No response. Third frame: They stole your beer! Fourth frame: An angry team tore up the dressing room. "That in a nutshell pretty much captured the Terriers," Gerry said. "I loved the team and fans, everything about senior hockey in Saskatchewan, and I would have kept going had the league not collapsed."

On another occasion, after an inter-locking game in Calgary, Bulitz told the team that there was to be none of their usual bullshitting in the dressing room, he wanted to get home as soon as possible. So Gerry hustled everyone out of the showers and onto the bus. Half an hour later, well on their way out of "cowtown", Gerry asked if anyone had seen Bulitz. After a quick search they discovered they had left the coach behind. It was too late to turn back and Bulitz would eventually find his way home to Yorkton by train. Needless to say, he was furious, but Glen Thorpe, a member of the team executive, suggested that perhaps this was a little payback, a little divine justice owed to Bulitz who was always, Thorpe said, second-guessing Gerry's decisions. "He was a bit of a back stabber as well, that's for sure," Thorpe added.

"Trying to play and coach simply didn't work," Gerry repeated. He felt he was in a conflict of interest. "How do you tell a player not to do what you've just done yourself," he asked? "Too often I got caught doing the same stupid things I was cautioning them about doing. It's a bit embarrassing to skate from the penalty box where you've just served five minutes for fighting to tell a teammate to exercise some self-control and not get into a fight. I felt hypocritical. After two years I told management I would play but not coach; and if the truth be known, we weren't doing very well with me as coach anyway. In addition to that, management was unable to pay me the salary they'd promised."

By this time, to supplement their income, Marg had established a children's clothing store, which she ran for three years. Unfortunately she discovered that most people who lived in Yorkton went into Regina to do their shopping so she was dependent on a clientele from the outlying area. That population base was simply too small to support the store. In addition people tended to shop by habit. Even though items in her store were priced competitively, people continued to shop at Woolworths, or any one of the other stores they knew and had patronized in the past. Gerry also took on extra jobs over the next six years, first as the assistant manager and later as the manager of a local hotel called the Holiday Inn, although it was not related in any way to the chain of the same name.

Senior provincial hockey was definitely not the NHL, but it was still rough, fast-paced and competitive and, for Gerry, presented its own challenges. The coach he was replacing had been killed in a car accident around Christmas, a tragic event for everyone associated with the team, and when Gerry arrived the Terriers existed essentially in name only. He soon discovered that he was expected to build a team from scratch, around a small existing core, by enlisting anyone from the community who was willing to play hockey for a few dollars per game. Included amongst their number were a teacher, a barber, a fireman, a beer salesman, a tire shop employee, a telephone lineman and a milkman. "No professionals," Gerry observed, "there was too much contact for them. We were an untidy and rambunctious lot."

The executive also assumed that Gerry's notoriety would attract new players. They encouraged him to go after imports, the name given to anyone who was from out of town. Most imports came from Manitoba, drawn to the teams in Saskatchewan with the offer of employment. Gerry recalled when Bobby Schmautz broke onto the scene. "He was from Saskatoon, and we thought about going after him but he was an unknown quantity and management wasn't willing to come up with the money to secure his services. Too bad, because eventually, when he made it into the NHL, he proved he had the heart and soul I loved in anyone who played for me."

Since hockey provided only a secondary income, there was little or no reason for team loyalty. Job security took priority and the additional ten to twenty dollars most players earned for playing a game of hockey was merely a supplement to their regular income. To make coaching more difficult, some players demanded additional money for road games. Otherwise it was simple; if it was a choice between snuggling down at home in front of a fire or travelling a few hundred miles over icy roads, they would rather stay home with their families. Why risk a road trip through a whiteout for a measly few bucks? On the other hand, Gerry had a trump card; as the long winter nights wore on and the darkness of the solstice closed in, there was always the "bushed" factor. Lacing up the skates was a way out of the house, a reason for a night out on the town and drinking beer with your buddies.

"As far as I was concerned," he commented, "I had decided at this stage of my life that if I were going to play hockey or any other sport, it was going to be largely for recreational purposes. And for the companionship. Hockey was no longer merely a spectacle; it was a collaboration that pretty much involved everyone in the community. I suppose it was a sort of a tribal event in which everyone participated in one way or another. You didn't have to be on the ice to be a part of the team."

There is little doubt that senior hockey was the foundation of hockey in Saskatchewan. The fan base was huge and knowledgeable, and the support incredibly enthusiastic. Fans hooted and hollered like no one else on the planet, probably to keep warm as much as anything else. Every small town had a team, mostly composed of locals. Bigger centres, like Yorkton, could afford to pad their rosters with a few imports which may explain why they had so much league success.

Without football in his life, hockey became a personal necessity, a form of therapy. Even though he was in his early thirties, he still desperately needed a diversion for his excess energy. Once released from coaching duties, and from whatever responsibilities and constraints that entailed, he was a free spirit. He could skate and play the game as he saw fit. "I guess I'd been on the go for so long that the prospect of inactivity scared the living daylights out of me. And I have to say, the rules sometimes got in the way of how I played the game. To put it euphemistically, I liked the physical side of play. The rough and tumble. I suspect today I wouldn't survive in any league at any level, unless I cleaned up my act, cut the fighting. And, where's the joy in that?" he asked.

At thirty-two, mid-way through his stint on the Senior Terriers, Gerry grew desperate to find an additional outlet for channeling his adrenaline overload. He turned to curling, a sport he had begun watching back in Winnipeg and had once described as "among the least appealing of all sports". Yet to keep active, he began playing two nights a week in a Yorkton club league. He was soon hooked. Playing the game was far more demanding, especially the strategy, than he had realized.

Then he met a group of farmers who came into the Holiday Inn every morning for a cup of coffee and a good jaw. As Gerry and the gang grew chummy, they talked him into playing on their team which meant being out an additional two afternoons a week. It is difficult to imagine curling providing Gerry with an outlet for his aggression but he enjoyed sweeping. From what he tells me and others say, he wielded a wicked broom. Throwing a rock was okay but sweeping, teasing the rock into the house, that was the real thrill. "There's an interesting balance in curling, he explained, between restraint or control when you're trying to curl the rock around a guard into the top of the eight or four foot circle, and when you're asked to throw a rock at weight to take out an opponent's guard sitting in front of the house. The take-out is explosive."

Accompanying an interview article by Reyn Davis in a Winnipeg paper, there is a bizarre picture of Gerry winding up for a slap shot using a broom on a curling rock. Poised on one foot and looking quite dapper, he is wearing a Fu Manchu mustache and goatee beard combination. He is playing third on a visiting Yorkton rink at a bonspiel in Winnipeg. Davis begins his article with, "Gerry James was once a hardrock. Now, he's a granite nut."

There might be a difference — only his geologist knows for sure — but James is in there pitching with 2100-

odd curlers throwing stones in the 82nd annual MCA bonspiel.

Don't expect to see those distinct rudiments that separated James from the boys in his hey-day in two worlds of professional sport

He's wearing glasses, and intellectual-type beard and pants with a smudge on one leg caused by the non-violent contact of his knee rubbing the ice when he delivers.

What little violence there is in curling, James extracts from sweeping. His sweeping is unquestionably his strength.

The one-time Bomber fullback and former Toronto Maple Leaf took up the game three years ago with his usual gusto.

"I've cut down a bit this season," he said after Thursday's last draw. "I'm only curling two nights a week. Last year, I was curling twice a week in a farmer's league, plus two more in the club draw."

Four draws a week is hectic enough for most curlers but James is still playing hockey. Fifty games a season is not unusual for James and his Yorkton Terrier teammates in the Saskatchewan Senior Hockey League.

"Curling was playing me out," said James, "it began to affect my hockey, so I cut my schedule in half by dropping out of the farmer's league."

James threw third rocks with all the grace of a disciple of the game. His southpaw delivery was long and orthodox.

The fluid motion of his powerful sweeping was highly effective and quite noticeable, especially in the sixth end when James coaxed Harris' last rock fully into the four-foot to nose out a Kjartanson stone and score a deuce.

...At 35, James still has plenty of time to master another game, which offers the kind of challenge he relishes. The flaming fury to excel still burns inside him.

Once again someone has taken measure of Gerry's need

to test himself. He was always searching for a way to prove himself and given that there were only two choices; doing it well or badly — the turf between was simply unacceptable — there was no choice but to strive for perfection.

※

Recently Gerry and I met up for coffee, and Gerry in a talkative mood volunteered a few anecdotes from his playing past.

"Would it surprise you," Gerry asked me, "if I told you that during my career with the Terriers I led the league in penalty minutes?"

My answer was an emphatic "No"!

"Look," he said, "here's how I played the game. But first you need to know that I never fought unless there was a reason. And during my latter days in the Senior League avoiding fights became increasingly difficult. I was the old gunslinger and all the young toughs wanted a piece of the action — me! Believe it or not, I was constantly skating away from guys looking to make a reputation for themselves. I didn't like turning my back but, hey, these hands were idle unless provoked. Besides, hitting someone hurts.

"Anyway, one night, I was caught up in a scramble in front of the Saskatoon Quakers' net, and without warning I was given a good stiff crosscheck from behind, right across my back" — which may help to explain why today he favours his back whenever he moves and why he is slightly stooped after a day in the garden. "I hated that," he continued, "the snap you feel right down your spine. I reeled around and instead of facing some tough guy I was looking down into the eager eyes of this puny runt. I mean he was small. As I say, I never fought unless provoked and this was one of those occasions. A just cause. I grabbed the punk's jersey at the neck — I always did this to keep the person off balance — and threw a punch. I broke the guy's helmet which you can probably guess is a little hard on the bones of the hand.

"Not happy with the result, I realigned him and gave him another pop, right on the end of the nose. The nose broke of course and blood shot out all over the place. What a mess. Any cut around the mouth or on the face bleeds excessively, usually indicating much more than the actual damage done. Anyway that nose remains distinctly bent till this day.

"The other player was Dave King. Whenever we get together these days we have a good laugh about what happened. He always points at me and says to anyone who is listening, this is the guy who bent my nose for me.

"As you probably know, Dave went on to have a fairly illustrious career as a coach: for the national team, the Calgary Flames, as the first coach of the expansion Columbus Blue Jackets, teams in Germany, Russia and Sweden, and now as an assistant coach with the Phoenix Coyotes. He's done well and I'm pleased for him. He's a good man.

"The funny thing, though, was Dave's dad, who was in attendance at the game. When he saw what a mess I'd made of Dave's nose, he jumped to his feet and immediately put a one hundred dollar bounty on my head. 'Any player who takes that SOB out,' he yelled from the stands, 'gets one hundred dollars.' He went wild, arms flailing, fists punching the air. As I sat in the penalty box, a parade of players skated by and warned me to keep my head up and eyes open. Soon I tired of this little exhibition and I lifted my hand and pointed to the large ring I was wearing, which doubled as a knuckle duster, and I could see each one of them flinch. Soon after that the league brought in a long-overdue rule against wearing rings during games.

Oh, and by the way, that night no-one earned Dave's dad's reward.

"On another occasion, we were playing against Father Bauer's Canadian National Team. Of course, they were all still competing for places on the squad and had a lot to prove. Most if not all of them played for university teams and supposedly had squeaky clean images. They were also in shape which is more than can be said for our lot.

"And I'd be stretching the truth if I didn't admit that everyone on the Terriers relished the competition. We were like dogs whimpering after a bone; some of the guys figured a team out of our ranks should have been representing Canada at the world championships, although to be honest we weren't good enough. For one thing, many of the players moved too often. To wherever the work was!

"Anyway, one of their players, Ray Cadeaux, speared me in the forehead. Again, blood, my blood this time, spurted out of the gash and covered the ice. I grabbed Cadeaux and threw him down, straddled him, bounced his noggin (gently mind you) a couple of times against the ice and then bled all over him. By the time the officials got between us and pulled us apart, someone had brought me a towel. To say I was a tad pissed off would be like suggesting there was a good chance the Pope might be Catholic.

"For the spear and cut alone, I figured Cadeaux should get a minimum of ten minutes if not a game misconduct, but instead I got the big minutes, probably for a combination of fighting and my past reputation. Admittedly, I had thrown a couple of punches but Cadeaux got nothing! Probably because he hadn't thrown a punch. I hadn't let him. I was so incensed I threw the bloody towel at the ref and he immediately tossed me out of the game. In the meantime, Cadeaux had fled to their team bus. During the intermission between the second and third periods, a couple of his teammates went to retrieve him and even though I had been banished from the game there was no way he was returning to the ice. He stayed cocooned in the team bus. I guess he figured I was raging mad and out for revenge no matter what. Come to think of it, he might have been right, but there was no way I could have got to him.

"As hard as it may be to believe, that was the first time I received a game misconduct as a Senior. Senior, by the way, is a bit misleading. Anyone of any age could play for us. Sometimes, young guys looking to make it in the NHL came to play in our league but always with the understanding that they could leave to pursue their dream at any time."

There's another incident that Gerry clearly takes delight in relaying. A brawl broke out in Yorkton but he'd just finished a particularly long shift and decided to stay on the bench. He was pooped. His legs were trembling and he was sucking for air. Most of his teammates, though, jumped the boards and entered the fray. The game had been a chippy affair, with the young guys from both sides wanting to prove they belonged. Ironically when order was finally restored, the only two players left on the Terriers' bench were Gerry and Barry Trapp. The ref then blew his whistle and motioned the two of them out on to the ice. As he skated up to the ref Gerry said, "You mean we get penalized for not entering the fight. Where's your sense of fair play?" Everyone on the other team had left their bench so the referee had to designate three players for them. "Then the six of us dogged it, circling the ice for five minutes," Gerry said, "each taking a turn with the puck. It was the only way we could kill off five minutes without a rest."

Then there was Rollie Wilcox who needed a lesson in teamwork. Rollie had played in the AHL and the WHL before he fell in love with a Yorkton girl, married her and moved to town for the Terriers' final season in 1971-72. In

Rollie's mind, he was descending the hockey ladder, Gerry speculated.

"There was no doubt he was a good skater," Gerry offered, "fast and quick, but every shift on the ice he seemed determined to prove this point to the rest of us. He was like a peacock out there, strutting his stuff. No doubt he was good and I suppose he had something to prove to his new wife but it annoyed the hell out of everyone else on the team.

"He was so preoccupied with himself that he ignored the rotation. This showboating became particularly difficult when he tried to kill a penalty all on his own, filling the full two minutes on his own; going through everyone else's shift; ruining line changes. One night in Edmonton, after one of these displays, he returned to the bench, looking for someone to relieve him, but no one moved. No one even looked his way. We all stayed put, our pants glued to the spot. Leaning against the boards, his leg muscles aching, Rollie didn't know what to do. Later he called a team meeting and lectured us on cooperation. No one made a peep. Not a word. Our lips were sealed. How else do you respond to someone who's that pig-headed?"

Marg said that during his first few years of coaching Gerry tried to encourage players not to drink the night before a game. "We want to be in shape at least prior to the game," he would suggest to them during one of his pep talks, but his words fell on deaf ears.

"No luck," she laughed. "That was like trying to stop their heads from swiveling to take a gander when a beautiful young woman took her place in the stands. All of them thinking how they were going to impress her. All experiencing a brief fluttering of hope. Flirts, the lot of them. And most of them couldn't wait for a break between periods to light up a cigarette. The dressing room was blue with smoke.

I think it was during this time that Gerry started to develop wrinkles and worry lines around his eyes."

Although he racked up a lot of penalty minutes, there is no question that Gerry was the team leader. His teammates were like family and they earned his respect or censure, whichever was deserved. The occasional bonehead play could stir his anger if he was in one of his uncompromising moods, but most of the time all that pent up energy went into playmaking or scoring. In spite of their bad habits, the Terriers won the Saskatchewan Senior League title four years straight, between 1966 and 1970, and went on after the playoffs (every team made the provincial playoffs, no matter what their ranking during the season) to compete in three interprovincial championships held to select the western representative for the Allan Cup.

One year, when three of the four teams ended the tournament tied with 2 - 1 records, the Terriers should have been the western representative in the Allan Cup finals. But St. Boniface, the Manitoba team, which had already been eliminated from the competition, went on a drinking binge the night before their final game and lost by such a colossal margin that the team the Terriers were guaranteed to beat for a place in the national final ended up winning the Western championship on goal difference. The St. Boniface coach, with that hangdog look that some men get when they know they've overstayed their welcome, later came to Gerry and apologized for his players and the score.

"I give him his due," Gerry said, "he made no excuses. As you can imagine, a lot of responses came to mind but you can't turn back the clock. I accepted his apology but I'd be remiss not to say we were disappointed. Sometimes Karma wags a finger in such a way that there is little doubt about the message. I imagine a mule kick to the family jewels would have had the same impact."

Two seasons before the league folded, Yorkton even went so far as to suggest that they wished to host a yearly round-robin tournament between the four western champions. This way they could reduce travelling costs which had become prohibitive. While at the local level owners worried and talked about survival, on the larger stage, the future landscape of every major sport was beginning to change. As with football, basketball and baseball, hockey was becoming swept up in a wave of optimistic commercialism and, coincidentally, the bottom line became more important than ever. This meant expansion. Profits and ledgers replaced score cards and a passion for the game. As hockey went corporate, attempts to prolong the life of smaller leagues faltered. Canada's game was beginning to change, not only on the ice but in "Board Rooms".

Glen Thorpe, a member of the Yorkton Terrier executive, mentioned in an interview that in his opinion you could not run a community sports franchise like a business — he, for one, had too much love for the game to think of it in those terms — yet that's precisely what the new breed of owner was doing. The business side of the equation was paramount.

Whereas Glen, for example, thought of Gerry as colour, the new owners of expansion franchises thought of players as a commodity, although they clearly saw the "value" in talent and charisma. Perhaps it was a matter of scale and focus but there can be little doubt that merchandising defined the new sporting ethos. A favourable interpretation of this trend was that it clearly expanded the options for emerging talent and extended the careers of some ageing players. Senior hockey may have benefitted as well, as teams became even more rooted in community and less dependent on "imported" talent. The motivation to play senior hockey shifted. The distinction between amateur and semi-pro and pro became more clearly defined. On the other side of the debate, there were those who believed sport was becoming too commercial, too driven by profit. Youth hockey, as in every other sport, had become the training ground for "Gladiators" in waiting.

In Yorkton, the executive was divided between Gerry boosters and detractors but everyone had to admit that he drew crowds and that the team consistently had a winning record.

"I remember one fan in particular," Glen Thorpe recalled, "a woman in her early nineties, who turned up for every single game and shouted out Gerry's name from the first faceoff to the last whistle. I'm sure she still haunts the bleachers, cheering him on!

"Gerry antagonized the opposition and defended his own team with equal zest. One night, early in a game, he got into a scuffle with Alan Ford, who played for the Regina Caps. Later Gerry came up against him along the glass in front of our fans. He puckered up and gave Ford a great big kiss. The fans loved it. He would do anything to incite the other players and to thrill his own fans.

"Oddly, even some of our own players resented Gerry for his antics. I think they were jealous; in some peculiar and twisted way I think his success in football and hockey offended them. You could never accuse Gerry of gloating or grandstanding but he had flair and that seemed to bother some people.

"Don't get me wrong, I really liked Gerry but he could get under a saint's skin. Near the end, he decided to hold out against the executive for a larger salary but we were losing money hand over fist by this time and it was a bad tactic on his part. Besides, we all knew he was putting in several hours a day training. His daughter had told us this: Don't worry, she said, he'll be there when the season begins. What annoyed some, I guess, was the gesture, his faking it, as much as anything else. They didn't like the joke, if that's what it was? Or the implied threat. Some wanted his head.

"They also didn't like the fact that they weren't included in his decisions or his social life, a problem Gerry would later face in spades while coaching the junior team. In some respects, certain people sat on the executive because they hungered for the association. They saw themselves as part of the brain trust, as part of the group in the know about everything to do with hockey. Being part of the inner circle was critical to their self esteem, their ego. In particular, they desperately wanted to be Gerry's friend!

"That said, if you really needed something, if the organization was in trouble, well, Gerry would do anything to help you out. I can't think of anyone I'd rather have on my side. If I wanted someone running my horses, well, it would have to be Gerry."

❧

The expansion of the NHL in 1967 to twelve teams combined with the announcement in 1971 of a new upstart league called the World Hockey Association tolled the death knell of minor and senior hockey across Canada. Owners of the original six NHL teams seemed dead-set against sharing players with their six new partners, which left the new teams hunting the backwoods of rural Canada for skilled players. The WHA, which up to this point was simply a proposal, a dream on paper, had no players signed to contracts. If this new league hoped to be in operation by the fall of 1972, they too were going to have to comb the minors and semi-professional leagues to fill their rosters. Both groups desperately needed to find a source of new talent if they were to succeed, and the WHL and the senior leagues scattered across the prairies provided the richest vein of quality players available. Wisely the WHA would eventually tap Europe to fill their ranks.

After poaching and signing a few marquee players from the NHL, Bobby Hull, Bernie Parent, Derek Sanderson, J. C. Tremblay and Ted Green amongst the first sixty-seven defectors from the NHL, the new league, albeit a bit lame, actually managed to get up and running for the 72 season. Simultaneously, senior teams across the country started to fold. By 1974, even the rock-solid, minor pro Western Hockey League, which had once been seen as a potential rival to the NHL, closed its doors. Overall quality suffered in all of the lower level leagues and attendance dropped dramatically.

"Yorkton was no exception," Gerry said, "we simply couldn't muster a team, not with players that anyone would want to pay to watch."

The Saskatchewan Senior Hockey League packed it in.

Once again the future looked bleak for Gerry and his family but, as usual, his instincts for survival kicked into gear. It may have been luck that guided or accompanied him but he is blessed with a belief in its certainty. If one avenue closes to him, another opens. The road may take a turn or narrow to a tight squeeze or prove to be a bumpy ride, but he will press on and find a way no matter what. Sometimes these avenues emerge out of tight corners or an alleyway and yet they become a way he is willing to follow. Risk is always part and parcel of the equation. This confidence may go back to his youth and arise from what his grandfather taught him about snaring rabbits. Or it may be part of the survival strategy he learned from defending himself against brother Don. What a long struggle that was to find peace. More likely, though, his faith in himself and his abilities is inherited from his mother.

During the summer of 1972, just as Gerry and Marg were contemplating a move, a delegation from the executive of the newly-formed Yorkton Terrier Hockey Club, an offshoot of the Senior Terriers, proposed to Gerry that he become the coach of the junior club. Yorkton had been accepted as an expansion franchise in the SAJHL (the Saskatchewan Amateur Junior Hockey League, later the SJHL) on June 25 and they needed a coach. Gerry was their choice.

13 / Coaching: Juniors & Pee Wees

Mike Ditka, the NFL Hall of Fame tight end for the Chicago Bears, Philadelphia Eagles and Dallas Cowboys, and later Super-Bowl-winning coach of the Chicago Bears, commented recently on a televised pre-game show (and I paraphrase) that coaches must live or die on the basis of their own successes or failures. Their *own* successes and failures, he repeated, no one else's!

Ditka was passionate about what he did, expected nothing but the best from his players, and, perhaps most importantly, as a player had already been where he wanted his players to go. He led by example.

No coach wants to be told how to do his job by an owner or management. Nor does a coach want to be fired for reasons beyond his control. No coach wants to be compromised by choices and selections made by people who don't fully understand the strategy of the game or who don't know instinctively the characters of the players being signed. Though the intentions of those in management are probably good and their love of the game unquestionable, their knowledge of the subtleties and nuances of team play is probably minimal. A coach should be fired because he or she "screwed up," not because some desk jockey purchased the wrong player or made a bad trade, often on a whim and a prayer. Coaches should not be victims of an owner's rash, devil-may-care decision to purchase a marquee player whom they hope will salvage the team or boost ratings with the fans. Often these players bring baggage with them that no-one can handle.

Who wants to be the victim of someone else's impulsive reactions and choices? One of the most unfortunate recent examples of owner interference and squabbling is reflected in the rapid decline of Liverpool FC of the Premier League in England. Once one of the most powerful and successful sporting franchises in the world, the Reds took a nosedive when they were purchased by a tandem of Americans, who clearly set out to buy a business not a football team.

Perhaps the oddest and most torrid on-again off-again relationship between an owner and coach/manager endured between George Steinbrenner, owner of the Yankees, and Billy Martin, at least five-time coach of the Yankees, who seemed to fall out of Steinbrenner's favour at the drop of a hat. Martin felt Steinbrenner's meddling and interference, especially his signing of Reggie Jackson over Joe Rudi in 1977, had a negative impact on the team.

While both men had egos as large as the state of Texas, certainly large enough to match the reputation and expectations of the fans from the "Big Apple," it could be argued that amongst owners Steinbrenner was an exception; he did have considerable knowledge of and passion for the game. Even so, Martin should not have had to accept a player "forced on him." Ironically Jackson helped the Yankees win several pennants but forgotten in the mix were Martin's rights and skills as a manager. He was the manager and the team's success (or failure as Ditka points out) was his doing. Based on his record and in spite of all of his crazy antics, most probably due to Martin's prolonged drinking bouts, he presumably knew better than anyone else what was best for a team he had been hired to lead.

By his own admission, Gerry's early assignments as a

coach proved to be fairly dismal, for many of the same reasons most coaches seem to fail these days. Management in Davos made promises they were unable to keep. With players away on national service and unavailable for practices and without a quality goalie he found himself caught between a rock and hard place. Within no time at all he realized the team's chances of winning the league were out of the question. Simply salvaging a place in the premier league would be a major achievement. That goal he accomplished, with little or no thanks from management who should have been giddy with joy at their placement in the 1963-64 season.

This travesty was followed by his experience first with the Senior Terriers and then, more significantly, with the Yorkton Terriers junior team.

While he led the Senior Terriers to three provincial titles, the position of player/coach made him feel like he was bellowing out commands in an echo chamber.

On the positive side, one of the executive members of the senior club owned a Dairy Queen in town and in 1970 proposed that Gerry and Marg lease and manage the operation to help supplement their income from the small seasonal contract with the hockey club. This offer was all they needed to keep them in town. The couple leapt at the offer. They had to. They had a growing family, they were living close to the poverty line and they had nowhere else to go. This arrangement, which paid them well, remained in place during most of Gerry's junior tenure. Fears that they might have to uproot their family to earn a livable wage were once again set aside. Gerry got to indulge in his passion for hockey.

On the negative side, Gerry soon learned that coaching for some members of the new junior executive meant his coaching by consensus. They wanted a say in all on-ice decisions, who played with whom, tactics, the whole kit and caboodle. This was an untenable arrangement.

Some members of the executive felt that their position entitled them to question Gerry's judgment at every turn. To be fair, though, these conflicts were limited to only a few members of the executive, yet those who did feel it was their prerogative to speak their minds were a proverbial pain in the butt. While their advice was undoubtedly given with the best of intentions, Gerry did not have the personality to accept any form of interference kindly. By his own admission, he was not receptive to "help or guidance" issued from those who, in his view, didn't have the slightest idea about the game of hockey. His term for them was "jock sniffers," guys who wanted to hang about the dressing room and talk to the young players, sometimes their own sons, about the sort of game they imagined themselves having played a hundred times in the Gardens or some other rink. Why appoint a coach, Gerry wondered, if you had no intention of listening to his advice? If the only word you trusted was your own?

In spite of the glasses that now rode his nose and gave him the look of a young college professor, Gerry was still raw and mulish. The timing of their invasion of his space, of sticking their noses in the door, couldn't have been worse. Their words came at him like a cloud of smoke on a clear day, obstructing his vision and smothering any hope of change.

When Gerry took the position with the junior club he had only recently come to the realization that coaching was something he had to do. He not only had the energy and desire to pass what he had learned about the game through his junior and pro careers, he also felt teaching the game was his duty or calling. Not to put too precious a description on this newly-found personal goal, he felt it was his future "mission" in life. It was a matter of survival, monetarily and psychologically. He discovered that he no longer thought of the game as a mere player but rather as a strategist.

In part, he realized he needed an outlet for his own energy and aggression, but more to the point, he was developing his own ideas and philosophy about coaching and playing hockey. He had begun to see and was intrigued by the complexity and the beautiful art of the game. Even though a cause of dismay for many, this was when the Russians came on the scene and entered the Canadian consciousness in what became known as the Summit Series of 1972. Whenever he had an opportunity to watch them, he realized Russian team play was like a ballet. Their practices were rigorous, a combination of art and athletics. If he could combine their art with the more physical tactics of the Canadian game, a side of the game he still embraced whole-heartedly, he felt he would have a winning combination. Everything in the Russian game happened at speed and with intensity. Gerry watched their practices and studied game tape. He loved what he saw.

All of this evolving awareness was fine in theory but at this stage in his coaching career, he hadn't a clue how to implement these exciting and innovative ideas. He quickly discovered that the junior Terrier players under his guidance were old enough and advanced enough in the system to have definite expectations about coaching methods. They knew the drills. They knew what to expect and what they wanted from a practice. Game routines were old hat. They would accept coaching idiosyncrasies but not wholesale changes to a ritual they had been following from the time they first laced on skates.

Suddenly Gerry was faced with a major dilemma; how to change the system while fulfilling the players' expectations. He soon learned that change came at his own peril. He was also worried not to give to those executive members already opposed to his coaching methods additional reasons for sacking him. During his first two-year stint with the junior Yorkton Terriers, he resisted the temptation to tamper too much with a deep-rooted if not inbred hockey culture. His new ideas fermented but for the most part remained bottled up.

Also, during this time, he told me, his face filling with amusement, as if this revelation has just dawned on him, he began to learn one other very important fact. "As a coach you are only ever as good as the players willing to take to the ice for you. If they are attentive and receptive to what you're telling them, that's good, that certainly helps; but if they lack talent, if they have no aptitude, savvy, gift for the game, call it what you will, well, then your chance of being a successful, 'winning' coach is probably doomed. You'd better appreciate all the other life-lessons these young men can learn from playing the game; and from what you have to say as a coach. You need to respect the lives you're about to influence. And you need to be a sympathetic guide to their futures."

In his seventies, Gerry's face is furrowed with lines of determination and, I believe, understanding. But what would he have looked like to his players thirty to forty years ago? His eyes or a curl of his lip or a toss of his head would have told the story, I imagine. He would have appeared a bit immovable, rooted, a tad stern.

Doubtless he would have spoken his mind; I can't imagine him not doing so. Yet he was not naïve; he knew how to survive. Beneath the surface, hidden in a pocket of his ever-active mind, new ideas fomented, ideas he knew would work if given a chance. Yet his instinct for survival told him to keep his mouth shut, at least until he could no longer tolerate unwanted and uninvited counsel.

First and foremost he had come to believe that his players must enjoy themselves. The game had to be fun! Even a team loaded with talent had to be having fun. Otherwise, he decided, without this benefit and result, what was the point?

In a way, he inverted his thinking. Competition was still important but was no longer at the forefront of his thinking. Oh, he still wanted his teams to win, you can be sure of that, but there was so much more of value to be imparted. "Hockey is a game," he insisted, "and therefore should be enjoyed."

Discipline, skill, physical development, commitment, strategy, teamwork, a sense of self-worth, curiosity, and trust, those elements which contribute to personal and collective growth were all still vital to his coaching philosophy, but there was more.

It is the "more" that he wanted to understand fully. He realized he had to prepare his players for more, much more, than just a future in hockey. Hockey, or any other sport for that matter, was a means by which to learn a whole set of life-skills; was a way to become a fully-rounded person. Hockey provided one context in which this awareness could develop, if his young apprentices were given the room to do so.

His two years, 1972-1974, as the coach of the new Yorkton Terriers junior franchise, were a mixed blessing. It would be unfair to say these were solely unhappy times but equally they were not as rewarding as he had expected them to be. For one thing, Tier 2 junior hockey was a repository for players who were younger or a little less skilled or less developed than their Tier 1 counterparts. The talent pool was not up to the expectations of some of the team executive. Gerry would do his best with and for his players, as I'm sure he expected the players would do for him, but whatever they accomplished would always come up short in the minds of those who for whatever reason saw their own destinies chained to the performance of the team. This vicarious association always puzzled and angered him. He wanted to be left alone to coach and he wanted his players to have the opportunity to hone their skills unfettered.

Tier 2 was also a place where those who wanted to keep their university options open could play without worrying about eligibility issues and professional commitments. Perhaps by making this decision these players were already thinking beyond hockey to a world of endless possibilities in which they could become lawyers, engineers, teachers, journalists, actors, businessmen, farmers, travelers, artists, chefs, pilots, politicians. So much was possible. Some, I suspect, were encouraged to think they could make a difference in the world. This was the "more" Gerry felt participation in hockey offered. It is the reason why he was instrumental in eventually establishing a scholarship program for players, first in Saskatchewan, and then throughout the Tier 2 system.

Gradually, as the Terrier team came together, camaraderie developed. Every team has a jokester and on the junior Terriers it was Norm Garbutt. "Norm was tall and lanky, built like a Lodgepoll Pine," Gerry said. In the piggy-back drill, Gerry would always pair him with the one other tall player on the team. Ideally you wanted two players of a similar size and build to do the drill together but these two looked like a giraffe as they limp-shuffled — legs separating, doing the splits — down the ice. They were always the last to finish.

As if to announce his arrival, when Norm entered the dressing room, whether for a game or practice, the first words out of his mouth were, "Anyone not here? Speak up!"

One day during the season the team had gathered at the home rink to prepare for the bus trip to Moose Jaw. After they had collected their gear together and Gerry had given them a brief pre-game talk, they boarded the bus and headed out of town. About thirty minutes into the trip they realized Norm wasn't on the bus. After whooping it up, speculating on Norm's whereabouts, hiding him in all sorts of unlikely spots, they agreed he had last been seen heading towards the can. By this time they were too far out of Yorkton to go back, so they continued on their journey. Gerry also realized he'd locked the dressing room door and there was no way out. Eight hours later, at about one-thirty in the morning, they returned home and immediately headed to the rink. There sat Norm, on a worn-out, old wooden bench, looking like a friendly and very patient — relieved no doubt — Basset Hound. As soon as they opened the door he asked, "Well, did you win?"

"No," they replied, and Norm smiled. They had missed him, he was sure of that.

These are the moments that leap into Gerry's consciousness with ease. Even though he felt he hadn't developed as much as he had hoped he would as a coach, his players clearly took a different view. Almost everyone sang his praises.

On the other hand, I think he feels he might have been a bit too subversive but frequently honesty challenges attitudes that have been held for far too long; that have become doctrinaire and are considered beyond reproach; attitudes that need to be exposed, aired and revised. Like laundry, ideas benefit from the sun and a gentle breeze.

In spite of the many frustrations he experienced during this first appointment to a junior hockey club, Gerry's record as a coach was quite respectable. In 1973-74, in his second season, the Yorkton Terriers of the SAJHL won 28 games, lost 19 and tied 3 for a .590 percentage. For a new franchise, this record should have been quite enviable. But it wasn't, at least in the minds of some of the executive. With their grumbling audible, Gerry quit as coach before the team had an opportunity to fire him.

No doubt he also had some choice comments for anyone who was presumptuous enough to offer him advice. One thing he had never managed to curb was his mouth.

Banning members of the executive from the locker room also put a few noses out of joint.

Everything has its end, yet in spite of his resignation and his memories of his final days with the junior organization, many players shared Tom Bast's response to surviving Gerry's reign as coach. In a letter written to Gerry years later, when Tom had his own family of four and was coaching in Red Deer, he wrote:

It's been a long time since we had contact. Frequently I see Tara (*Marg and Gerry's third daughter*) and ask about you. Linus (*Linus Westberg, a contemporary of Gerry's and former Sports Director of a Yorkton TV station*) told me that you will be in Yorkton as a special guest during the World Junior Trials. Rumour has it that you have been voted as the most popular coach in Yorkton hockey history. As a rookie with you in 1972-73, you were not the most popular coach then but without a doubt the most effective.

In looking back at my hockey career, I should have followed your advice and stayed under your coaching guidelines longer. The brief time I spent with you was most rewarding and I say honestly that you were one of the best coaches I have had.

At the present I am still playing hockey at the age of 49 and still enjoy the thrill of the game.

My life is full of activity with many coaching assignments, hockey schools, golf schools and a very active and growing business....

Very best regards,

Tom Bast

PS One of the many hockey players fortunate enough to have had you as a coach.

Obviously Gerry was pleased to receive this letter and testimonial but, more to the point, it endorsed the focus he had brought to the game: the pleasure the game offered and the opportunities it engendered. Clearly hockey had contributed to Tom's rich and productive life.

❧

With his coaching career on hold, Gerry turned his attention to the Pop Shop franchise he had purchased. Marg had taken a position as a dental technician. Both had sought alternative sources of income when their lease on the Dairy Queen had run out mid-way through Gerry's second year with the junior Terriers. But through all of these ups and downs, he was still thinking hockey. During lulls in business, and there were plenty of those in the pop business, he said, he read and reread and then made notes based on Lloyd Percival's *The Hockey Handbook*.

Gerry had met Percival at his Sports College in Toronto when Gerry needed rehab on a painful arm injury he had received while playing for the Leafs. Percival did wonders for the injury. Gerry remembered asking Percival how long it would take for him to mold his body like Tim Horton's. Percival replied: "Forever! I hate to disappoint you kid but you don't have the body of Tim Horton. No amount of work will help you attain that goal." This frankness impressed Gerry and he decided to read Percival's book.

Percival was one of the first people to study sport scientifically and *The Hockey Handbook*, published in 1951, was one result of that study. Even so, one NHL coach, Dick Irvin Sr., rejected the book at the time as "the product of a three-year-old mind." But the Russian hockey patriarch, Anatoli Tarasov, appreciated its contents, adopted many of Percival's methods and applied them rigorously to teach his players. He even wrote to Percival saying, "Your wonderful book which introduced us to the mysteries of Canadian hockey, I have read like a schoolboy." While Percival struggled against the complacency of the Canadian hockey establishment, Russian and European coaches seized on the book as the first authoritative, analytical treatment of hockey fundamentals and based their own training methods on the principles Percival described.

Gerry was captivated by Percival's writings. Here was someone talking about the game he loved in constructive terms. As he sat in his shop on a sunny, summer afternoon, dreaming about what was possible with this new knowledge, he decided that if no one was willing to pay him to coach, he would volunteer his services.

A local Yorkton Pee Wee team leapt at his offer. A big-time coach for free, they thought. For Gerry this was to become one of the most enjoyable and enlightening experiences of his life. His memories of this time are palpable, as if he is standing on the ice at the moment of telling, seventeen pairs of enthusiastic ears listening to his every word; seventeen pairs of eyes watching his hands draw diagrams in the air, showing them where he expected them to be and when during a game; showing them how they should work together. "Don't doubt who you are for a moment, and trust, trust everyone else on the team," he told them.

The Pee Wee team was a Triple "A" travelling team which meant that for their age group, ages 11 and 12, they were the pick of the crop. In essence, they were an all-star team. They were in a six team division, including Weyburn, Estevan, Melville, Swift Current, Moose Jaw and Yorkton, that travelled and billeted on weekends throughout the southern region of the province. What Gerry loved most about this team was their keenness, their raw passion for the game. Both players and parents gave him their unqualified support. Here was the blank slate he had been longing for.

If coaching the junior Terriers team had become a bit of a poisoned pill to swallow, coaching the Pee Wees was the perfect antidote. This group of youngsters had no preconceptions about coaching methodology. Where he had felt more and more constrained or handcuffed with the junior team, he now felt totally liberated by the Pee Wee program.

From the get-go, Gerry explained to his young team that they would be working in three units of five: three forwards and two defensemen. Through a combination of Percival's book and from what he remembered of the Russian system and his own analysis of games from ten rows up in the stands, he had come to the conclusion that fixed units within the team made good sense, not only for play but for practices as well.

I mentioned to him that many of the top managers of English Premier League football teams — Ferguson, Moyse, Redknapp, for example — often observed at least part of a game from the stands, probably because from a higher vantage point they got a better view of play and the success (or failure) of the formations they were using. On occasion, when things didn't appear to be working, you would see them come down out of the stands and realign players.

"Seems reasonable to me," Gerry responded. "You see the field of play so much better from above."

As Gerry explained his system to his young band of disciples, he told them that the three groups would be known as the Jameses, the Youngers, and the Daltons, all named after gangs of brothers from the old American west. They seemed thrilled to assume these roles. It was as though Gerry were sharing the secret plans for a major train robbery or bank heist with them. It built a new excitement into the game and gave them a greater sense of belonging. Play and acting out roles became a part of the learning process.

The plan worked like a charm. Each gang became as tightly knit as a woollen sweater. Not only did they quickly learn to work together but they exerted pressure on each other to cooperate. After all, they were members of the same gang, riding through this dream of hockey together. The peer pressure made coaching that much easier. Gerry could work with an entire string all at once, emphasizing team play. He developed a play book which all the players had to know: D1, D2, and D3 were all different ways of moving the puck up the ice. If one player messed up then the entire line suffered. In part this was the Russian influence. Gerry had noted that as long as the game permitted it, the Russians worked in units of five. They always tried to have the same five players out on the ice. For him, this made sense. The more you played together, the more you developed an empathy or second sense for the movement of your line mates.

Gerry also employed other ideas he had learned while he was coaching in Europe. He brought in a figure skater to help the team with their power skating. He had noticed that speed skaters and figure skaters all generated much more power on their skates than most hockey players. Loreen Kuspira, the rink manager's daughter, showed Gerry's players how to use and keep their edges, going both ways. Skating backwards became as important as skating forwards.

One figure skating exercise Gerry employed, "shoot the duck," was particularly useful, in a couple of ways. A balance exercise, the players would squat down, sit back on their haunches and glide on one skate, while the other leg was kicked forward, up and off the ice. To add to the difficulty and to help maintain equilibrium, Gerry would have his players hold their sticks out in front of them at shoulder level. They would do this eye-popping exercise going for-wards and backwards.

Once they became proficient at the drill, after everyone had taken a tumble or two, he would have the entire team perform the movement before a game. When their oppo-nents saw this exhibition, they wondered, "What the hell is that!?"

"They were gob-smacked and a little intimidated," he told me as we sat on his deck in the afternoon sun.

I can imagine this little pageant, demonstrating balance, strength and flexibility, having quite an impact on a young opposition. A little sideshow performance preceding the larger drama wouldn't do Gerry's team's chances any harm.

Another standard drill Gerry used was an under and over exercise. In this routine, he set up sticks, at the two blue lines, balanced between and on top of two pylons, about a foot and a half off the ice. At the centre line, on shorter pylons, at a height of about six to ten inches off the ice, he set up another two pylons and stick. The object was to slide under the two blue line gates and jump over the centre gate. When the players asked him to demonstrate exactly what he wanted them to do, he took off, made what he thought was a perfect slide under the first gate only to bounce his head off the ice.

"I took a pretty good whack without a helmet," he said. "Almost knocked myself out!" When the laughter died down he vowed never again to show off his own skill package. The boys, of course, had no trouble with the task. "But heck," he said, "they were smaller!"

He also used a basketball court to simulate hockey situ-ations. They would do walk-throughs so movements made sense to everyone. Perhaps one of his most successful passing drills was having two groups going on goal in opposite di-rections at the same time. This way the players not only had to be aware of their own line mates, but they had to keep their heads up for the players coming the other way.

"I'm a strong advocate of never turning your back on the puck," he said. "That leads to all sorts of problems. So we spent considerable time on blocking shots, using a shinny puck because it's soft, and doesn't hurt. As much. I'm surprised when I watch the pros these days by how poorly they block shots. I don't think it's a skill given much attention at the lower levels. It may have something to do with all the extra equipment players are wearing these days. They develop a false sense of their own safety."

All in all, Gerry's year with the Yorkton Pee Wee team was a revelation. They were great kids! The team won the majority of their games, usually quite handily. At one stage, when scores were becoming too lopsided, he told his players they had to make a minimum of five passes before they took a shot on their opponent's goal. If they lost the puck, they had to restart their count.

"On another occasion," he told me, "we were leading in a game 4 – 1 and when I looked up at the clock there were three minutes and a few seconds remaining in the game. Then the other team scored and when I looked back at the clock suddenly there was five minutes remaining in the game. People tried all sorts of questionable tactics against us. We won the league but Weyburn beat us in the playoffs and went on to represent our league in the provincial finals.

"To win against us in the playoffs, a home and away total goals series, Weyburn employed a snot-nosed kid no taller than Jiminy Cricket as goal judge. He sat directly behind the goal and could barely see over the boards. He signaled goal on a couple of shots our goalie had stopped. This young whippersnapper said the puck had crossed the goal line before our goalie caught it. He would have needed x-ray vision to see that happen. Even though the puck was clearly in our goalie's glove, there was no way we could protest these decisions."

Gerry was very much the stoic about this result: "Perhaps we didn't play well enough to deserve the victory," he suggested.

What Gerry cherished most about his year with the Pee Wees was what he learned about coaching.

"I held classroom sessions and used a blackboard to illustrate puck movement," he said. "And I always had a clipboard with me that the players could consult before we began a practice. They knew what we would be doing before they went out on the ice. I also learned that if I were patient and they could see the benefits of doing what I was proposing, well, then even practising became enjoyable, for everyone. Calisthenics were fun, whether in the gym or on the ice, because all of them could see the value of conditioning. For me, the entire enterprise was like winning the lottery."

Life lessons don't usually come this readily, at least I don't think they do, and don't customarily come tripping our way so willingly, like gifts given thoughtlessly. Serendipitous moments are often when we are truly blessed. Gerry had received such a gift. The Pee Wees had taught him how to be a coach.

14 / Surviving the Game

At the end of the Pee Wee season a group, led by Jerry Hudy, a turkey and cattle farmer, representing the Melville Millionaires junior team, came courting Gerry. Many of the Pee Wee parents tried to convince him to stay on in Yorkton with the youngsters he had just coached through such an auspicious season, but Melville was offering him a salary and a job. As difficult as it was to part from the Pee Wees, Gerry still had a family to support, although his two eldest daughters, Debbie and Tracy, had moved out on their own. One went voluntarily, the other departed after a dispute with Gerry, not something he is willing to talk about, although he does mention that even today they struggle to talk to each other. The rebel had raised a rebel.

For the next five years, from the 1975-76 season to 1979-80, Gerry would be the highly successful coach of the Melville Millionaires of the Saskatchewan Junior Hockey League (SJHL). Only in his final year with them would the winning percentage of the team fall below .500 to .492. Otherwise, the team had winning seasons, one year achieving a record of 42 wins against 15 losses and 1 tie. Much of his success as a coach he owed to the skills he developed with the Pee Wees.

But, and Gerry is quick to point this out, in addition to many very fine players, he had Brian Propp in his lineup. He considers him the finest player he ever coached. Propp returned the compliment. In an email dated January 19, 2011 he wrote:

I'd be happy to comment on Gerry James and his coaching in Melville. First of all, I was a young 15 year old playing in the Jr. B league. I had great line mates with Kelly Dean and Dwayne Tuberfield. Craig Stokes was a defenseman and Larry Mazur our goalie. We had a number of older leaders on the team but for me it was a new experience.

Gerry James was ahead of his time in coaching because of his conditioning methods and team play books. I believe that he learned those from the CFL football league. Gerry gave our team a package of team plays, from break outs, neutral zone play, offensive and defensive plays, to power-play and penalty killing plays. Everyone on the team had to know the plays by different numbers so that our defense-men could call out a number and everyone would know the breakout. It was like a quarterback play book. That really helped me adjust to the older league.

Gerry's conditioning drills in practice were extreme and I'll always remember wearing the army weight belts while we practiced. It built up our conditioning so that we were in better shape than players on all the other teams.

Gerry always wore different hats and caps to games and was very colorful. He demanded a lot from the players but also treated us all very well and especially guided me as a young player. He gave me a great opportunity to play in all situations which helped my confidence and taught me how to play a great two way hockey game.

I always look at Gerry as the coach who gave me a great start in my hockey career. I have great respect for him. It was nice to see him at the Melville Millionaire 100 years of hockey event in 2008. Tell him I say hello and wish him my best.

Thanks, Propper

During his career Brian Propp became one of the all-time great players in the NHL. In 1999 he was named to the MasterCard Canadian Junior All-time Team, which included Mario Lemieux, Guy Lafleur, Bobby Orr, Denis Potvin and Bernie Parent, a starting lineup to warm any fan's heart.

I imagine Brian Propp is a lot like Gerry, his old mentor, when it comes to tooting his own horn. He's quick to credit others for his own successes. In team sports that's the way it should be, but it is worth remarking that as a rookie on the Melville Millionaires Brian Propp shattered the SJHL scoring record with 76 goals and 92 assists for 168 points in 57 games. Gerry, of course, would attribute this rather amazing feat to Brian's innate skills, and Brian would likely give a bow to his teammates and coach. "Pass it on."

I suspect such respect is a marriage of the best qualities of all of them.

Brian Propp went on to play over 1000 games in his fifteen year NHL career, mostly with the Philadelphia Flyers (although he did have short spells with Boston, Minnesota and Hartford), and to score over 1000 points. Playing alongside Wayne Gretzky and Mario Lemieux, he helped Canada win the Canada Cup in 1987. In 1993, while playing in Switzerland, he helped Team Canada win the Spengler Cup. Some of the parallels between Gerry's and Brian Propp's careers are intriguing. That the two have such respect for each other is not unexpected.

What is surprising, although probably far less so than I seem to want to suggest, is that the beginning of this branch of Gerry's story has its origins in what is often referred to as Saskatchewan's smallest city: Melville. Legally, Melville doesn't even qualify for municipal status but that doesn't appear to have stood in the way of someone at some point declaring the place a city. Perhaps because there is a hint of the maverick in this unilateral declaration, Marg and Gerry speak of the "city" of approximately 4000 people with great affection. The couple was surprised by how quickly they fitted in.

Melville is a railway hub, with buildings and houses on a smallish scale, which the couple preferred. It is a town of necessity. Unlike Yorkton — and this is not intended to be judgemental — Melville has utility; and a function of utility is the common ground, the comfort and sense of belonging, that people who live there feel. The network of rails that runs from the hub out into the prairie emptiness, beyond the outskirts of town, is their baby. Even in this day of satellites orbiting willy-nilly about the earth, the rails keep our terrestrial lines of transport and communication open.

K.C., Marg's and Gerry's elder son, was so impressed with the railway — what young boy hasn't been caught up in the spell of powerful diesel engines shunting boxcars around a yard — he applied for a job with the CNR. The railway also passed through Yorkton so he had been twice bitten by this commotion of sound and movement, like a choreographed dance on rails. Following in his father's footsteps, K.C. told a little white lie about his age. Even though he was only seventeen, he was hired by the CNR and has worked for the railway in Melville for over thirty years. Now an engineer, a job he prizes, he continues to live in the larger centre of Yorkton and make the commute up Highway 10 to work.

What Gerry remembers best about Melville are the people. They were generous and totally unpretentious, but, more importantly, they were the most enthusiastic fans he had ever encountered. First of all, they were knowledgeable, they knew how the game should be played and Gerry loved that; second, their passion was amazing.

"As a player, if your hair didn't stand on end, you weren't alive. The rink, filled with devoted and boisterous fans, was a madhouse," he said, just as he imagined ancient Rome's coliseum was for the chariot races. Games often drew capacity crowds, especially for the epic struggles against Yorkton.

The annual major hockey event was the back-to-back holiday brou-ha-ha held on Boxing Day and New Year's Day between the two neighbouring towns. These clashes were always sellouts. In both rinks, the cheering from the fans raised the rafters. You could almost feel the building breathe, in and out, with each rush of either team up and down the ice towards goal. The rivalry was crazy and fun. Pandemonium ruled the day.

During his first year, from May to September, Gerry supplemented his income from coaching by working at the local municipal golf course. This part-time job suited him perfectly. While he liked the extra distance his drives got off the frozen turf towards the end of September, he relished the winter ahead. He was particularly happy about assuming responsibility for coaching as well as scouting for the junior hockey team. The good citizens of Melville did all in their power to make the James family, Gerry especially, feel welcomed and comfortable.

The rink itself, built in the old hangar-style out of large timbers and metal, was quite beautiful.

"You wouldn't expect that," Gerry said, "but it had character. Every year, it was lovingly painted. Most of the seating, for over two thousand fans, was at both ends, high up, where everyone had a good view of the action, coming and going. At either side there were about ten rows of traditional seats.

"All in all," Gerry and Marg concluded, "it was a great place to play and watch hockey."

For the first year, Gerry commuted the twenty-five miles (about forty kilometers) from Yorkton to Melville, but once the family was able to find a large enough home they relocated. For the first time they felt as though they were in a state of arrival rather than departure. The question was whether or not Gerry could get accustomed to the idea of a permanent home. In the second year, Marg took a position as a dental assistant.

To earn extra income over the next four years, Gerry would buy smaller, older (at times almost derelict) houses and renovate them over the summer, during his time off. Once again he mentioned the scale of the town, how it suited his eye. He enjoyed manual labour and managed to turn enough of a profit from each remodeling job to keep bread on the table. "At that time coaches were paid pretty poorly. When I left Melville, I was only earning $15,000 a year, barely enough on which to get by, especially when you don't receive benefits and a retirement package. My son earned more working for the railway. I'm not complaining, but essentially we were just making ends meet."

While Gerry still had an executive to whom he was accountable, no one interfered with his running of the team. Free to attempt new coaching strategies, Gerry was in heaven. Occasionally he was offered advice but it was given in the right spirit; he wasn't being told how to do his job. Thus, what happened on the ice pleased everyone. The team performed well, attendance at the games was good, which meant revenues kept everyone happy, and the young players were learning to play the game.

Well, most of them were.

Gerry told the story of Bob Morrell, a nice kid and potentially a good player, who was a little slow to learn from the lesson he was about to receive. Bob, who was a defenseman, broke his hand in a game early in the season.

"Sorry coach," Bob said, "I can't play, my hand is broken."

Always sympathetic, Gerry told him, "Bob, you'll play."

So Bob continued to play, responding in the way Gerry

respected and expected his players to do. Over the next few weeks Bob's plus/minus dropped from -20 to -5, largely because he now passed the puck.

Every time he moved his fingers or tried to grip his stick, pain shot through his hand and he quickly realized the faster he got rid of the puck the less his hand hurt. Everything about his game improved. Gerry was delighted. Bob had seen the light! Gerry figured his coaching was finally working. But as Bob's hand healed, he started to carry the puck more and more and pass less. Soon he was back to a -20 playing his same old undisciplined game. Even so, everyone on the team was contributing and dedicated. They were a joy to coach.

Gerry gave Bob credit for heart. "In spite of the pain, he held up his end of the bargain. You can't ask for anything more," Gerry suggested.

For Gerry enjoyment was critical. "The energy you muster to do more than should be humanly possible can be staggering when your enthusiasm isn't bridled," he observed. Even though the Millionaires were a Tier 2 team, the quality of the hockey was gold standard; a pleasure to watch.

After his first three seasons in Melville, Gerry felt secure in his role as coach. If he needed help, there was always someone ready to pitch in, without complaint. When he was away scouting, Jerry Hudy would take over and run the team. Gerry felt as though he were part of a larger family.

But as he entered his fourth year, the executive brought in someone else to manage the club, on the pretext that this would free Gerry to do more "bulldog" work scouting players. Gerry felt slighted and his dream of owning and controlling his own team became more and more appealing. No matter how well he was treated, he couldn't get the idea out of his mind of having complete control over the team and its and his destiny.

Perhaps everyone desires this sort of unlimited freedom even though our bodies and our circumstances constantly remind us of how bound we are to the needs of others; to our own expectations; to time itself.

Although no one said anything specifically about the quality of play, in his fifth year as coach the team was soon mired in the middle of a mediocre season. "No coach is better than the players he's got. And we were poor that year if not a bit of a dead duck. No one was to blame here, these were good people, good kids, but talent is hard to come by."

So, just as he reached a personal comfort zone, a combination of doubt and the temptation of ownership cropped up. The Yorkton franchise was in turmoil and for sale. As he considered the prospect of becoming an owner, Gerry realized he would be coach, manager and the executive body, all rolled into one. No-one could say squat, zilch, zip about how he ran the club. It would be his show to run. This suited him perfectly. As the season ended, in April, Gerry, with Jerry Bulitz as his partner, jumped at the opportunity to purchase the faltering Yorkton franchise.

As this episode in his story unfolded, the irony of his decision confounded a lot of people. As the coach of Melville he had done everything in his power to mock his old team, including winning most of what could be termed their "derby games". The rivalry between the two teams always drew a standing-room-only crowd and the winners of these games exercised their bragging rights. Gerry was quick to get in his jabs. At every opportunity, he found a way to stick it to his old team.

Three years earlier, when a motion had been made to the governors of the league to close down the Regina Silver Foxes franchise because they weren't competitive, Gerry entered the debate by remarking that the league should keep the Silver Foxes around so that the Yorkton Terriers could muster a few wins. He couldn't resist the temptation to taunt his old masters. His competitive nature once again reared its head. Egging them on, he made sure he was quoted in the local paper. He still had something to prove to his old community. After all, he remained their only winning coach and they had rejected him. They had dissed and dismissed him, somewhat unceremoniously. Now it seemed to his Melville supporters that he was abandoning them for the enemy. They wondered why he would want to return to a place where the executive had treated him so poorly.

There was no question Gerry angered — pissed off would be more precise — the entire city of Melville when he decided to buy their arch rivals, the Yorkton Terriers. There was no doubt that Gerry misread the mood and thoughts of the Melville team executive; they had no intention of sacking him, quite the contrary. Perhaps Gerry was forearming himself against disappointment by distorting reality, because the truth was the executive to a man was delighted with him as coach and begged him to stay on. But when Yorkton made it clear that they thought of him, along with Jerry Bulitz, as the perfect candidates for the new owners and coach of their franchise, he packed his bags.

❧

Yorkton was in trouble. Morale was low and team play was poor. Consequently, fan support was much weaker than it should have been. In Gerry's mind, if he put a decent team on the ice, attendance at home, as well as on the road, should go up. During his previous term as coach, he had twice managed to take the team through to the playoffs, in spite of all the bitching and backbiting; and the crowds had been reasonably good. They had drawn on average eight to nine hundred fans to a 2600 seat arena. Now, he figured, should he put together winning seasons, "they would come, in droves." There's nothing like a winner, or so he thought, to draw an audience. Also, the city had built an inviting new arena complex called the Agriplex.

As extreme as his return to Yorkton seemed to some, Gerry was determined to prove two things to those who were responsible for pushing him to resign as coach his first time around: they had made a huge mistake, he was a winner; and he knew a hell of a lot more than they did about the ins and outs of running and, more specifically, coaching a hockey team.

He wanted to prove that Watching "Hockey Night in Canada" once a week didn't qualify his critics as coaches. Listening to the "hot stove" sessions on television between periods didn't qualify them to pass judgment on his qualifications or to offer advice. As far as he was concerned, this pigheaded crew was too cocky. Hanging around the arena like young rink rats, breathing in the stone-cold, spirited air did not imbue them with hockey wisdom. While Gerry retained his zeal for the game, he felt his youthful passion had been reinforced by a more complex and mature dedication. Simply stated, he understood the game better. He was not a brawling charlatan as some seemed to want to characterize him. In many respects, hockey defined his personality. Hockey was in his soul and had been deep-rooted there from the time he took his first spin on the ice at the outdoor rink in Winnipeg.

Back in Yorkton, as one of the new private owners, Gerry led the Terriers to their first playoff competition in six years. On their last road trip against northern division teams, they had victories over the top three teams. In one of their final games of the season, they came within a whisker of beating the first place Moose Jaw Canucks of the southern loop. Yet all was not as happy and as blissful in Yorktonland as one would have expected from a winning franchise. "Grumpy" had entered their den.

On the ice that first year, the team fared reasonably well. They had a winning record, 32 wins, 26 losses and two ties to finish in third place. They lost in the semi-finals to Estevan, away, in the seventh game, 4 to 3. There was certainly no shame in what turned out to be a major turnaround season. According to Gerry, Yorkton was now playing a Gerry James style of hockey.

As Gene Krepakevich observed in his *25 years with the…Yorkton Terriers*, a history of the club:

> But James wasn't resting…above all James was a man of no contradiction. People either loved him or hated him. Gerry James didn't care which of the two it was.
>
> James exuded an air of unswerving confidence. His ability to turn the Yorkton Terriers, the league's perennial doormat, into a championship club, was never doubted.
>
> Perhaps his confidence in himself was responsible in determining the Terriers' destiny.

Krepakevich went on to attribute this success as follows:

> The majority of his early years had been spent in sports. He was on a winning Memorial Cup team. He had been the youngest CFL player at 17— playing for the Winnipeg Blue Bombers. As halfback and place-kicker, he had captured the league scoring title three different years and he won the Schenley Award, emblematic of the Most Valuable Canadian Player in the CFL, twice.
>
> James also played professional hockey with the Toronto Maple Leafs, earning the distinction of being the only play-

er ever, to play in the Stanley Cup and Grey Cup finals, all within six months.

Yes, the "man" had arrived.

When the team didn't quite perform to Gerry's unrealistic expectations, Krepakevich wrote "Sports has a way of humbling even the best of us."

Interestingly, throughout Krepakevich's description of James's era at the club, I sense a hint of envy and distaste. I know the two men didn't like each other but Krepakevich, it seems to me, was both excited by and disappointed by the Terrier's success under Gerry's leadership. How curious and tragic this deeply felt ambivalence. How sad when we are unable to celebrate someone else's achievements.

Performance off the ice was another matter. After just one year, the two new owners agreed to dissolve their partnership. Each man threatened to buy out the other but Gerry prevailed. Part of the problem was that their office, not much larger than a kitchen pantry, was crammed into a corner of the arena and they couldn't escape from one another. A place where both men should have been happy, in which they both should have felt like the masters of their own destinies, felt like a jail. With filing cabinets jammed up against the walls and their desks pushed together, they sat there, face to face, day in and day out. They couldn't agree on anything although Bulitz kept his nose out of the coaching side of things. From their senior men's team days, he knew better than to cross Gerry when it came to anything related to on-ice activity. But soon they were quarrelling about financial matters and management issues. They argued about who should write cheques and who should receive them.

On a more basic and childish level, they started to go after each other personally. Bulitz quickly learned how to get under Gerry's skin. From the minute Bulitz arrived at the office in the morning, he began clicking his ballpoint pen, in and out, in and out. Click click, click click. Simple but effective. "And the most irritating part of it," Gerry said, "he never used the damn thing." Ironically this is the sort of tactic Gerry would have resorted to had he been able to figure out how to annoy Bulitz, although his turning up every day was probably enough of an irritation.

"He wanted to get on my nerves," Gerry said. "And he succeeded."

This developing bitterness coupled with lukewarm reporters, a few of whom seemed to be constantly on the attack, pushed their relationship to the edge. One of the two owners had to go. Bulitz was the one to yell uncle.

In spite of all of these off-ice distractions, Bob Burak, who had been the Yorkton Terrier goalie for three of his four years as a junior, stated publicly that, "The high point of my SAJHL career had been the 1980 - 81 season." For the last two of his four years in the league, Gerry James was his coach — one season in Melville, the other in Yorkton.

Lin Orosz, a staff writer on a local paper, wrote: "The Lord created the earth in six days and then he rested. Gerry James had made the Yorkton Terriers into a hockey team after four exhibition games, and reflecting on last year's hockey team, some fans couldn't decide which task was the greater of the two."

The team was a hit and the players were responding to Gerry's coaching philosophy.

Another solid member of the team during the first two years of this new era was Joey Kocur whom Gerry had moved up from defense to right wing. "Like me," Gerry pointed out, "Joey could not skate backwards fast enough to play on defense."

Joey was a farm boy from Kelvington, a small town situated about ninety miles north of Yorkton. He came from a terrific family, Gerry recalled, very supportive of the entire team. Weather permitting, Joe senior and his wife Rita made the long trek down to Yorkton to attend every home game. Joe seldom said much, at least about what was happening on the ice, but one night, after the game, while Gerry and Joe were having a drink together in the Blueline Club at the rink, Joe asked Gerry why his son Joey got into so many fights. He seemed concerned. Gerry said he didn't know. Joe shook his head and that was that.

A year later, well into the new season, Gerry and Joe senior were once again sitting in the Blueline Club. Joe looked up at Gerry and asked, as if he had raised the subject first only just yesterday, why wasn't Joey fighting anymore? Again Gerry said he didn't really know. It wasn't a subject he had discussed with young Joey. Again the father seemed concerned, as if something were now missing in Joey's game.

Gerry suspected that Joey had heard that he had better improve his scoring stats for the scouts if he planned to move up to Tier 1 and then on to the NHL. The league had passed a new rule stating that if you fought you couldn't play the rest of the game. If you accumulated a certain number of game misconducts, then you got suspended for at least a game. If you weren't playing, there would be no stats to examine.

The kid Gerry had thought a bit lazy and spoiled proved he had the goods by scoring twenty goals. Eventually he became one half of the Bruise Brothers, playing on right wing for Detroit, opposite Bob Probert on left wing. As pleased as Gerry was for Joey's success, the moment he treasured most was his memory of Joe senior's puzzling expression of concern about Joey's willingness to fight. Gerry never did figure out which part of Joey's game had pleased Joe senior the most. He was a good man but reticent. Perhaps the answer was simple. Joe senior wanted to see his son play hockey, not sit in the penalty box.

While his players were showing restraint, Gerry was getting into trouble with the league and civic authorities. At an away game in Weyburn, a man in the stands emptied a cup of hot chocolate all over Gerry, who prided himself on his sartorial elegance.

At that time there was no protection between the benches and the fans. That worked both ways. Gerry leapt from behind the bench into the stands and gave the culprit a good thrashing. Shortly thereafter the police arrived. In addition to his reputation for being a bit of a hothead, they had all the evidence they needed to lay an assault charge against him. When he appeared in court a few months later, in mid-spring, the judge asked Gerry if he was in the habit of beating up on seventy-year-old men?

Gerry responded with his own question. "If you are seventy does that give you license to throw hot chocolate over other people, just because your hockey team is losing? Whatever happened to sportsmanship?"

"Just answer my question," the judge said.

Gerry was struck dumb.

"No," he said.

"Okay," the judge said looking down from where he sat on his judicial perch, "I appear to have made my point. From this time forward there will be no more beating up on old men, no matter what the circumstances. Am I clear? Behave yourself!"

He gave Gerry a conditional discharge.

Gerry contended the judge was as generous as he was because he knew how much the Weyburn fans enjoyed the sideshow. "Now," he told me, "when I shut my eyes all I recollect as I stood there and looked up at him was his grizzled hair and his mouth twisted with mischief. I have a hunch, just a hunch mind you, he might have been a Yorkton supporter."

The complaint, the scolding, the courtroom banter all appeared in the sports reports of the local media. The next time the Terriers played in Weyburn, Gerry added an umbrella hat to his coaching ensemble.

The year following the incident the league insisted all rinks install plexi-glass around the players' boxes.

This measure did not stop Gerry's interaction with opposing fans. As in his days as a pro, he was happy to get into a trash-talking duel with players, officials and fans, no matter where they sat. He carried on verbal battles with anyone willing to take him on, whether on the ice, on the opposing bench, or in the stands. When drunken fans grabbed the plexiglass behind his bench, he rapped their knuckles with a stick.

On another occasion, a little later in his career, Gerry told the General Manager of a team in Humboldt that the next time they played each other his team was going to whip Humboldt's ass. Unfortunately, after the first period Humboldt was up by three or four goals. The General Manager, feeling smug, scoured the rink, found Gerry, and made a point of taking the piss out of him. Not to be outdone, Gerry chased the man around the rink, caught him and not only emptied a garbage can on to him but shoved the garbage can down over the poor man's head and shoulders, in the process breaking his glasses. After the game the RCMP took Gerry to the station to lay charges but the manager never turned up and Gerry was released. Again he had escaped repercussions for his short fuse.

In spite of his behaviour or perhaps because of it, his teams were a success. His antics, admittedly too frequent for the tastes of some, and unquestionably extreme in the minds of most, inspired his players. He had chutzpah, brass, balls, and the players admired and appreciated that.

For Gerry his actions were a simple matter of cause and effect; his eruptions a consequence of the laws of necessity.

As the sole owner of the Terriers, he led his gang of young charges to three successive playoffs — which included two finals and, finally, a provincial championship in 1983. All this happening in the span of three years. A remarkable record by any reckoning. Yet again the mood of supporters started to waver. Surprisingly and ironically, they seemed to take some pleasure in his failure as the coach of the South Division All-Star team. As Gene Krepakevich suggested in his history of the Terriers, after losing three out of four starts in the role, fans suggested that perhaps Gerry was a jinx and should forego further nominations to the position, especially if he was going to continue to load the team with Yorkton players. Gerry pointed out that it wasn't him who lost the once-a-year competition, that perhaps the malcontents should look to the players, but the grumbling and mumbling continued. No matter what he did, happiness, like a shadow on a cloudy day, appeared to elude many Yorkton fans.

Attendance over the first three years was respectable although not overwhelming, about twelve to thirteen hundred paying patrons per game, but as the fourth season rolled around, on the heels of the year the team won the championship, people seemed to grow blasé. Winning had become habit and habit led to resignation. There is nothing worse than being resigned to win. Fans started to take the team for granted.

To compound his problems as owner, the fee for the use of the rink was raised dramatically by the city council, to the highest user-fee by far in the league. This was the price the team had to pay for winning the provincial championship. Gerry pleaded his case with council and the Manager of the Agriplex. He argued that they were making it impossible for the franchise to survive, that the increased rent ate into the small profit he was making. Council was unconvinced. They thought he must be making money, hand over fist, a prospect they appeared to resent. That the team was a success was irrelevant. That winning a championship reflected well on the city mattered not a hoot. They were more concerned that Gerry might be profiting from this success and they wanted their share. They jumped to this conclusion even though few of them attended Terrier home games. Certainly the mayor of the day never showed his face in the rink although he made an "issue" of purchasing the first season ticket each year, a gesture he hoped to parlay into votes at the next civic election.

Maintaining the franchise in Yorkton finally reached a critical point. The rules of basic economics applied. If the team was going to survive, they either needed to draw larger crowds or the city fathers needed to drop their levy on ice time. That or Gerry would have to sell or move the team. He wasn't going to work for nothing. I should point out, though, that many of the city fathers didn't consider what Gerry did to be work. As far as they were concerned, he waved his wand or sprinkled fairy dust over the players and the team won.

By December of the fourth season (Gerry's third as sole owner) Linus Westberg, a good friend, suggested to Gerry that the situation was desperate, verging on calamitous, and called for some sort of dramatic promotional gimmick to increase attendance. Gerry was at a loss but Linus thought he had a great idea. He bet Gerry, over the airwaves, that his Yorkton team couldn't beat his old Melville club by more than two goals. At the time the Terriers were the best team in the league and the Millionaires were struggling near the bottom. If the Terriers couldn't beat the Millionaires by more than two goals, then at the end of the game Gerry would have to wheel Linus around the rink in a wheelbarrow. If the team won by a greater margin than two goals, then Linus would have to wheel Gerry around the rink. The bet was on.

The fans came, close to three thousand of them, a good representation from both cities. It was never clear who they were supporting, Gerry or Linus, but while the Terriers won, they won by only one goal. Victory was bitter-sweet. Gerry had to wheel Linus around the rink. Slip-sliding his way across the ice, he ended the show by dumping Linus unceremoniously into the net. No one had left the arena and they definitely enjoyed the spectacle.

On another occasion Linus tried to help Gerry along by adding to the legend: "Gerry was and still is quite a character," he wrote. "I can recall one of many incidents. It was a live telecast after a Yorkton – Melville game in Yorkton where Yorkton beat Melville on that occasion. In the interview following the game, I made the comment that his coaching left a lot to be desired. He, of course, did not take criticism lightly and said in return, 'And you, Linus, are a *horse shit* sportscaster' or words to that effect and walked off the set, leaving me quite startled. But the fans ate it up. The phones rang off the hook. Most wondered why I put up with the guy. Gerry was great copy!" From Gerry's perspective, Linus was equally great copy.

But without some sort of special attraction, some gimmick, attendance fell off. In retrospect, Gerry said he wished he could have afforded to hire Linus full-time to help with promotion. But finances were tight.

"Ironically," Marg observed, "winning had become boring and the fans stopped attending games. In fact, we often drew better crowds when we were losing." Following a loss, people gathered in the coffee shops up and down main street and bitched. With each loss, with each post-mortem, their expertise bloomed. Everyone became an expert. The air was blue. "At times," she said, "it seemed that fans had become so enamoured of losing, they were disappointed when the team won. Winning 'streaks' were insufferable. Unspeakable. Literally. What could you say about winning? Everyone went mute in the face of success and refused to turn up for games."

As soon as Gerry had become the principal owner of the club, Marg took over control of the Booster Club and the souvenir booth. Between the two of them, they clocked a lot of hours at the Agriplex; Marg knew as much as Gerry did about what needed to be done if the franchise was to survive.

Finally, as his fourth season as owner came to an end, a season in which the Terriers won the league and lost the championship, Gerry reached the end of his tether. Fans continued their bellyaching after the loss to Weyburn, a decidedly inferior team they felt, and yakkety-yakked about how they would have played the series, all the time muttering advice for the coach. But Gerry had a much more serious issue to cope with. He had explained repeatedly that under Council's rental terms the franchise was unsupportable. Yet they refused to compromise on their extortionate ice fee. They controlled the ice and as far as they were concerned Gerry either accepted their terms or he could take a hike. With all the assurance of a novice poker player, Council was convinced Gerry was bluffing. He wasn't!

So why the surprise, why the howls when he actually did pack up and leave?

"I didn't want to leave Yorkton," James said a few days later, just hours after the Estevan Bruins of the same SAJHL announced he would be their new coach and general manager. I didn't have a choice," the former Terrier owner-coach offered. "I could no longer remain an employee of the city, contributing approximately $35,000 last year so I could have a 'hobby'". He added that what the Terrier organization had done for the city went "unnoticed" and "unappreciated".

As we can see from Krepakevich's report in the club's history, Gerry would have preferred to stay in Yorkton. In essence, City Council had forced his hand, had forced him to sell. This complaint was borne out by subsequent owners and by the executive put in place when the team eventually went public again in 1985. Each successive managing body discovered they couldn't make ends meet while paying the excessive fees the city taxed the franchise for ice time. Each management team in turn, whether private or public, tried to get the lease lowered and each failed.

When Gerry took the position of coach in Estevan, he was accused by many in Yorkton of ransacking the Terriers but there is one thing to keep in mind. In the spring of 1984, when he accepted the job in Estevan, he still owned the Terriers and the players' contracts and playing cards, and his decision to sell several of them to Estevan was not only his prerogative as owner but also made good business sense. He could earn back some of his losses, in particular some of the exorbitant fees he had paid for ice time. Plus, as Krepakevich observed, Estevan's new coach would have a team with a Yorkton flavour, a team schooled in a Gerry James's style of hockey.

Gerry's decision to sell his players to Estevan did not sit well with the brains trust, with the czars of city hall, in Yorkton. The fact that he happened to benefit at both ends of the arrangement appeared to be an abuse of the spirit of the regulations, if not downright immoral. There was something inherently unfair about the transaction — the community was suddenly faced with losing their prized hockey team, not to mention a revenue source — which galled them. Yet technically and legally Gerry did not plunder the team at all, as some complained. He merely made a business decision, the sort of choice any one of them would have made under the circumstances. More importantly, the players themselves had strong feelings about what had transpired.

Gerry's announcement that he would be moving to Estevan, shocked many of his players. They indicated they would not return to the Terriers for the 1984 -85 season if Gerry wasn't in Yorkton. Greg Thomson called Gerry "the heart and soul of the Terriers"; Serge Poulin referred to him as the "backbone of the team"; while Mike Macmullen was more personal when he said "he made a man out of you, whether you wanted to be a man or not"; and Rick Bourassa put it bluntly, "if he's not back, I won't be either." This sentiment was echoed throughout the team. Brad Thompson predicted the future accurately when he said, "Yorkton's gonna miss Gerry James."

They did. Interestingly enough, old-timers tell Gerry this is the case even today, more than twenty-five years after his departure. They tell him, "The Yorkton Terriers have never been the same. They have never played with such energy."

I suspect there are far fewer fights and out-and-out team brawls as well, but that is another issue. Gerry was not only a good coach he was a strong motivator. Estevan recognized these strengths and at the all-star game that year they offered him a position with their club, but only if he was unable to come to an agreement with Yorkton City Council. One could argue that Yorkton was blinded by greed. They wanted a winning team that would pay for their new Agriplex, at any cost. The toll on Gerry and Marg, apparently, was incidental; was a necessary sacrifice. The couple could grind themselves down to the bone in exchange for the greater good. While there was much they loved about Yorkton, they refused to be town chumps. For Gerry and Marg the move to Estevan meant survival and a lot less aggravation. Both felt strongly that their relocation was positive even though they would once again have to work with a management team.

15 / Once A Coach...

Estevan hugs the border with North Dakota. Promotional materials from the city boast the sunniest and clearest skies in Canada. No mention is made of the cloud of coal dust kicked up by the local mines. Nor the flue gas, fly ash and greenhouse gases belched into the atmosphere by the coal-fired power plants. Amongst the farms and ranches, woven into an otherwise dry and arid landscape, oil rigs churn away like giant grasshoppers. Six thousand wells are located within a 160 kilometre radius of the city. During winter the temperature can drop to an average of -14° C and in summer, on muggy hot days, the mercury can settle around 27° C. Just warm enough to be uncomfortable. The other two seasons are brief and unpredictable.

"Energy City" as Estevan has come to be known doesn't sound too hospitable, but Gerry and Marg soon came to love the place. "The people," Marg said, "were special, but with all that ash and cloud floating in the air you wouldn't want to hang your laundry out on the clothesline for the day. Not unless you wanted to add to your grey mood."

When the "new" Estevan team put up the impressive record of 44 wins against 18 losses and 2 ties to win the league during Gerry's first year as coach, the 1984-85 season, and then went on to win the provincial championship against Weyburn, the Weyburn coach said he wasn't at all surprised. He figured his team had lost the league and the championship to two teams from two different cities. Hardly fair, he pointed out. They had ganged up on the rest of the league.

True enough, Gerry had built his new Estevan team around a core of five players from his old Yorkton team and that team had won 46 games the previous year. The reality, though, was that no matter how skilled the players, performance did not happen in a vacuum. A good coach gave a team eloquence, an expressiveness, it otherwise lacked.

Mind you, as with any team, Gerry inherited a character or two. Darwin "Dewey" Sommerville, son of a farming family from Brandon, was one such original. Dewey was six foot five and weighed approximately 245 pounds. In those days he was big by hockey standards. He also wore a size 15 skate. I imagine him being like a giant Douglas fir from the west coast, roots spread in the middle of a flat prairie grassland.

Gerry's first formal business with Dewey was as a "no show" at training camp. Gerry had heard lots of stories about Dewey but being AWOL did not fit his MO. When Gerry finally tracked Dewey down, he found him in jail. Apparently he had been in the pub and someone had teased him about the size of his feet. His roots. That was more than just cause in Dewey's mind to start a rumble. After Dewey had straightened out his critic and accomplices, the police asked him to "cool off" for a couple of nights in the lockup. When Dewey finally showed up for training camp, Gerry made it clear that being an instigator would no longer be his role if he wanted to make the team.

Dewey, who most of the time was far too bashful to say anything to anybody, looked at Gerry and said, "They shouldn't have said anything about my feet."

What Gerry soon learned was that Dewey could handle the puck reasonably well and that no-one but no-one would go near him when he was on the ice. Happily, Dewey actually responded enthusiastically to the idea that he was being asked to "play" hockey. Space opened up around him, almost as if he projected a force field that repelled other bodies. This gave Dewey an advantage which more than made up for his lack of skills. He could free wheel. And he did.

Gerry was also fortunate that he now had a Board, guided by Tom More, which gave him free rein on the ice. Tom, who had been instrumental in bringing Gerry to Estevan, was always available to talk and Jean Goertz, who was secretary and treasurer, signed cheques whenever Gerry dropped by her home unannounced and in need of cash. "We laughed," he recalled, "because invariably I caught her in her old blue and tattered housecoat. My timing was impeccable. Often she was on her way out. To lunch. To a meeting. And yet, she was always there. Jean, Tom and Dr. Doug Blue were good and reliable allies."

The second season in Estevan was a duplicate of the first. The team won the southern circuit but lost in the provincial finals. Importantly for the executive, Gerry and the team he put on the ice had cleared off $60,000 of indebtedness. The team was operating in the black for the first time in years. Once again Marg and Gerry had worked their magic on a failing franchise.

The next two years were less rewarding. In his third year the team ended up mid-table but made the playoffs. For most of the new executive, this was a disappointment and not the sort of downward skid they had expected. Gerry attempted to tell them that until they put a sound scouting system into place, the team would suffer. "You need to keep an eye out for up-and-coming talent. You need to know who to enter on your list," he explained. "It was impossible to be both coach and scout."

But the executive was unwilling to spend money on

scouting; they couldn't understand why he was unable to travel about the countryside, when he wasn't otherwise occupied with coaching, in search of young talent. Once again attendance dropped and the financial picture began to look a bit bleak.

In November of 1987, Moose Jaw was looking for a new coach. Gerry knew the team had problems and that moving there might be unwise, but he was no longer confident about his place in Estevan's future plans.

Before making the decision to move shop again, he first went to the Past President of Estevan, Dr. Doug Blue, a man he liked and trusted, to get the lay of the land. He wanted to know his status with the Estevan club. Quickly it became apparent that what he suspected was true. He was not on a sound footing with the new executive and Dr. Blue recommended he seriously consider the job in Moose Jaw. To a man the executive of Estevan thought Gerry was overpaid even though he had had a couple of his most successful campaigns at the helm of the Bruins. Unfortunately, in their most recent run, the team was languishing near the bottom of the table.

In December 1987, Gerry and Marg moved out of the apartment they had lived in for the past three and a half years and headed down the road to Moose Jaw. Gerry had an eerie feeling this was not the best move but his instincts told him he was damned if he did and damned if he didn't. He was tipping into an unmapped country. Like darkness, the unknown can be exciting; can pull you into its vortex, as long as you don't fear it. Perhaps mistakenly, Gerry knew no fear. He wasn't going to run.

When the club signed Gerry on, they included Marg in his contract. She was to be the new office manager. The executive would soon drop the General Manager and ask Gerry to assume responsibility as both Coach and GM. This meant Marg's services became doubly important when it came to the day-to-day business side of things.

Marg was shocked with what she discovered about the office routine. For instance, the phone bill was over one thousand dollars a month when they took over the club. Everyone connected with the franchise, it seemed, felt it was their right to drop in to the arena and place a long distance call to wherever, whether it had to do with club business or not. "They could have been calling Timbuktu to order camel dung for their gardens for all I knew," Marg said.

Quickly the couple cracked down on this practice. Soon the phone bill was down to fifty dollars a month. Furthermore, when the club had been purchased from its Winnipeg owners, approximately two hundred Moose Jaw locals had contributed one thousand dollars each to finance the take-over. Four years later, they were all still reaping the benefits of their investment — free tickets to all the games with their rear ends parked in the best seats in the arena. Again, Gerry and Marg put a quick end to this drill. Everyone was going to have to pay to watch the Moose Jaw Warriors in action.

A loss of privileges angered everyone. Most of the old guard blamed Gerry for the team's dismal performance. No-one appeared remotely concerned that the team lacked talent. Nor were they willing to spend money to seek out new talent. That the city was on the edge, often within forty-eight hours of losing the franchise, didn't bother most of the original investors.

Driven to succeed, to keep the franchise viable, over the summer of 1988 Gerry and Marg canvassed the town for financial help. They got it, but not without a struggle, and not without alienating the entire executive.

Gerry lasted one season in Moose Jaw, from December 1987 to November 1988. Even though Moose Jaw was a larger city, with a population of around 35,000, and was surrounded by an abundance of good fishing lakes and rivers — Gerry loved fishing — this was not a happy time. Gerry was not there to sit back and fly-fish the rivers or soak up the benefits of the spa waters. Nor was he there to retire. He soon learned that the club had financial problems and team morale was poor. In short, the players were uninspired and low on talent — with a couple of exceptions, Lyle Odelein and Theoren Fleury, the latter of whom was undoubtedly the most difficult, not to mention hotheaded, player Gerry had ever coached.

Gerry had played with Theo's father, Wally, a man he had a high opinion of, as a senior on the Yorkton Senior team, but young Theo was cheeky, bordering on rude, and a challenge. He would not listen. Once on the ice, he ignored line changes and positional play. He was his own master. For Gerry this attitude was unacceptable; he had been raised and taught to view hockey as a team sport. "All I can tell you is that Theo was a pain in the ass. But skate! Boy could the kid skate.

"He was both fast and quick, and his lateral movement on ice was second to none. When he first came out onto the ice during practice, he left his laces undone, probably to strengthen his ankles. This was likely a trick he learned from his dad."

While Theo was growing up, Wally maintained the rink in Russell, Manitoba, and Theo got a lot of ice time. He had used the time well because he skated like a dream. Regrettably, Gerry pointed out, he was also a selfish player, something Gerry found impossible to abide.

For the first time, a team coached by Gerry James finished with a losing record: 27-42-3.

One incident from this period remains acutely poignant in Gerry's mind. The team was returning home from an evening game in Brandon. The Trans-Canada Highway was covered in about six to eight inches of heavy, wet slush. The driver was doing a yeoman's job of keeping the bus in the deep ruts left by earlier traffic when suddenly something nudged the vehicle off course and out of the tracks. Soon the bus was slip-sliding sideways towards the edge of the road. The driver quickly spun the wheel and steered the bus down the bank into a gully twenty feet deep, and then up against a farmer's fence.

"Without rolling the damn thing!" Gerry said. "His quick thinking saved us. I hate to contemplate what would have happened had we done a couple of rolls. Of course, all of the players remembered what had happened to a team from Swift Current on their way home from a road trip. Their bus had spun out of control on an icy road and rolled three or four times, killing several players.

"To a man when our team got off the bus you could read the relief in their faces. Quietly and gravely they thanked the driver and counted their blessings. No question, for each one of them this was their first brush with their own mortality. I don't mean to be heavy-handed about this experience, but suddenly hockey had a different priority in their lives."

Reminiscing about his time in Moose Jaw, Gerry had the following to say. "The biggest problem in Tier 1, and this runs throughout the league, is that the best players don't trust the weaker players and take on too much responsibility. This is not a question of character. Those who have an instinctive sense of the game, the ones likely to push on with their careers, want to shine; they don't want to be hauled down by the pack. So they begin to compensate. They begin to stray. When they see a mistake unfolding on the ice, they move to correct the problem. But when they do they leave their own position exposed. Of course, the system is compromised and the original error is compounded. The whole thing collapses. Any vestige of positional play disappears out the window. In a way, because they are strong characters, they want to help, but in doing so they create a weakness throughout the system. And without a system, you don't have a team, at least a functional team. It's like playing chess without a plan. Sacrifice the pawns aimlessly and the king is in peril.

"This is the major problem I inherited when I arrived in Moose Jaw, in addition to poor management, a lack of attendance and the fact that the team was losing money. For me, the issue was trust. The players lacked trust, which in my view will always destroy a team. You see this over and over in professional sport. I admit this might explain why I had a problem with Theo, although as we all learned later, from Theo himself, he had additional demons to deal with. His entire story saddens me."

After he was released by the Moose Jaw Warriors, fired for the first time, a future for Gerry James in hockey seemed highly improbable. For one thing, he had priced and talked himself out of the market. Clubs could retain the services of a young, up-and-coming coach for much less than they would have to pay him. Usually these aspiring coaches were not married and therefore had none of the financial obligations a man with a large family had. Nor did they feel tied down. Their only commitment was to their careers which made them much more pliable and receptive to direction from owners and upper management.

As Gerry and Marg gazed dreamily into their hockey futures, Gerry had no option but to accept the reality that his time was over. To take less than he deserved to do the job properly meant compromising financially and sacrificing his values.

⁂

Everyone who plays in a sport under an inspiring and caring coach benefits, of this there can be little doubt. Some go on to attain greater heights in the sport itself while others apply what they've learned about teamwork, to their personal goals. Gerry can look back and take pride in how well all his players did. Some went on to successful university careers, others went into business and professional careers and a few made the leap to the big show and had careers in hockey.

Those who played professional hockey include: Dave Brown (Philadelphia, Edmonton and San Jose); Joey Kocur (Detroit and New York Rangers); Lyle Odelein (Montreal, New Jersey, Columbus and Chicago); Theo Fleury (Calgary and New York Rangers); Mike Eagles (Quebec Nordiques, Chicago, Winnipeg Jets, Washington); Blair Atcheynum (St Louis, Nashville and Chicago); Alan May (Washington, Dallas and Calgary); Frederic Chabot (mostly minor and European hockey but he did have short stints with Montreal and Los Angeles); Chris Lindberg (Canadian National team, Calgary and Quebec but spent most of his time playing in Europe); and Brian Propp (principally with Philadelphia). Like any good coach, he had the distinction of cutting a player who later proved how fallible Gerry's judgement could be. Gerry cut Kelly Buchberger, who not only had a successful NHL career in Edmonton and Los Angeles but has distinguished himself as an assistant coach with the Edmonton Oilers. Rob Daum became head coach at the University of Alberta and Brent McEwen coached Tier 1 junior teams and university hockey in Saskatchewan. He also had a successful coaching career in Europe. Don Walchuk, who Gerry asked to come out and play for the Millionaires, declined his offer. He explained to Gerry that curling was his passion and he hoped to make a name for himself in that sport. In addition to winning briers, Don went on to become a world champion curler.

One final observation. Gerry's Melville team still holds the record for most goals in the SJHL in a season, 479; and for the most short-handed goals in a season, 30. In any world these are impressive statistics.

Do the achievements of others reflect back on the man who in some way provided a model for their growth and development? If so, and I think they do, the rough and tumble side of the game is certainly a part of Gerry's legacy. His ex-players have tallied up some pretty impressive numbers in the penalty box. But this simplistic characterization of Gerry and his protégés is shallow and probably exaggerated. Teams do not win championships by being thugs and bullies. A Gerry James-coached player is probably tough and determined but those qualities coupled with success argue for a far more complex set of values such as trust, cooperation and compassion. Significantly, most parlayed what they learned from playing hockey into impressive careers and lives, on and off the ice.

҂

As a coach Gerry liked to quote Lloyd Percival, the fitness expert, from his *The Hockey Handbook*, on the relationship between parents and their children in any sporting activity. Towards the end of his coaching career, Gerry made a point of submitting that list of ten points to the parents of his players. What follows is largely in Percival's words although Gerry has paraphrased him in a couple of places.

Gerry prefaced the list by saying: Hockey is meant for everybody — players, coaches and parents. If we are to play better hockey, everyone must help, but especially the parents. A youngster spends a lot more time with his parents than he does with his coach, and their influence on him is bound to be greater. In a way, they are his first and most important coaches, so the job of improving hockey is more theirs than anybody's. Maybe your child will be a great athlete one day, and maybe he won't, but he will be a better athlete if you follow these rules. And if you follow these rules, he'll have more fun participating in the sport of his choice.

1. Make sure your child knows that win or lose, you love him. Let him know that you appreciate his effort and that you won't be disappointed in him if he fails. Be the person he can look to for support and reinforcement.

2. Be completely honest with yourself about your child's athletic capability, his competitive attitude, his sportsmanship and his level of skill.

3. Be helpful, but don't coach your child on the way to the game or at the breakfast or dinner table. Non-stop advice and criticism isn't helpful.

4. Teach your child to enjoy the thrill of competition. To be "out there trying". To be constantly working to improve his skills, to take the physical bumps and come back for more. Don't tell him that winning doesn't count because it does and he knows it. Instead help him to develop a healthy competitive attitude, a feel for competing, for trying hard and for having a good time. Enjoyment is first and foremost.

5. Try not to live your life through your child. Most of us both win and lose. We've all been frightened and, on occasion, we've had to adjust our expectations. Don't expect any more or better of him. Don't assume he feels the same way you do, or that he has the same goals. Don't push him in the direction that will give you the most satisfaction.

6. Don't compete with your child's coach. A coach may become a hero to him for a while, someone who can do no wrong, and you may find that hard to take. Or your child may become disenchanted with the coach. Don't

side with him against the coach. Talk to him about the importance of learning how to handle problems and how to react to criticism. Try to help him understand the necessity for discipline, rules and regulations.

7. Don't compare your child with the other players on his team. Try to be honest with him. Don't lie to him about his capabilities as a player. If you are overly protective, you will perpetuate his problems.

8. Get to know your child's coach. Make sure that you approve of his attitudes and ethics. A coach can be very influential and you should know what his values are so that you can decide whether or not you want them passed on to your child.

9. Remember that children tend to exaggerate when they are praised and when they are criticized. Temper your reactions to the stories he brings home.

10. Teach your child the meaning of courage. Some of us can climb mountains but are afraid to get into a fight. Some of us can fight without fear but then turn to jelly at the sight of a bee. Everyone is frightened of something. Courage isn't the absence of fear, courage is learning to perform in spite of fear. Courage isn't getting rid of fear, it's overcoming it.

Hockey can be fun, but it isn't always fun, any more than school or work is always drudgery. It depends on the attitude of the people involved — the players, coaches and parents. We must realize that young people are naturally curious and eager to learn. We can teach skills and technique to young players that will contribute to their enjoyment, to their development as players and to the general improvement of the sport.

❧

Recently, on a Wednesday night, Gerry and I attended the practice of the Parksville Pee Wee Generals, a team coached by Grant Hicks and Jim Hykaway. Grant was running a pass and release drill off the boards when he noticed Gerry and me standing in the bleachers behind him. He came over to greet us and immediately Gerry was on his case. Gerry wanted to know why Grant was running three-on-one breakaways. Grant hesitated, then fumbled out a reply that had something to do with penalty killing. Gerry responded, "Waste of time. Three on ones rarely happen. If ever. Not worth the time."

Everything he explained made good sense, but from what I could see, all the kids were doing something, were active, and they were clearly enjoying themselves. This in itself seemed a major accomplishment. Keeping seventeen eleven- and twelve-year-olds occupied is a major feat.

Gerry also remarked to Grant that he was impressed by how well the kids skated, especially one. "*She's* one of two girls on the team," Grant pointed out, "and she's by far our best skater."

After a couple of skating drills the practice ended and we all gathered in a very smelly dressing room, all sweat and no fresh air, so the kids could meet Gerry and Gerry could tell them a couple of anecdotes from his own career. I felt like I was suddenly caught in a time warp. It didn't seem to matter to these kids that Gerry had played the game over fifty years ago or that he was a wizened old codger from days before even their parents' memories began. He had the good sense to bring along a couple of his own hockey cards from when he played with the Leafs and Grant awarded them to the players who were able to guess the number Gerry wore on his jersey. He had their attention. Gerry had four numbers, 19, 16, 11 and 6 over his career with Toronto, so nailing down the correct number even for those in the know would have been difficult. "Numbers in the old days," he explained, "were handed out based on when you started playing for the team."

I wanted to add to Gerry's explanation what Larry Robertson had told me, that originally numbers were assigned by which berth you slept in when you travelled by train. Upper berths got the higher numbers, lower berths got the lower numbers.

A couple of delighted kids went home with a signed card each.

When they saw his Grey Cup ring, though, that's when the mouths dropped. Quickly they grabbed their cell phones and began snapping pictures of the ring. Then one kid wondered aloud if he could try the ring on and soon they had formed a scrum around Gerry and they were all slipping the ring off and on. Chests swelled, eyes brightened. Obviously what mattered for the kids was this brief brush with fame. They clearly liked Gerry, his gruff manner and gentle awkwardness as he shifted on his mechanical knees. Somehow they knew he was one of them.

A short time later Gerry attended a General's playoff game and when I called and asked him how things had gone, he sounded a bit disappointed. "What shocked me was how poorly they skated. At first I wondered why and then I realized they didn't know where they should be on the ice or what they should be doing. Clearly positional play is important but you can't let that affect your skating. I used to tell my pee wee players to skate their hearts out, go for it, and then tell them later where they might think about going. It's skating without the puck that's key to hockey, not standing like a stone statue and waiting for the puck to come to you. Skate, skate, skate," he said. "Do you think I should phone Grant?"

He paused.

"I think I should phone Grant!"

The coach has never left the man. Nor has the kid from those outdoor rinks back in Winnipeg. I think I see him slipping on his skates and taking a spin around the rink. He is being chased by Gordie Howe and Rocket Richard. Bobby Orr has joined in on the play, Brian Propp has his stick on the ice, ready to take a pass. Sidney Crosbie and Wayne Gretsky fly down the wings. Bobby Baun just shouldered Stan Mikita into the boards. Frank Mahovlich yells from his seat in the Senate that hockey is truly Canada's game. The anthem sings out from the organ, followed by a rising riff of scales. Dave Keon and George Armstrong break in on goal. Jean Béliveau turns away, gracefully, always gracefully from the corner boards, and tells Gerry, "You should stick to football. Football is your game." Gump Worsley leans on his net again, his elbow resting on the top pipe of the goal, daring someone to shoot.

The game is on.

16 / West Coast & Retirement

I'm trying to imagine what Gerry must have felt when he was fired for the first time in his life. Was it guilt? Impotence? Humiliation? Somehow I doubt it. More likely it was anger and a sense of betrayal. Relief is another possibility, I guess, although if what you have been doing is definitive, is precisely what you were hired to do in the first place, that response seems unlikely. Mind you, it is important to recognize that Gerry was somewhat naïve. In spite of all of his blow and bluster, he still is. In his world, honesty pretty much trumps everything. I suspect he was surprised by the way he was treated. He would not have seen or paid much heed to the ways in which his actions offended or antagonized others. In his view, what he said or did to upset others was a natural response to stupidity or selfishness. He left little room for compromise. Presto, the only surprise is that he had not been fired sooner.

In the past he had always seen the inevitable coming. This time, though, in spite of all the signs to the contrary, he held onto his conviction that he was doing his best for the Moose Jaw team. He felt there was enough talent on the ice to make it to the playoffs, which the team did at season end, without Gerry, but the players needed time to mature. The executive was not about to give him or his players that time. It is probable his head was on the chopping block and the axe hovering above his neck even as he began his second season with the team.

Gerry's stature as a sports icon was secure, or should have been, so I can't imagine he felt failure. But there are no guarantees so perhaps doubt started to gnaw away at what was only a veneer of certainty. Self-confidence can erode quickly when left swimming in a persistent corrosive. Hockey politics, as caustic as any human pastime, especially as you climb the ladder from Tier 2 to Tier 1 and so on, can eat out the heart of the most committed enthusiast.

To be suddenly disconnected from what had defined him since he was a young boy must have been wrenching. Over the next few months, from November of 1988, when he was fired, to June of 1989, Gerry lapsed into a serious depression. This is not a topic he is willing to discuss, probably because he still sees it as a sign of weakness, but Marg knows better and says those months were the most miserable in their married life.

No matter what she said or did, Gerry disappeared into a dark and remote place. Outrage bubbled beneath the surface. As Marg talked about this brief period in their lives I noticed how white Gerry had become. I know he felt embarrassment if not shame even though what happened to him had nothing to do with any mistake or failure of his own making that I can see. Maybe whatever guilt he was feeling — and for some reason I feel there was some — had more to do with how he treated Marg during this period of introspection than with anything connected to hockey and how he was treated.

Marg said, "When you don't have a job you feel like you've lost your independence. You're no longer your own person. I guess we were lucky that by this time all the kids had left home. Imagine trying to explain to a young family why their father is lurking about the house, day in and day out. Why he isn't going off to work. In that sense I guess we were fortunate."

Over the next few months Gerry wrote away to every team in the NHL offering his abundant services as a scout. No one responded. He lacked connections and he knew his success in Tier 2 junior hockey would not have even registered with the "big boys." Suddenly he had an additional reason to feel disappointment and rejection. He was out of the loop, essentially a non-entity on the hockey map.

Through a particularly cold winter he spent much of his time pacing the streets of Moose Jaw and, when he tired of that, he visited the library. Lost in thoughts he refused to share with anyone, he tramped two miles into town through deep snow in the dead of a prairie winter. Temperatures that winter were not bitterly cold, Marg recalls, but the sky seemed interminably gloomy. For hours Gerry sat staring at pages of print, absorbing a new world of ideas, places and people. He began to read ravenously, about anything and everything. I don't think this was an act of indulgence, a reaction to feeling sorry for himself, I think he was genuinely attempting to figure out why he was always the victim of these little, in-bred conspiracies.

Hockey was, and probably still is, a hive of petty politics. People want the glory that comes with a winning franchise but they refuse to pay the piper. At first, while they are happy to have a new coach in their midst, invariably, it seems, they lose trust in that person without ever stopping to consider the possibility that their own lack of support is the source of what they judged to be a failure. As quickly as their noses go out of joint, they rotate coaches in and out with the hope of finding the warlock with the right spells or magical potions. Coaches are the easy scapegoats.

For the first time in their lives Gerry and Marg were living on unemployment insurance. The couple stayed on in Moose Jaw because they felt they had nowhere else to go, thus prolonging a cycle they needed to escape. Day by day they felt increasingly trapped. The worst thing, Marg says, was that Gerry stopped talking, to her and to everyone else. For six months, they glided through their lives in a state of suspension.

As adults, when we suffer the anguish of a loss, we tend to linger in the past, too often expecting a reprieve. We live in regret rather than embracing the next adventure, the next opportunity. I think this may have been Gerry's problem. Hockey had always been a part of his life and now he wanted to press the replay button. Instead he needed to get on with the next chapter in his life.

Then one day, during the late spring of 1989, Marg read an ad in a local paper: "Caretaker Manager needed for Regina apartment complex." Luckily Marg knew a bit about the business. While Gerry had been coaching in Estevan, she had worked part-time as a bookkeeper for a property management company. She wrote off in response to the ad and the next thing they knew they had moved out of Moose Jaw and were managing an apartment building in central Regina. Importantly, they were no longer dependent on the government dole. This brought back a feeling of dignity. Living on the dole had not sat well with either of them.

Gerry threw himself into the job. Even though they were just scraping by, he set about fixing up the place as if it were his own. The restoration work he had done in Melville came in handy. He planted a garden at the entrance and repaired all the visible eyesores. He wanted the tenants to feel pride in the place where they lived.

Four months passed. Then one afternoon, Ambrose Reschny, who owned a property management company that managed the building next door, walked into their lives. He came up to Gerry, introduced himself and wondered out loud if Gerry and Marg would be interested in caretaking a co-op building his company managed in south Regina. His clients were fussy and lazy and he hadn't been able to find anyone to do the job to his and his clients' satisfaction. As Gerry knelt in his new garden, Ambrose made a grand gesture with a sweep of his hand and told Gerry how impressed he was with the improvements he had watched Gerry make over the past couple of months to the grounds and building they now stood in front of. He offered the couple accommodation in the co-op building and, to Gerry's surprise, a decent monthly income.

A deal was struck and Gerry and Marg moved into the co-op where they lived for the next year. "Even so," Gerry observes, "as a caretaker there is always a feeling of impermanence. You don't own your own home. In the back of your mind, you feel like a nomad. A drifter."

Neither of them was comfortable with this sort of lifestyle so they decided then and there that they had to establish a goal, a goal to save up enough money to buy a piece of property and eventually build a retirement home. "There is no question in my mind," Gerry says, "that this helped to solidify our relationship."

"Such as it is," Marg says, laughing. "Fifty-seven years with the same man can seem like several lifetimes. Fifty-seven years. Imagine! Who would have thought?"

Suddenly sports no longer dominated their lives. While Gerry missed the camaraderie, the competition, the crowds, he was ready for a change. The decision to dedicate themselves to saving enough money to retire to a home they owned, Gerry says, in a place of their own choosing, was one of the best things he and Marg ever did as a couple. They faced the challenge with all the tenacity Gerry had displayed in his athletic careers.

"I put my head down and went for it!" Gerry says. "I don't think I have ever been as focused or as obsessed."

There was a tacit understanding between the couple that

everything they did over the next few years would lead to this goal.

There would be no wavering. They put their social lives on hold. They did not travel. They gave no explanations and made no apologies. They lived inside a bubble, and were determined that for once nothing was going to pop it.

People forget that until well into the 1970s most professional athletes were earning a range of incomes comparable to all of their contemporaries, whether those contemporaries were mechanics, salesmen, lawyers, loggers, doctors, builders, fishermen, farmers, whatever. Playing football or hockey was a way to earn a living. No-one in sports earned the stratospheric salaries of today's athletes. Granted, it was a great way to pay the bills but that's all it did. "On our salaries," Gerry explains, "you weren't searching for an investment broker to hide your earnings from the tax collector or stash extra cash in an off-shore account. We weren't buying yachts and waterfront homes in Florida. Most of us worked at second jobs in the off-season. What many people don't realize is that until the 1970s the CFL paid players better salaries than the NFL. But by today's standards, they were still miniscule."

In 1989, after searching with friends for property in Winnipeg, Gerry and Marg eventually bought a lot in Nanoose Bay on Vancouver Island. This new development was where they were to build their future home. They had visited the island after attending Expo '86 in Vancouver and liked the climate, the vegetation and the rawness of the place. What they needed most, emotionally and for stability, was a plot of land that spelled out "new beginnings." Above all they liked the price so they made the purchase.

This steep sloping patch of granite and dirt on the edge of a golf course was covered in grand old trees — balsam, Douglas fir and arbutus — the last of which they would eventually have milled for flooring. For the time being, salal and Himalayan blackberry, sword-fern and Oregon grape flourished beneath the canopy of larger trees. In the future this would become a mixed garden of ornamental grasses, rhododendrons and indigenous plants.

In the meantime, they had set about putting away enough money to build a house. Moving away from the prairies would be difficult but the prospect of a new life in a totally different part of the country was exciting and rejuvenating.

They settled into their new routine with reawakened conviction. Daily chores were done with a self-belief that during their last days in Moose Jaw had all but evaporated. After a year and a half on the job, some of the old glow had returned to Gerry's view of the world. He had found a cure for his malaise outside of sport.

In 1991, Ambrose came to them with a new proposal. A challenge. He had just assumed responsibility for a CMHC apartment complex in Weyburn and he desperately needed the sort of expertise and commitment he knew Gerry and Marg would bring to the project. The complex included six rapidly deteriorating buildings set on nine overgrown acres.

It was a large complex with a lot of problems, serious problems, but after Ambrose's presentation and somewhat desperate plea for their help, the couple felt they were up to the test.

Within a short time, they were on their way to Weyburn. After two years in Regina, they were ready to return to the relatively peaceful life of a small city. Weyburn — the name reputedly coming from a corruption of the Scottish term "wee burn", referring to a small trickle of water, a creek or brook — sits beside the Souris River. Flood control measures have turned the river system into a series of ponds and wetlands attractive to water fowl. In short, it is a pretty place situated south of Regina, midway on the road to Estevan, familiar country to Gerry and Marg. Once again they were back in the heartland of oil and wheat.

When the couple first set eyes on what was to be their home for the next three years, they could not believe Ambrose had consigned them to such a dump. They had been sucker punched. Their new home was a slum. Everything about the property spelled seedy and scruffy. It looked like a place on which the sun had set years ago. Everywhere there was the smell of foreclosure. This really was going to be an "earn as you learn" project, Gerry says. To be fair, Ambrose had not embellished his description; if anything they had failed to listen. They had been teased by the challenge and the opportunity to add to their nest egg.

Each of the six buildings contained twenty-four units, making a total of one hundred and forty-four units. A total of thirty-one of those were rented out. Thirty-one out of one hundred and forty-four! Only three buildings were in use, the other three were vacant and derelict. Most units in those buildings had been stripped of stoves, refrigerators, dishwashers, microwaves, any appliance or fixture that was not nailed down, when tenants vacated them. To compound Gerry's and Marg's problem, within a few weeks of arriving, they had evicted tenants living in three of the occupied suites. They had just arrived; now they seemed to be moving backwards.

The place was a minefield of rats, garbage, dog shit, waist-high grass, discarded junk, you name it. Maintenance had not been done on the buildings in years. Gerry quickly discovered this was the case with every unit in every building. How people could live in such squalor puzzled him, but not one to be put off by a little dirt and rubbish, he began scrubbing, scraping, and scouring; steam-cleaning, disinfecting, and painting. "When you are up to your eyeballs in filth, people become suspicious of each other," Gerry says. "There may be some merit to the old adage about cleanliness."

Outside, he mowed the grass, weeded, cut flower beds into the sprawl of lawn, and planted dozens of trees, mostly juniper and poplar, although he added a few fruit trees into the mix.

Today, two decades after they left, one of the original tenants writes to tell them she is still picking apples from four of the trees.

Once the grounds had been cleaned up and the nine acres had begun to look more and more like a park, people became inquisitive. They wanted to know more about this place called Greystone Manor that was situated within walking distance of the downtown core. With paint had come a new name and a totally different reputation. Prospective tenants wanted to see the apartments. Within one year, Gerry was beginning his restoration of the third building and Marg had rented out every suite in two buildings. Buoyed by their success, they pushed on.

By the end of their third year, the couple had worked themselves out of a job. Gerry had moved on to the restoration of the fifth, and four buildings were full. They were taking a waiting list. CMHC, not in the business of property management, had found a buyer for the complex.

Now was the time to move to Vancouver Island although they did so with reluctance. They had both become attached to life in Weyburn. For Gerry the move was abnormally difficult.

For two years he had been involved in coaching a floor hockey team of Special Olympians. They had enriched his life immeasurably. For the first time in years, he found a way to channel his energy back into sports. What he had not expected was the extent of his commitment. These young athletes shared their lives and thereby entered his life in a way that he had never experienced before. The unqualified joy they received from putting on a uniform and running up and down the floor was infectious. They understood what it meant to compete, and the competition was hard and vigorous, but never did it boil over into anger or self-pity. There was no time for that. They were caught up in the rush of anticipation. He became emotionally connected to them in an unexpected way, as if a taproot or electrical current ran between them.

"Sometimes what was simple for me was incredibly difficult for them and yet they faced each and every hurdle with a strength and resolve I had never witnessed before. Not even amongst the most competitive of athletes. Including me. They get into your life, with such positive energy," he says, "I don't know how else to describe it."

❧

In 1994, Gerry and Marg moved to Vancouver Island where they took on one last management project. They remained on this job for three years, adding to their treasure chest, and then moved to their new home in Nanoose Bay in 1997.

During this period of his life is Gerry still one of those people ceaselessly arranging the details of his life or has he given in to the mayhem that surrounds him, satisfied to bring a modicum of shape to what lies within his control? The answer lies somewhere in the middle I think. He no longer feels compelled to master each and every situation, as he did as a coach, but he does all he can to bring a semblance of order to what he can influence.

What has he learned, I wonder? I think it is the value he

places on his curiosity — his need to know himself — his need always to know more.

❧

As we get older, time tends to telescope. While some events seem more distant, others appear closer. One certainty is that as we age time passes more quickly. We go from "Are we there yet?" to "Don't tell me we're there already!" In our bleakest moments, the end of time, if there is such a thing, seems imminent. Otherwise, it's business as usual. No time-piece or calculation can change this wavering perception. We seem wired genetically to respond differently at different ages to the passage of time. Our hair grays or falls out, our skin wrinkles, stomachs fall, all at different paces. While time may be the most constant nonspatial phenomenon of all human constructs, it seems remarkably fickle. Duration may be continuous but its measurement seems anything but, especially when filtered through the human imagination. We all contemplate our place in time but our interpretation of it sometimes is, well, downright confusing.

Where exactly are we on the continuum? Perhaps the proverbial blonde joke best illustrates my point. A blonde asks someone what time it is, and they tell her it is 4:45. The blonde, with a puzzled look on her face, replies, "You know, it's the weirdest thing, I've been asking that question all day, and each time I get a different answer." I know exactly how she feels.

A few years ago I got into a conversation with an old friend, Sean Roden, a successful football coach with the Nanaimo Redmen, a feeder team for the national champions, the Vancouver Island Raiders. Sean is a fine and dedicated coach. During our conversation, I mentioned my friendship with Gerry and suggested that maybe Sean's players might enjoy meeting him. Not only would they have the enviable experience of meeting a genuine football legend up close but I was certain that Gerry would enjoy meeting and talking with them. I believe strongly in this sort of bridging between generations. The naming and knowledge of those who have gone before us, a roll call of sorts, is a part of that process. I figured Gerry might be able to give them some tips based on his playing days with the Bombers and Roughriders. Sean, to his credit, thought this was a good idea and we arranged for me to bring Gerry along to one of the team's pre-season practices.

On a beautiful, sunny August evening, Gerry and I arrived at Pioneer Park on the northern boundary of Nanaimo. As we strolled across the rugby pitch toward the football field, we watched youngsters of all sizes, shapes and ages practising under the watchful eye of Sean and his fellow coaches. All the drills they were running appeared to be well-organized and everyone seemed totally engaged in what they were doing. Both Gerry and I were impressed; no one was slacking off. Sean greeted us and after he had completed a particular exercise he asked all the players to gather round. He introduced me and then said a few words about Gerry, mostly things I had told him during our earlier conversation. He mentioned the obvious, the Grey Cups and the Schenleys, but not much else. What was clear immediately was that he hadn't bothered to do any additional research of his own on Gerry's background. He was impressed by the statistics and story I had told him, but none of this information had translated into anything concrete. I could have been talking about the man on the moon.

Sean ended his brief recounting of Gerry's achievements by encouraging anyone who was interested in doing so to ask Gerry a question, either about his own playing days and career or about something they were doing in their own game. Gerry and I would wander amongst them, Sean suggested, and the kids could break away from whatever they were doing to talk to Gerry.

At this point we entered a time warp or temporal wilderness. I kept trying to gauge the young athletes' response to our being there. None of the signs was encouraging. The kids shuffled a lot and looked around, somewhat bewildered, at teammates. Occasionally they looked at Gerry. What were they seeing, I wondered? I tried putting myself in their place. What they saw was a man in his early seventies who was having difficulty standing up on his recently reconstructed knees. There was absolutely no way these kids could possibly visualize Gerry as a past running back, let alone a star, in the CFL. What they saw was an old man inside a body which they could not possibly imagine scoring eighteen rushing touchdowns in a single season. At best he looked like a favourite grandfather. No one was being disrespectful, not in the least; in fact, they all seemed like fine young men getting ready for a season of football.

Gerry's story was old, like those objects in the attic or like a song from a different era or a word that's going out of use. At that moment, time was compressed. Simultaneously, Gerry remembered taking to the field at Kelvin in the 1950s, and the young men saw stretched out before them their own heroics on the fields of the future. They saw a beautifully thrown spiral tracing a path downfield for a touchdown, or they saw a critical block that released a runner for a significant gain, or they saw catching a pass along the sidelines in the last minute that resulted in a field goal to win a tight game.

What Gerry and I saw was a loss of patrimony, or the

lack or the loss of tradition. I'm not going to say that the game is only as strong as our memory of the past because I don't believe that's true, but who we are in the moment, and I believe this to be true, is for all time. That includes all of us, from the beginning to the end. Having that awareness and living with that knowledge is a good part of the battle. The great players understand this and carry within them the solidarity that makes their accomplishments appear indistinguishable from all others — past, present and future. We have yet to name adequately that unique quality. We call it genius, courage, reading the game, IQ, whatever seems to assist us with naming the unnamable. I could have told the young men before us that day that Gerry's football IQ was off the charts but what would that have meant?

Retirement is a good thing, if we are comfortable and secure, but discovering in our old age that what we have done throughout our life is unappreciated, well, that's disappointing if not depressing. Nothing in life should be lost. Perhaps nothing is. But that awareness in no way compensates for the hollowness felt at the centre of one's core when you find yourself on the slag heap. The fact is, succeeding generations simply choose to forget or simply don't care to know or don't think to know. They are, rightfully so I guess, absorbed by what they are doing themselves. They are focused on their own pursuits.

What happened the day of our visit to the Redmen was both sad and encouraging. Not one kid stepped forward with a question or comment. Gerry said later that he felt forgotten, almost invisible. In a way what he said sounded like something the homeless might say. Standing in the middle of a football field, on what at one time for him had been sacred ground, he suddenly felt as though he didn't belong. He was a displaced person, an old man benched on the sidelines.

He remembered later that he had behaved similarly when during his early career a man offered to show him how to improve his conditioning. Gerry had responded to this gentleman by saying he was happy with the shape he was in. "In fact," Gerry said, his face flushing, "I think I told him, 'I'm perfect the way I am.' How could I have said that," he asked? There was no acting here, this was raw confession. Words can become their own source of punishment, as can memory.

On the other hand, what we saw from the kids that lovely warm evening was inspiring and outstanding. These men, and in their teens they are men at least in terms of physical maturity, were bigger, faster and in better condition than Gerry and his contemporaries were. "Imagine," he said, "a man of six feet four, weighing well over two hundred and fifty pounds, running a forty yard dash in 4.4 seconds. Such a specimen can keep up with any running back or receiver. Every weekend on NFL broadcasts we see men of over three hundred pounds moving with amazing agility. The game's changed. The strategies have changed, all because of increased speed and size.

"Many of these kids will be much better players than we ever were."

As Gerry says this, I'm not sure the comparison matters or is true. I realize that what frustrates Gerry is that he can't get out on the field and share with them what he does know. At least in his last years as a hockey coach he took to the ice with the players and was able to demonstrate moves and positioning while balanced on his own two blades. Now, physical limitations make that impossible.

As we left the field at twilight, we turned and took one last longing look at the choreography of the practice. We both hoped to see some of these kids playing college or professional football. As ever, the game was still exciting to watch, suffused as it is with anticipation and the unpredictable, with joy and an unqualified sense of fulfillment.

Perhaps what we had experienced was a Zen moment. There is elegance in forgetting yourself, in being open, in being. I know Gerry is interested in alternative ways of seeing and I suspect he may already be viewing this encounter with humour as well as nostalgia.

❧

Our Redmen experience and Gerry's observations about the size of contemporary players came back to mind recently while I was watching an NFL game on television. I listened in disbelief to the announcer saying that one of the offensive lineman was six feet eight and weighed in at three hundred and eighty-five pounds. I was flabbergasted and impressed. What chance did his opposition lineman, a mere six feet two and two hundred and eighty pounds have against this giant. The lineman the announcer was talking about seemed to dwarf his teammates and move quicker than most.

Then as I watched what I considered a sizeable running back move into this behemoth's shadow, the little fellow truly disappeared. Not to be outdone, the colour commentator responded with the personal dimensions of another lineman who came in at six feet five and weighed well over four hundred pounds. I suspect he might be closer to five hundred, replied the first announcer. The two linemen they were discussing were Titans. The league is filled with them. What amazed me was that both men were agile, almost graceful, and neither looked obese. At least, I certainly wouldn't be caught suggesting they were. These are the sort of numbers that make coaches salivate.

Gerry's point, though, is well taken. As long as field dimensions remain the same, the tactics in today's game have to be different. In a way the game has become unrecognizable. Big men with speed refocus everyone's attention. As with the atom, the "split-second" has been split yet again. Don't blink or you could get trampled under sizeable feet.

⚜

When Gerry heard that my sister's grandson, Jacob, had started playing hockey, Gerry asked for Jacob's address and sent him a signed copy of one of his Toronto Maple Leaf player cards from what is known as the "Lost Series."

In 1956-57 one of the major player card manufacturers forgot to include Montreal and Toronto in their series. How they could forget to print cards of the entire rosters of two out of only six teams in the NHL is impossible to fathom — but they did. Is there something symbolic if not sinister in the fact that it was the two Canadian teams they forgot? Three decades later the demand to fill the hole had become so great and the potential profit so attractive that the manufacturer searched out all the old teammates, had them sign releases, and finally issued a card for each player, Gerry included. Issuing it as the "Lost Series" and not the "Forgotten Series" was also astute, but I digress.

Jacob, who is around eight, was over the moon when he received Gerry's signed card and immediately put it away with all of his other treasures. I imagine things like his favourite Dinky toy model (do they still make Dinky toys?), the skull of some rodent, a prized rock from a remote holiday beach, a ribbon from sports day at school, a soccer or baseball pin, a picture of his first girlfriend, a figurine of Darth Vadar, a few marbles (do kids still play marbles or am I dating myself here?), his favourite comic book, that sort of thing.

A few weeks later, Gerry received an envelope from Jacob and inside it there was a note of thanks and a copy of Jacob's own card which he had made especially for Gerry. On the back it gave his birthdate and other incidental personal information and said: Future first round draft pick, 2020 — which happens to be Jacob's year of eligibility. He did not sign the card because he is not yet confident about his writing skills.

Apart from Jacob's optimism and obvious passion for the game, there was something else precious going on here. Perhaps Gerry had done his job as coach again and inspired another young hopeful to excel in a sport both love. An important pact had been forged. Trading cards can do that.

ॐ

When I ask Gerry about the recent controversial hit by Boston Bruin's Zdeno Chara on Montreal's Max Pacioretty, he makes the following observation. In his mind there is absolutely no doubt that Chara meant to hit Pacioretty from behind and to do injury.

"Players today don't respect the game. In my day heavy hits and fighting were just as much a part of the game but the game came first. You didn't train yourself to fight by taking martial arts courses in the summer so that you would have the upper hand on your opponent. For a lot of fighters in the game today, hockey skills are secondary, probably because they couldn't make it in the league with their hockey skills. This is a subtle but important distinction. Chara's hit was dirty and premeditated. On the other hand, Pacioretty should have known where he was in his own rink. He should have known the stanchion was there. As a player, you always know the danger spots in your own rink. You have to, especially if you are a player who attracts the more physical side of the game. You make a point of learning the danger spots in all of your opponents' rinks."

He also agrees with Don Cherry that the crackdown on fighting in the league has resulted in many more serious injuries occurring. "There is much more stick work today and there are many more cheap shots than there used to be. No one ever got hurt by a punch, not seriously, but a crosscheck into the boards from behind can do serious back damage, break a neck or cause a concussion."

⯎

Reading, listening to all sorts of different types of music, going to theatre, attending art exhibitions — many hitherto unknown worlds have opened up to Gerry over the past few years. One change in his life that I admire is his insatiable appetite for knowledge, at least up to a point. On a few occasions I have recommended certain books to him and offered to loan him copies, but if they were authored by women he refused to borrow them. When I asked him why, he said he doesn't read female writers. When I repeated my question he said he's not prejudiced, he's not a misogynist, it's just that he doesn't believe women can write about men or about what men think or like. "How," he asked, "can they possibly know how I think?"

He's not even sure he knows how he thinks or how other

men think let alone how women think. Therefore, how can women know what he, as a man, struggles to understand? For him this is a serious question. How do individuals as well as the sexes think? I imagine he finds Schultz creeping into the minds of Snoopy and Lucy a bit weird.

Likewise, he doesn't believe that men can write about women and what they think. He firmly believes the two sexes are wired differently. When he's reading a book by a male and comes to a part that purports to reveal the female mind or to a passage that is narrated from a woman's point of view, he skips to the next paragraph or section. Here I have a serious problem with his logic but there is no way around what has fossilized on the inner sanctum of his brain.

"Once," he admits, "I thoroughly enjoyed a particular work of detective fiction, skipping the female parts as usual, only to come to the end of the book and discover the author was P. D. James. I was so pissed when I saw P. D. was female, I threw the book down on the floor. I felt like I'd been tricked."

"Did she get the male thoughts and actions right?" I ask.

"Yes," he answers, "until I knew she was a woman. Then I was confident she must have been wrong."

We smile.

Gerry is not unaware of the irony of his position. After all, as we have seen, his mother negotiated his first contracts and was very successful at doing so in a male world. I want to ask him if he thinks she simply bamboozled the Smythes and charmed others with her female guile and logic or did she actually succeed in the world of male thinking?

"I know," he says, "none of this make sense."

As his confidence crumbles he adds, "One of my greatest regrets is that I never thanked my mother for the wonderful job she did negotiating those early contracts."

We are sitting on his back patio.

"I don't come off so well here, do I?"

"Not really."

"But that's the way I am. Or was."

"You've changed your mind?"

"Perhaps."

Gerry can be an enigma, filled as he is with a medley of contradictions, a position which gives him considerable pleasure. But speculating on his attitude to women could be fruitful or a fool's game. I fear the latter is most likely and remain silent. Let that door close.

Later, after he's read what I've written, he makes a point of letting me know that he has started to read women writers and he is amazed by how much he is enjoying their work. Either I've been had or we've broken another barrier. Of course, there is always the possibility that he is embarrassed by what he sees on the page and is guiding my hand in showing this sudden change of heart. Rather than cursing what he fails to understand, he simply redirects the topic of conversation.

❧

Gerry loves to stir the pot. I suspect this has always been the case. The incidents that dotted his career on the ice, on the gridiron and behind the players' bench were not premeditated. He did not set out to get someone, at least as a pre-game strategy; those encounters arose out of frustration, a sense of fair play — believe it or not — or downright annoyance.

In short, it has always been easy to become the proverbial burr under Gerry's saddle. Mind you, he can always find an explanation or rationalization for what he does and says.

According to his neighbours he is a generous and kind-hearted man, but beware the hapless golfer who strays out-of-bounds and into his garden to retrieve a ball.

While the original "No Trespassing" sign he nailed to a tree was clearly visible, the message printed on it was un-readable — perhaps for good reason — unless you were standing well within the boundaries of his property. Some felt this was a deliberate incitement and became so incensed they decided to chip their balls off his property, often taking a shrub in the process. The irony of what he had attempted to do was wasted. Most who complained were disgusted by his liberal use of "purple" prose.

A lot of people avoid him by reputation, in spite of the two knee operations and a bad back, even though the most one can expect is a good tongue-lashing. Otherwise he is fairly harmless. He does have a slingshot and an abundant supply of pebbles, but he reserves these mostly for the deer nibbling on his hostas or azaleas. From first hand experi-ence, I can tell you, sure shot he ain't!

❧

In recent years Gerry has made a conscious effort to diversify his interests and generally enhance the quality of his life. He is aware of some huge holes in his experience and knowl-edge. These are not the regrets of a man suddenly aware of his mortality but rather a genuine realization that while fly-ing high in the public eye as a sportsman, he was actually missing out on the exchange of ideas and the beauty of art and music. Success as an athlete should not preclude what-ever else life has to offer. He wants more, not of the physical sort, but spiritually (in the broadest sense of the word) and philosophically.

He and Marg are comfortable. They've been married for close to sixty years, they have a large supportive family and he is as focused on a couple of hobbies, the world of wines and his garden, as he ever was on his athletic endeavours. He reads voraciously, wanting to learn as much as possible in the time left to him. He reads fiction, history, biography, books on current events and some philosophy. It's not that he regrets his life as a Bomber or Leaf, far from it, they've both been a source of great reward and pride, not to mention privilege; no, what he wishes is that he had lived a more balanced life.

I'm not sure this would have worked. Time spent studying or attending university would have been time spent away from football and hockey. There is only so much room in one's psyche for each obsession.

Recently, Gerry tells me, the Blue Bombers announced that they were going to celebrate their eightieth anniversary by inviting past Blue and Gold greats back to the city to participate in the opening ceremonies of the season. There is a feeling in Bomber town that the franchise needs to rebuild if the team is going to return to the old glory days. Fans not only expect a revival of the team's fortunes after missing the playoffs in 2009, they expect a winning season and a return to the playoffs. The Bud Grant and Cal Murphy eras are difficult to put out of mind if you are a Bomber fan and while memories are unlikely to bring them their wish, parading a few legends before the fans and in front of the current roster should be at least inspirational. So thirteen past legends, ten players and three coaches, were asked to attend a celebratory dinner on June 30 and to join the festivities for the opening game of the 2010 season — on Canada Day.

"Great idea," Gerry says, and then he gives me this quizzical and somewhat hurt look.

"But you weren't invited. You're not one of the ten?"

"No, and it did hurt, not to mention piss me off.

"All of the legends chosen by the Hall of Fame Committee deserve to be there, there's no doubt about that. I was particularly pleased to see Buddy Tinsley's name included amongst the legends. You may remember him. He was the one who almost drowned in the centre of the field, in the 1950 Grey Cup game against Toronto? While the other players huddled up, he was lying face down in the mud, in the middle of the field. He had been knocked out during the preceding play.

"When the team noticed Buddy wasn't in the huddle, they looked around, saw him and rushed to his aid. It's a famous story. They turned him over and saved his life. He would have drowned. Two years later, there I was playing right halfback behind Buddy at right tackle. Immediately he came over to me and said, just follow me kid and I'll make you an all-star. And he did.

"What he said was true. Buddy was huge, for those days, six feet three or four and two hundred and fifty, sixty pounds. I couldn't see around him so I did as he told me to do. Right up his back. You couldn't slip a blade of grass between us, I was that close. He was largely responsible for the great season I had in 1954. I was so green. Without Buddy, well..."

Through his own particular lens, Gerry has sighted an image I can't quite get him to translate. But it is obviously one that brings him pleasure.

"While I didn't like Bud Grant very much," he continues, "largely because of his treatment of and attitude towards Canadian players, he was a great coach, and definitely deserves to be on the selector's list. So do all the others. What I don't understand is why in the supplement to the *Winnipeg Free Press*, 'Celebrating 80 Years of "Your Winnipeg Blue Bombers,"' my picture appears on the front cover wearing my old number, 98, and three questions out of the '20 questions to test your Blue Bomber knowledge' use my name, and yet I wasn't selected as one of the legends? Seems odd and slightly ironic to me."

When I ask him why he thinks this has happened he says he suspects it might be because he divided his loyalties between football and hockey. He wasn't as dedicated to football as he should have been, at least in the eyes of his football bosses.

For me it is difficult to imagine anyone more devoted or faithful to the game, whichever of Gerry's games is being discussed. I wonder if the selectors' limitations have crept into the selection process. If Gerry's right, his omission from the list is not surprising. Most people can't deal with those who excel at more than one activity. I also wonder if his somewhat abrasive nature, as Al Abbott implied, might not provide the explanation. Gerry didn't go out of his way to endear himself to people. He had little patience for swaggering behaviour, a weakness he contends is far too common in sports these days.

"My God, after a back or end makes a catch or scores a touchdown these days, they strut around the field like young peacocks. I often expect plumage to suddenly appear and fan out like they are about to go into some sort of mating dance," he says.

He has often made his views on this sort of boastfulness known. Honesty is one thing but sometimes he might have cut a bit too close to the bone.

Another issue that sticks in his craw is that he has never been invited to present the Eddie James Trophy to the running back who gains the most yards in a season in the Western Conference.

"I'm available," he says, "and not far out of reach. Sometimes I feel like I've been banished to a remote island in the

Pacific, where I'm lounging under palm trees, out of touch with the rest of the world. Come to think of it, I have relocated to an island in the Pacific but so what; even here we have cell phones and email. This trophy was named after my dad, honours his name and contribution to the sport, and on at least one occasion I'd like to present it to the winner. I may be deluding myself, but I think fans and players alike appreciate a sense of history."

"There is no question football has a history," I reply.

Gerry James is a big part of it, I think, but I decide not to say so. Why make him feel uncomfortable with intimations of fame.

Since his knee operations Gerry hobbles a bit. He now feels an uncertainty in his legs that surprises and annoys him. Even so, three times a week he and Peter Brooks climb Notch Hill, approximately a thousand foot climb from the base up through arbutus groves, firs and Garry Oak stands, across wild flower meadows, to one of the most breathtaking views on Vancouver Island. From one of the granite outcrops at the top you can see Nanoose Bay, Georgia Strait and the mainland. The nearer vista includes a patchwork of islands including Maud, the Winchelseas, and Jedediah.

If you care to linger, you can sit on a bench around which two trees have grown, incorporating a plank that was placed there years ago between their upward thrust into the sky. Someone's foresight. Either way, for many a rest at the top is a reward for the climb.

But Gerry and Peter rarely pause to rest or to take in the view, even on the sunniest of days. A certain fanaticism drives them to turn, legs still pumping, and return downhill. The act replicating a life. Neither man knows how to rest. The descent along the rocky path is a little more difficult on mechanical knees but Gerry being Gerry, this is a challenge; he still has much to prove, if only to himself. Each time he makes the ascent, he clocks his new time against his previous day's time. And he notes Peter's time. Competition, even here and at seventy-six, is stamped on his core.

The other four days he works out in his home gym, lifting weights; or he plugs away in his garden constantly fiddling with the placement of plants, always searching for the perfect mix of colour and form; always taxing his body and mind. His back aches without relief. To a certain extent this is a fitness regime that he has followed all his life but it is also a way of proving himself, of keeping in contact with a life force that he is determined to celebrate to his last breath. Although like a lot of other older people he feels marginalized, he also feels blessed and grateful.

To walk and talk with Gerry is to feel alive.

There are few if any explanations that satisfactorily account for any of our desires or experiences, but as Gerry and I stroll amongst his grasses — I spot Miscanthus Giganteus, blue fescue, blue oat grass, silver feather grass, Japanese blood grass, pampas grass, maiden grass to name only a few — I realize there are expressions of the individual spirit that are undeniable. Whether it's a run off right tackle into an open field, or a body check that redirects the flow of play, or the introduction of a rhododendron amongst a garden of exotic grasses, I have come to believe that Gerry's compulsion, no matter what it is, is invincible. In a way, each one of us is a replication of the big bang; Kid Dynamite is proof of that.

Acknowledgements

Many people helped make this book possible. I am most grateful to Gerry and Marg James, for their friendship and for their willingness to talk about their lives together. Even as we struggled through differences in opinion and memory, they remained in good humour. Usually.

I was unable to acknowledge two provincial organizations within the body of the text for inducting Gerry into their respective Sports Halls of Fame, Manitoba in 1982 and Saskatchewan in 1994. I know how appreciative Gerry is that both provinces bestowed upon him their highest honour for an athlete. He is truly pleased by this recognition. That these two honours are not mentioned in the main narrative is my fault.

Gerry's mother kept a scrapbook of his early successes and Marg added to it, the contents of which have helped immeasurably. Often they cut off the byline and rarely did the actual name of the newspaper and the date of publication appear anywhere on the photocopy of the scrapbook I received from the Manitoba Hall of Fame. However, I count my blessings that this document has been safely stored in the Hall's archive. With the help of the internet I was at least able to date many of these documents. I regret that I'm unable to credit some of the authors or sources more specifically. I am hugely indebted to all of the many fine journalists who wrote so enthusiastically about sports from the 1940s forward. With apologies to those I have missed, these talented scribblers included: Jim Hunt, Hal Sigurdson, Linus Westberg, Jack Wells, Jude Kelly, George Mac-Farlane, Arnie Tiefenbach, Al Vickery, Laurie Artiss, Ted Bowles, Bob Moir, Vince Leah, Maurice Smith, Hal Walker, Red Burnett, Gordon Campbell, Tex Coulter, George Dulmage, Alan Ryder Thomas, Don Hunt, Gord Walker, Bob Hesketh, Hal Pawson, John Brown, Jack Matheson, John MacDonald, Gorde Hunter, Jack Meeks, Jim Coleman, Milt Dunnell, Wilf Smith, Stan Houston, Ted Reeves, Al Ritchie, Bill Good Sr., Jim Brooke, Lin Orosz, Jim Vipond, Bob Frewin, Scott Young, Rick Winston, Rob Vanstone, Rex MacLeod, Jim Kearney, John Robertson, Don Blanshard, and Reyn Davis.

I am equally in the debt of the newspapers for which they wrote: *Winnipeg Free Press*, the *Winnipeg Tribune*, the *Toronto Star*, *Globe and Mail*, *Toronto Telegram*, *Hamilton Spectator*, *Edmonton Journal*, *Vancouver Sun*, *Ottawa Citizen*, *Montreal Gazette*, *Yorkton Enterprise*, *Yorkton This Week*, *Calgary Herald*, and the *Regina Leader-Post*.

In total I read well over a thousand articles and was constantly surprised and delighted by the insight and quality of the writing.

Bob Ferguson's *Who's Who In Canadian Sport* helped to get me started. John Chaput's *Saskatchewan's Sports Legends* was insightful and useful, as was Bob Irving's *Blue &Gold*. Lloyd Percival's *The Hockey Handbook* provides a priceless examination of hockey. This small book should be required reading for anyone interested in playing or coaching hockey. Along with Paul Patskou, Roly Harris and Paul Bruno, Kevin Shea's *Diary of a Dynasty* provided some invaluable insights into a decade of Leaf teams and players. Gene Krepakevich's *25 Years with the Yorkton Terriers* raised questions and answered some about Gerry's years as a coach in the Saskatchewan junior hockey system.

Al Abbott, Alison North and Jack Robertson, friends of

Gerry's from his years growing up in Winnipeg, all provided interesting anecdotes about the boy. Jack was one of Gerry's closest accomplices. There were many more individuals who volunteered to give me information but I was afraid of information overload.

Ex-players from Gerry's years as a coach made themselves available but I thought a couple would be sufficient to reflect the whole. I'm grateful to Brian Propp for his quick response to my query.

Larry Robertson, statistician for the CFL and NHL, took a keen interest in my project and offered some wonderful tidbits of information, material I could not have found on my own. I thank him for our few long telephone conversations and for sending me an extract from Scott Young's *The Leafs I Knew*.

Marilyn Bowering and Michael Elcock assisted me when we talked about Marilyn's research into the Bombers, in particular into Jack Jacobs. Alan Safarik's enthusiasm when I was starting the book gave me a great boost.

Others who helped with the research include: Astrid Lange, who tracked down the Tex Coulter article for me, and Joanne MacDonald at the *Toronto Star*; Meghan Sturgeon-Archer at the Canadian Football Hall of Fame and Museum; Lynn Crothers, Steve Pona, Mike Aporius, and Steve Lyons at the *Winnipeg Free Press*; Craig Campbell at the Hockey Hall of Fame, who turned out to be a big fan of football as well; and Andrea Reichert at the Manitoba Hall of Fame. All were kind and generous with their time.

I am grateful to the Hockey Hall of Fame, the Manitoba Hall of Fame, the Canadian Football Hall of Fame, and the *Winnipeg Free Press* for the use of photographs held in their archives.

Thanks to Randal Macnair and Christa Moffat who

agreed to publish this book under the Oolichan imprint and to Vanessa Croome for the cover design.

My thanks to three old friends who have given me editorial advice along the way. Bob Kroetsch read an earlier draft and provided encouragement when it was needed. Bill New has read several drafts and has provided many pages of helpful suggestions. And Edwin Webb, who will want to strike out that last conjunction, has done a wonderful line edit and offered constant useful and constructive criticisms throughout the writing of this book. Their patience, support and friendship are much appreciated.

And Pat, last but certainly not least, I thank for her love and inspiration.

Ron Smith is the author of numerous books of poetry, fiction and a play. His recent children's book, *Elf the Eagle*, was short-listed for the BC Book Prizes and the Saskatchewan Young Reader's Award. He retired from teaching at Vancouver Island University in 1998 and was the inaugural Fulbright Chair in Creative Writing at Arizona State University in 2005. In 2002 he received an honorary doctorate from UBC. He has given readings and lectures in England, Italy, Albania, the States and across Canada. His poetry was translated by Ada Donati and published in a bilingual edition entitled *Arabesque e altre poesie* in Italy by Schifanoia Editore. He lives in Nanoose Bay, BC.